T0320883

Multiculturalism and Advertising

Multiculturalism and Advertising

Indian and European
Enterprises under Globalization

ANURADHA BHATTACHARJEE

OXFORD

UNIVERSITY PRESS

OXFORD
UNIVERSITY PRESS

Oxford University Press is a department of the University of Oxford.
It furthers the University's objective of excellence in research, scholarship,
and education by publishing worldwide. Oxford is a registered trademark of
Oxford University Press in the UK and in certain other countries.

Published in India by
Oxford University Press
2/11 Ground Floor, Ansari Road, Daryaganj, New Delhi 110 002, India

First Edition published in 2019

ISBN-13: 978-0-19-945356-6
ISBN-10: 0-19-945356-X

Typeset in Adobe Garamond Pro 11/13
by Tranistics Data Technologies, New Delhi 110 044
Printed in India by Nutech Print Services India

Contents

Figures and Tables

Figures

Tables

"L'humanité est constamment aux prises avec deux processus contradictoires dont l'un tend à instaurer l'unification tandis que l'autre vise à maintenir ou à rétablir la diversification."

(Claude Levi Stauss, *Race et Histoire*, 1952).

"Mankind is constantly faced with two contradictory processes, one which tends to establish a unification, while the other seems to maintain or restore diversification."

(Claude Levi Strauss, *Race et Histoire*, 1952).

Introduction

This book, at the broadest conceptual level, looks at the rise of multicultural symbols as the outcome of what is popularly termed as "globalization". Globalization of course is not new. In the past, religion and conquest, empires and trade routes had already indelibly contributed toward it. What is different about globalization taking place today, however, is the bewildering speed and capacity of modern-day technology, culturally neutral, one might add, that seemingly propels globalization at a rate that unnerves countries and societies. In this book, I have chosen one tool of measurement as it were. This is advertisement. Because advertisement, in my opinion, is the interface between two important aspects of globalization: trade and the spread of a global, more inclusive culture.

The book devotes itself primarily to an empirical investigation of a large number of advertisements and how this is a metaphor for the most visible part of the globalization process—the widespread proliferation of common symbols particularly in the area of consumer goods—both for elite and for less elite consumption. More specifically, this book argues with data from a study of more than 5,000 advertisements both at the high end such as luxury cars and lifestyles such as perfumes to mass consumption that globalization has brought about an increasing acceptance of multicultural images, symbols and texts reflecting perhaps a larger unity that is shaping the world.

Let me add, however, this book is not about globalization per se. There are of course many differing views on globalization. Its supporters, on the one hand, describe it as an irresistible and welcome force that brings the best the world has to offer. For them, globalization is, *au fond,* a continuation, albeit in an intensified and accelerated form, of the perduring challenge of modernization. Its critics, on the other hand, term it as a "juggernaut of untrammeled capitalism", which is leading the world to a particular type of homogeneity, West-centered (if not actually America-centric), and pushed by Western capital and media that creates a kind of "McWorld" where Western goods, capital, and ideas prevail. My own belief is that this is a debate we have visited in the past. This book submits that an equally strong case can be made to suggest that globalization has been a two-way process, and that the civilizations of the East—the Chinese and Indian to be more precise—with such discoveries as the compass, paper, the zero and the decimal system—provided the initial impetus for developments that made globalization possible.

This book does not attempt to go into the merits or otherwise of globalization. It deals instead with a variety of empirically grounded perspectives on globalization pari passu with the internationalization of culture. More specifically, the book takes into account a comparative and statistical analysis of advertising in two geographically diverse commercial regions—Europe and India—to suggest that in spite of our differences, we are moving, at least in the corporate world, to an intercultural ethos, an index to the rapid globalization process at hand. It focuses, in particular, on the character and range of multicultural advertising in France and Germany of the mid-1990s, cross-referencing this with a similar examination of Indian advertising of the same period. This period is of specific interest because "never before in history have human cultures been exposed to such a massive reciprocal confrontation and never before has the cultural dimension of human action been directly addressed as the core resource for production and consumption."[1]

Historically speaking, this was the time when the Union of Soviet Socialist Republics (USSR) was disintegrating, East and West Germany were merging, the European Union (EU) was forming into a single market and the emerging economies of China, India and Eastern Europe were integrating with those of the United States (US)

---

[1] Alberto Melucci, "The Process of Collective Identity", in *Social Movements and Culture*, eds Hank Johnston and Bert Klandermanns (Minneapolis: University of Minnesota Press, 1995).

and the EU to form a more visibly global economy. Yet another important phenomenon taking place during this time was that owing to saturation in their own markets, many Western companies were turning toward the developing countries of the South for joint ventures and partnerships. As a result, investments by multinational corporations (MNCs) in the South during this period became even more significant in monetary terms than official development aid. For example, whilst the US foreign aid declined from 11.4 billion dollars in 1990 to 9.7 billion dollars in 1993, the outflow of US foreign investment rose from 423.2 billion dollars in 1990 to 548.7 billion dollars in 1993.[2]

All these events, the book postulates, would soon lead to the emergence of a worldwide affluent, consumption-oriented class in the South whose lifestyle had far more in common with their counterparts in the West than with those living in the South. From a sociological point of view and as Scheve and Slaughter point out, this class of people constituted a new life force for the global economy by creating new demands for commodities produced by the "West".[3] Yet the point I argue here is that global trade in the future will be driven, not by the major industrialized countries of the West nor regional trading blocs like the EU but by the emerging economies of the South. This is based on the premise that global economic growth is triggered by the creation of regional trading blocs and the desire for economic growth and industrialization in the developing world, both of which factors were given special momentum by the signing of the Maastricht Treaty in Europe and economic liberalization in many of the developing countries during this period. The objective of this book is to see how much of this is real.

To study the impact of this worldwide trend, I have chosen the examples of France and Germany in Europe and India in South Asia. An important reason for comparing the East and the West is that very few studies to date have examined the roles of European and

---

[2] C. Thomas, "5 Development and Inequality", *Newsweek*, June 26, 1995, 3.

[3] Kenneth F. Scheve and Mattew J. Slaughter, "A New Deal for Globalization", *Foreign Affairs* 86, no. 4 (2007): 34–47.

Asian companies in designing and implementing advertising campaigns for non-domestic markets.

France and Germany—old and established members of the European Union with cultural blends attractive to international marketers—were purposely selected to provide insights into the differences, no matter how subtle, among nations that are normally thought to be similar because of their geographical and cultural proximity. To what extent does the post-Maastricht Europe signify not just a single market but also a common set of consumer needs and wants? Can consumers in this market be targeted with the same approach—what a German Union Investment Banking advertisement of this period euphemistically described as "Euromarketing"?

What makes South Asia, a developing region grouping some of the poorest countries in the world, particularly interesting, in my view, is that in 1991, four countries in this region—India, Nepal, Pakistan and Bangladesh—abandoned their inward-looking domestic oriented import substitution model in order to embrace an outward-oriented market liberalization model.[4] The success of these countries' newly launched economic reforms, however, depended primarily on their ability to find new markets, both in the developed and developing world. But given the slow growth of the world economy, and the formation and expansion of such giant regional economic blocs as the North American Free Trade Agreement (NAFTA), the EU, ASEAN Free Trade Area (AFTA) and Mercado Comun del Sur (MERCOSUR) and the desire on the part of these blocs to increase intra-regional trade, it seemed impossible that these newly emerging countries would be able to succeed in their efforts. On the contrary, they faced the rather bleak prospect of being marginalized in the international economy.

India, within the larger framework of South Asia, was chosen for the simple reason that this region is Indo-centric. India not only shares frontiers with every other country in the region but as the world's second most populous country with more than 1 billion people, it also accounts for about 70 percent of the population of

---

[4] R. Gilpin, *The Political Economy of International Relations* (Princeton, NJ: Princeton University Press, 1987).

the eight countries that make up the subcontinent's premier regional organization, the South Asian Association for Regional Cooperation (SAARC). The nascent post-liberalization Indian market, prophetically described by *Forbes* magazine in its 1994 (23 May 1994) cover story as the "best emerging market of all" seemed therefore, in my view, to merit a separate category among the developing countries that were in transition, as it were, from a low income to a middle one, by the sheer dint of its size and potential.

Ironically, however, at the time it made its rather dramatic shift toward liberalization in 1991, India was not only one of the most statist and inward-looking of the Third World countries but also one of the poorest and most agrarian.[5] The long colonial rule had left behind a society with 16 percent literacy, practically no domestic industry and over 90 percent living below what we would today call the poverty line. A nation that had once been among the world's richest and which, as late as 1820 had accounted (in the estimate of the late British economic historian Angus Maddison) for 23 percent of global gross domestic product (GDP), had been reduced by 1947, into one of the poorest, most backward, most illiterate and most diseased societies of the world. The period of transition that India faced following liberalization of its economy was rendered even more complex by the fact that the world in which it had to now find its place was itself in a state of transition due to shifts of power—economic, political and military—particularly in those countries that since the end of World War II had laid down the rules and controlled the institutions by which most areas of global interaction were governed.

A late capitalist society, India's post-1990 paradigmatic turnabout in foreign policy is best explained by the post-Cold War global political-economic developments. Ironically, even though, India, as part of the non-aligned group of nations, had been calling for an end to the Cold War for years, when it did end, it was least prepared for the consequences. India was not only broke but had two raging insurgencies on its hand and a government that was not fully stable.

[5] G. Alam, "India's Technology Policy and Its Influence on Technology Imports and Technology Development", *Economic and Political Weekly* 20, no. 45–7 (1985): 2073–80.

With the collapse of the Soviet Union and the gradual incorporation of Eastern Europe into the West European economy, India found itself suddenly de-linked from two of its most vital markets. Faced with rising inflation and a balance of payment crisis, the "cornerstone" of Prime Minister Narasimha Rao's economic policy became "liberalization, privatization and globalization (LPG)". India took a massive loan from the IMF even while agreeing to IMF's condition to open its markets to foreign investment.[6]

What is particularly interesting in this case is that following its shift from a closed economy to a liberalized one (the shift, interestingly, has survived way beyond the foreign exchange crisis that was its immediate trigger) in 1991—"more and more Indians" as pointed out by Kemper and Appadurai "were now engaged in forms of consumption that resembled the cosmopolitan cultural forms in other parts of the world."[7] This trend, as this book suggests, is best reflected in advertising because most companies, at least in the early phase of their entry into the Indian market, would tend to target these "very rich and consuming" classes since they were the ones that could afford to buy luxury cars and other premium products.

Two decades is a reasonable time span to gauge the impact of globalization. In this book, we will subsequently look at many issues in both historical and futuristic perspectives. But first, a few words on its structure and coverage.

The Book's Structure

This book has two separate but interconnected sections. The first begins by exploring, very briefly, how societies developed into rival communities culminating in the establishment and consolidation of nation states in modern Europe. These values were then taken out of their home-countries through conquest and colonization where

[6] Nikhil Sinha, "Doordarshan, Public Service Broadcasting and the Impact of Globalization: A Short History", in *Broadcasting Reform in India—Media Law from a Global Perspective*, eds M.E. Price and S.G. Verhulst (New Delhi: Oxford University Press, 1998), 22–40.

[7] Arjun Appadurai, *Larger Modernity at Larger Cultural Dimensions of Globalisation* (Minneapolis: University of Minnesota Press, 1996).

radically different cultures had to come to terms with each other—from domination to adjustment while going through a period of intense hostility, sometimes even genocide. In short, the first part traces the development of culture from the individual to the family, clan, tribe, right up to the nation state. The book thereafter posits the thesis that these are now being superseded by the growth of supranational institutions (the United Nations (UN) and its sister bodies, the EU, Association of Southeast Asian Nations (ASEAN) and others). It emphasizes, in particular, the enormous gains in the global economy premised upon, among other things, the multilateral trading regime that was put in place, initially under the aegis of the General Agreement on Tariffs and Trade (GATT) and the Free Trade Agreements (FTAs), bilateral and regional, to deepen and widen the benefits of an open, liberal and multilateral global order. Some, in the French intellectual tradition, have written about the resulting cultural image of the "other", who is different, or at least appears to be different, leading to prejudice and stereotyping. Yet the point I argue here is how institutional structures have grown in recent times to "connect" and to "unite" countries and communities across the world.

The second part of the book is an extension of sorts of the discussion touched upon in Part I about what some view as a growing threat of or already existing "clash of civilizations". As the Cold War ended, Samuel Huntington was among the first political scientists to ask what the resurgence of non-Western peoples with their own distinctive cultures portended for international relations. If civilizations clash, as Huntington feared, religious exclusivism would aggravate conflict, lapsing into tribalism. However, the point the book makes is that since the nineteenth century, religious pluralism has grown steadily alongside the contrary drift toward fundamentalism. Favored by the unavoidable interchanges of the global age, pluralism may yet prove to be the more enduring trend.

The book touches upon certain important aspects of twenty-first century realities such as: the end of the Cold War, the blurring of national boundaries in the information era, the advent of Islamist terrorism as a pan-global force, the dramatic rise of China and India in a changing global order and the global consciousness of soft power. All these elements have been variously described here. In particular, the book poses and discusses, through analysis of a large corpus of advertising, a few key issues in contemporary globalization debates such as: are nation states getting hollowed out with the rise of enormously powerful non-state actors (Chapter 5)? Should global companies adapt and localize their products in different countries (Chapter 6)? Is globalization generating increasing homogeneity or heterogeneity (Chapter 6)? This point is of special relevance as a major challenge faced by marketers is whether to use the same advertising themes everywhere based on the assumption that there exist global consumers or communities with universal values—or to customize strategies to suit different cultures (for example, McDonald's Mc Aloo Tikki in India). Chapter 7 calibrates the extent of multicultural penetration in some detail across a wide range of product categories to underline the increasing trend in international trade toward commonly understood symbols, visuals and texts. Since advertising is an important commercial tool where returns are carefully monitored, advertisers, it is assumed, will only use those images, symbols and texts that find a resonance with the consumer. Chapter 8 describes the rise of the global South, that is China and India in what has been commonly described as the "Asian century". Chapter 9 analyses the potential of the emerging Indian market through statistical data for conceptual and analytical thinking about consumer India's purchasing power in contrast to the more advanced Western nations of France and Germany to see whether or not liberalization has contributed to the birth of a new breed of capitalist elites. Chapter 10 analyses the economic, cultural and political changes sweeping India over the last two decades. Chapter 11 examines States' behavior in today's globalized relations with a study of relations between India and China. The simultaneous rise of these two Asian giants in the twenty-first century represents a geopolitical event of historic proportions. Rarely has the global system witnessed the re-emergence of two major powers simultaneously—States that account for 40 percent of the world's population, have ancient histories and dominate the geographic region within which they are located. This chapter is an attempt to understand both Chinese and Indian perspectives in the light of India's initiative to strengthen ties with the region, in particular with Japan, ASEAN, Vietnam, Australia and South Korea. Chapter 12 lays the groundwork for assessing the prospects of greater regional cooperation in South Asia, which remains to this day, India's closest and most vital sphere of strategic action. Yet the region continues to present challenges at several levels. India's ability to play a more engaged role in the global arena is now commensurate with its capacity for ensuring a modicum of stability in its relationship with its South Asian neighbors. A unified South Asia, the book argues, inhabited by nearly one-fourth of the world's population and a staggeringly vast and empowered middle class, has the potential, like the post-1993 single European market, to become an economic powerhouse provided it can overcome all that divides it. Chapter 13 focuses in great detail, for reasons, which I will elaborate later, on how advertising is used to sell automobiles in France, Germany and India, using at least twenty different variables and spanning over two decades, to contrast the selling strategies in the three countries.

An important take-away of this book is that, contrary to common assumptions, global homogenous markets exist primarily in the minds of international marketing managers and advertising professionals. Even people with similar lifestyles do not behave as a consistent group of purchasers. Youngsters and yuppies (young urban professionals), rich people and graying populations do have economic and demographic aspects in common. They cannot, however, be targeted using the same arguments or appeals because their values are different. In other words, even if across countries certain groups can be defined by ownership of the same products, the motives for buying these products vary so strongly that for developing effective marketing campaigns across countries, these lifestyle definitions are not useful (convergences and divergences in buying motives and their relationship with culture are discussed in Chapter 13). As the old marketing paradigm puts it—there may be global products, but there are no global people. There may be global brands but there are no global motives for buying these brands (this topic is dealt with in some detail in Chapter 6).

At the root of many assumptions about convergence, as the book notes, is universalistic thinking. By the term convergence, people often mean "Westernization", whereby "Western" usually is associated with being "American." Most global advertising agencies and many multinational companies, in fact, have Anglo-American management. Their universalism generally makes them think their values are valid for the whole world and should be shared by all.[8] As a result, they focus more on the similarities (these are often pseudo similarities) and ignore the differences. In contrast, Asians are more particularistic and tend to focus more on the differences rather than on the similarities. Lack of knowledge of individual countries and their culture also endows people with a distorted perception of one another (see Chapter 2 on prejudice and stereotyping). Universalism or lack of knowledge can also be the cause of mistaking the habits or values of one European or one Asian country for all of them. For example, taking the United Kingdom as representative of Europe or categorizing all European countries as hierarchical societies.[9] Hence, even though consumer needs and wants under globalization are converging everywhere to a large degree, there still exist important differences between countries, even those countries in Europe that share a common border, and these, in turn, can influence advertising strategies (this topic is covered in Chapters 5, 6 and 13). Finally, universalism has also led to Anglo-American marketing theories being applied worldwide. Not only have these theories been exported to other cultures, but practitioners and academics have often enthusiastically copied practices and theories from the US without realizing that not all these concepts and theories have the same relevance in their own countries. This has happened in all regions of the world, both in Europe and in Asia. This is not due especially to American Imperialism (or ethnocentrism) but to the fact that advanced marketing and advertising practice originated in the US (see Chapters 4 and 6).

The book emphasizes, in particular, the fact that with the transition of developing countries toward post-scarcity societies (see Chapters 8 and 9), culture will assume greater and not lesser significance in the future. For comparing post-scarcity societies, where ownership across countries for new commodities has reached maximum convergence, culture and not national income will serve as an explaining variable for understanding differences. This is because as people around the globe become better-educated and more affluent, their tastes will not

---

[8] N.J. Adler, *International Dimensions of Organizational Behavior*, 2nd edn (Belmont, CA: Wadsworth, 1991), 47.

[9] J. Rossant, "Old World, New Mandate", *Business Week*, January 31, 2001, 49.

converge but diverge. This is in contrast to the general assumption held by sociologists that consumer behavior across countries would converge with converging media, technology and national wealth. Indeed the common assumption has been that with increased wealth, people's values will change. The expectations were that with increased openness and capitalism in China, the Chinese would turn to Western values. Instead, the Chinese are rediscovering the teachings of Confucius, which for centuries, provided moral guidance to the Chinese people. The Chinese, in other words, want to become modern while retaining their core values.[10] This does not mean, however, that there can be no convergence on core universal values, wants or needs across countries. The last chapter on automobiles (Chapter 13) emphasizes the underlying theme prevalent throughout this book, that of "unity in diversity" among peoples and nations and cautions against a narrow and parochial similarities only (universalistic) or differences only (particularistic) approach.

Having said this, a few limitations of the book also need to be acknowledged here. First, although I have attempted to look at numerous variables in order to understand advertising in three such diverse countries as France, Germany and India, considering how multifaceted an art advertising is, many other variables or characteristics could also have been taken into account, the absence of which may have somewhat limited the scope of this investigation. Second, the number of countries included inhibits to a certain extent, the generalizability of the findings. Third, even though common signs and/or symbols that firms use to connect their brands with consumers across the globe have been identified, the book does not delve into their associations. Fourth, the use of visual metaphors—animal figures, religious objects and signs, and aesthetic codes—may need a more detailed analysis than has been possible here. Fifth, the arguments reviewed are obviously not conclusive and leave a certain number of issues unresolved. In particular, the complex phenomenology of cultural identity in an evolving globalized world requires a far more extensive and nuanced treatment than has been possible here. What this book has tried to do, however, is to offer a glimpse of alternative ways of

---

[10] P. Mooney, "Learning the Old Ways", *Newsweek*, May 27, 2002, 29.

thinking about the complex cultural issues thrust upon us by the contemporary globalization process. Because there is controversy over whether global media industries create uniform desires and habits, globalization, for advertising and marketing, is one of the most widely discussed concepts in recent years.[11]

Some of these constraints notwithstanding, I hope this book, given its practical orientation, will be of special interest to academicians and practitioners, not so much for its abstractions as for its empirical evidence not always found in international marketing and consumer behavior textbooks. Indeed, a salient feature of this book is the inclusion of a large number of case studies. I hope, in particular, that the book will provide a better understanding of some of the variables or cues that consumers may search for in their buying decisions.

Values As a Tool

This book approaches consumer behavior across cultures by reviewing some of the existing theories for comparing national cultures to see how certain groups or cultures are similar or different from one another (see Hofstede's cultural model). This approach—even though it includes the risk of overlooking some unique aspects of distinct cultures—is still widely considered as the most practical approach common to cross-cultural and other comparative social studies.[12]

The most important aspect of this book is the examination of values as a tool for understanding the impact of culture on consumer behavior. Values, widely considered to be the building blocks of culture, generally signify ideas about what a group believes to be right or wrong and which, transmitted in a gradual yet dynamic process over time, serve as social guidelines for appropriate behavior in

---

[11] Mike Featherstone, "An Introduction, Global Culture", in M. Featherstone (ed.), *Consumer Culture and Postmodernism* (London: Sage Publications, 1993).

[12] G. Hofstede, *Cultures Consequences: International Differences in Work-Related Values* (Beverly Hills: Sage Publications, 1980).

specific situations. As a rule, values are relatively difficult to identify since they are embedded in tacit lifestyle preferences.

I have used the evaluation of value systems to understand the cultural commonalities and differences between the three countries studied and I have used a practical data-based (statistical) analysis for corporate use, such as a market survey, to provide empirical evidence. The three cited cultures—France, Germany and India—are active participants in the global marketplace, each with its own unique way of doing business. While Germans place a high value on equality among individuals, French and Indian cultures place a high value on hierarchies or power distances between people. While the French and Germans value certainty in everyday life and have difficulty in coping with unanticipated events, Indians have a greater tolerance level for ambiguity and change. While the French and Germans are relatively direct in their communication, Indians are more subtle.[13] Managers and advertising practitioners who understand the socio-relational, verbal and non-verbal contexts of these cultures are, in my view, in a much better position to design a more effective business strategy.

A stratified random sample of about 5,000 advertisements for consumer products in leading print magazines of general interest in France, Germany and India, namely, *L'Express, Paris-Match, Der Spiegel, Stern* and *India Today* and limited to a period of six months has been taken into account to see if a study of advertisements can help us calibrate how much globalization has helped the spread of multiculturalism in France, Germany and India. Based on a select analysis of samples, this study provides an innovative methodology by which the sampling can be optimized.

It is to be noted here that although the cited magazines are comparable in terms of their content, they differ significantly in terms of their advertising volume. For example, the French *L'Express* and *Paris Match* contained fewer advertisements than their German counterparts, perhaps due to the fact that newspapers/magazines in Germany are considered as the leading media vehicle with print advertising exceeding that for television by a ratio of two to one. Therefore, a few more

---

[13] G. Hofstede and M.H. Bond, "The Confucius Connection: From Cultural Roots to Economic Growth", *Organizational Dynamics* 16, No. 4 (1988).

issues of *L'Express* and *Paris Match* were added so that the three nations could be represented equally in terms of their advertising volume.

The advertising corpus in all three countries has been analysed in terms of (i) linguistic codification (headlines, subhead, tagline/baseline/logo, body copy); (ii) visual codification (imagery); (iii) combined verbal/visual codification. The data collection method takes into account 13 criteria or parameters and is quite rigorous. The set of parameters pertaining to both image and text are: (i) title of advertisement—does it use any foreign element?, (ii) slogan, (iii) product name, (iv) other (text), imagery in the advertisement—does it use any foreign, (v) characters, (text), (vi) animal, (vii) landscape, (viii) object, (ix) symbol, (x) text in the image, (xi) general composition, and so on (see Table 7.1). This format has been applied to 19 groups of products ranging from high-end products such as luxury cars, fashion, leisure-related activities and lifestyles like perfumes, watches to low-end mass consumption items such as personal and household products, and food and beverages to arrive at certain broad conclusions, statistically based. The 19 product categories that have been studied are: (i) perfume; (ii) cosmetics and toiletries; (iii) high-end fashion; (iv) watches; (v) pens; (vi) food and beverages; (vii) travel and leisure; (viii) automobiles and related products; (ix) computers; (x) telecommunications; (xi) technical products; (xii) housing/furniture; (xiii) industry and commerce; (xiv) finance and insurance; (xv) health; (xvi) humanitarian organizations; (xvii) energy; (xviii) media; (xix) other.

Hofstede's Cultural Model

Although a large number of models have attempted to explain cultures and their underlying values (e.g. Hampden-Turner and Fons Trompenaars, 1993; Kluckhohn and Strodtbeck, 1961; Milton Rokeach, 1973; Abraham Maslow, 1954; Edward T. Hall, 1981, 1990; Schwartz, 1992, 1994; GLOBE study, House et al., 2004; Hall 1976). Dutch anthropologist Geert Hofstede's model of national cultural differences derived from a study of IBM employees conducted between 1967 and 1973 in more than 50 countries is undoubtedly the most well-known. However, not without its limitations, this cultural framework has shaped marketers' thinking over many decades.[14]

1. Power Distance (PDI), the first cultural dimension identified in Hofstede's research, concerns the degree to which a culture accepts the fact that power is distributed unevenly in a society. Members of high power distance cultures are expected to show proper respect to their superiors. Low power distance cultures, on the other hand, are characterized by more participation in decision-making. Hofstede's classification shows Germany with a score of 35 to be the least accepting of power inequality. In contrast, India and France with respective scores of 77 and 68 rank higher in power distance. This means that hierarchy is a part of the business culture in these two countries.

2. Individualism (IDV), the second dimension, is indicative of cultures that put emphasis on individual achievement in contrast to the group. In contrast, collectivist cultures value loyalty to the group, distinguishing between in-groups and out-groups (for example, family and organization). In Hofstede's research, this cultural dimension was also shown to strongly correlate with power distance, which means that individualist cultures tend to have a preference for lower power distance. A notable exception is France—a relatively high power distance culture where status differences go hand-in-hand with an emphasis on individual rights. France, in fact, with a score of 71, has the highest IDV scores among the three countries. India, on the other hand, with a score of 48, ranks below the world average of 50. The Indian culture is generally very relationship and group-oriented and communication is often indirect in contrast to individualistic cultures where parties want to get to the point fast. Germany, with a score of 66, ranks somewhere in between. While collaboration is important in this country, people are also entitled to make their own decisions. The German language, in fact, is quite literal, with individual words having very precise meanings (for

[14] D. Luna and S. Forquer Gupta, "An Integrative Framework for Cross-Cultural Consumer Behavior", *International Marketing Review* 18 (2001): 377–86.

example, there are no fewer than eight words for "comfort", each reflecting a slightly different shade of meaning). Having been conditioned by their language, Germans are fairly formal and direct. On the job and in business dealings, they are known to be absolutely obsessed with facts and precision.

3. Uncertainty avoidance index (UAI), the third of Hofstede's value dimensions, describes the degree to which members of a society are willing to accept and deal with ambiguous situations. In societies with low uncertainty avoidance, on the one hand, there is an acceptance of situations, which favors risk-taking (for example, starting a new business venture). India, with a score of 40, has a medium tolerance for change and risk. Germany, on the other hand, with a score of 65, much above the world average (51), is seen to have a high aversion to risk-taking and uncertainty. As for France, with a score of 86, it has the highest uncertainty avoidance scores among the three countries.

4. Masculinity (MAS), the fourth dimension, deals with cultures that reflect a dominance of tough masculine values such as assertiveness, competition and material success. In contrast, feminine cultures focus on personal relationships. Compared to masculine cultures, firms in feminine cultures place a relatively stronger emphasis on overall employee well-being rather than bottom-line performance. An important aspect of this dimension is role differentiation. In masculine cultures, household work is generally less shared between spouses, and men also tend to make all major purchase decisions; Indian culture has medium scores for masculinity (56), somewhere between France (43) and Germany (66), which, with slightly higher than world average score, is considered to be a very masculine society.[15]

A fifth dimension identified by Hofstede and Bond a few years later was first termed as "Confucian dynamism" and then renamed "long-term orientatation" (LTO).[16] This dimension is associated with the

[15] Geert Hofstede, "Marketing and Culture", Working Paper 90-006, University of Limburg, Maastricht, the Netherlands, 1990.

[16] Source: Adapted from "Top Countries for Ad Expenditures for 2000", Zenith Media, *The Economist*.

way members exhibit a future-oriented perspective as opposed to a short-term point of view. India, in contrast to the West, is characterized primarily by long-term values such as planning, perseverance and setting up of long-term goals for long-term rewards. It has a high score of 61. This suggests that personal relationships based on mutual respect and trust and built over a period of time are viewed as crucial to conducting business in this country.

Although Hofstede's model is generally considered as the primary frame of reference for studying cultural differences across countries, there is nonetheless an important caveat to his analysis. An obvious weakness is that the data are relatively old despite the study's replications over the years. Societies in Asia are moving fast and the dimensions described are not set in stone. In other words, the differences between Western and Asian cultures are not black and white. Perhaps in the pre-Cold War period when the number of people emigrating around the world was relatively few, the breakdown of the East and West could apply. However, if we contemplate the way the world has changed since, we may safely conclude that a duality of cultures and societies no longer applies. Indeed, one of the underlying features of culture is precisely its evolving nature. Consequently, it would be too simplistic to label all Asian cultures as collectivist and Western cultures as individualistic. With economic liberalization, many Asian countries, in fact, have embraced a much more individualistic style of living. While it is not my intention to contest here the theories introduced by Edward T. Hall (1981), Hofstede et al. (1980), it needs to be pointed out nonetheless that some of these definitions may require re-examination in light of the cultural amalgamation that exists in today's world.

Quo Vadis?

This book raises several questions, the most important one being: Are we heading toward, what I have called, a "larger unity", at least in the cultural sense? Is this common only to open societies? Do open societies have a greater propensity to overcome prejudice and stereotyping? Culture, in my view, is very often the expression of frustrations with an uneven distribution of wealth, power and influence in a society and not its underlying cause. And by the development of a globalized culture, there are certain fundamental challenges. The broad conceptual framework of this book attempts to deal with some of these challenges, prejudice and stereotyping to name a few. I have placed special emphasis upon the arena of international economy and trade, which is the driving factor behind globalization. I have dwelt at some length on the cultural aspects of globalization, which is one of its fundamental components—so fundamental in fact that some thought the next Armageddon would be a "clash of civilizations". Perhaps the perceived Americanization of global culture will lead to opposition from those cultures that see globalization as Western inspired and a threat to their way of life. Yet the point I make here is that if indeed globalization is adding to the pressures that are said to be eroding the borders of national economies and fostering religious exclusivism, how does one justify the long-term trend toward regional and global integration and the survival of such supranational institutions as the EU, North Atlantic Treaty Organization (NATO) and the World Trade Organization (WTO)?

The WTO, of course, tried to establish a rules-based global trading system. In reality, however, it could not, despite its efforts, wholly overcome the lacerating differences between developed and developing countries. For sure, openness to trade did play an important part in lifting developing countries to higher levels of growth and welfare. In the main, however, the liberal global order was "liberal and rules-based" only in a small part of the world, the West. It is here today that following America's election of a new president, Donald Trump—who has made it clear that his policies will be guided primarily by national considerations—that populism and nationalism have once more emerged,[17] reflecting an apparent rejection of the Washington Consensus,[18] which put free markets, global free trade and investment at the heart of economic success. This rejection was not due only to the global financial and economic crisis

---

[17] The Trump government, in fact, had announced that it did not view the world as a global community but as an area for "competitive advantage."

[18] The Washington Consensus refers to the economic orthodoxy, which puts free markets and global free trade and investment as the guiding principle of economic success. In the post-1990s, there was often a conflation of free markets with liberal democracy as the proven recipe for successful nationhood.

of 2007–8, which widened financial grievances across the advanced industrial democracies, the original patrons and beneficiaries of the Order—it is equally a cultural rejection, a rejection of globalization that enriched corporate America, contributing to the creation of a global elite but not benefiting the average American worker. The backlash against slow economic growth has now taken the form of anti-immigration, nationalism and populism resulting in the stunning Brexit referendum, the ripples of which were also felt across other European countries—in Italy, Iceland, Spain, the Netherlands, Austria, Hungary and even core nations like France and Germany in what looks like an acknowledgement of the failures of the European Union, from out-of-control immigration to the coddling of radical Islamism.

In the contemporary world there appear, in fact, to be two compelling and seemingly contradictory forces at work. On the one hand, globalization is leading everywhere to the triumph of liberal, free market capitalism. The technological revolution spawned by it is bonding humanity much closer than ever before in the history of mankind. Through the virtual media, there are today vastly greater opportunities to directly experience and learn about other cultures and their ways of life. This has resulted in a growing appreciation of the very best that every country and culture has to offer. At the same time, paradoxically, this proximity is also leading to fear of loss of identity, which is now manifesting itself in rising intolerance of ideas, beliefs and even ways of life different from ours.

Behind all these developments lies the fact that globalization characterized by the mobility of people, capital and idea and accelerated by the rapid development of communications and technology has weakened traditional forms of authority everywhere, from Europe's social democracies to the despotic states of the Arab world. At the same time, it has also produced an array of unpredictable new international actors that have seized upon the sense of alienation and dashed expectations that define the political mood in many parts of the world today.

Do these trends, in particular the resurgence of ultra-right and xenophobic tendencies, suggest the failure of multiculturalism? The coming months and years, no doubt, will test that theory. However, rationally speaking, although it has become almost conventional wisdom to argue that the populist surge in the United States, Europe and elsewhere marks the beginning of the end of the contemporary era of globalization, circumstances today are so different that the analogy does not really hold up. What is clear, however, is that among the challenges we now face in this ever more interconnected world, there is one whose urgency stands out. Our national and international life must be reshaped so that the affluence of some no longer depends on or coexists with the poverty of others.

Where does India belong in this rapidly evolving landscape? India, as an integral part of a resurgent Asia, is and will remain an influential actor in the new World Order that is now emerging because of its demonstrated capabilities of an economic, regional and maritime player in its own right (see Chapters 10 and 11). At the same time, this cannot be the whole India story. I firmly believe, in the midst of all this churn, open and plural democracies like India—whose essence is encapsulated in the memorable words of the ancient Rig Vedas sloka—"Ekam sat vipra bahuda vadanti" ("Truth is one but sages call it by different names")—are far better equipped to deal with the new World Order that is emerging. Even as the world, deeply interconnected on the one hand, and deeply conflicted on the other, gropes for a solution to successfully manage the multiplicities that rapid technological change has forced on us, it is India, that must strive to lead through example. It is against this background that the book focuses on the possibility of increasing multiculturalism brought about by the latest phase of globalization as a driver of international trade.

PART I

1

What Is Culture?

Before attempting to evaluate the impact of culture on advertising and marketing per se, a by-product of globalization, let us first take a brief look at the definition of culture.

"Culture", as defined by Colette Guillaumin, is the entire social heritage of the human race—"the totality of the knowledge and practices, both intellectual and material of society... [it] embraces everything from food to dress, from household techniques to industrial techniques, from forms of politeness to mass media, from work rhythms to the learning of the familiar rules".[1] Or as the anthropologist Edward Taylor put it way back in 1871, "culture is that complex whole which includes knowledge, belief, art, morals, law, custom and other capabilities acquired by a man as a member of a society."[2] In other words, it is "everything that people have, think and do as members of their society."[3] More specifically, culture encompasses a system of values, norms and practices shared by a group of people which, when taken together, constitute a design for living.

---

[1] Colette Guillaumin, "Culture and Cultures", *Culture* 6, no. 1 (1971): 1.

[2] Source: Wikimedia Commons. From *Popular Science Monthly* 26 (1884), 145 (Public Domain).

[3] Gary Ferraro, *The Cultural Dimension of International Business*, 3rd ed. (Englewood Cliffs, NJ: Prentice Hall, 1997), 16.

Another popular definition of culture comes from the religious historian Bruce Lincoln who describes it "as the prime instrument through which groups mobilize themselves, construct their collective identity and effect their solidarity by excluding those whom they identify as outsiders."[4] Some other scholars, however, prefer a concept of culture that more readily accommodates hybridity and convergence instead of exclusion and difference. Sociologist, Jan Nederveen Pieterse, for example, defines culture as "behavior and beliefs that are learned and shared: learned so it is not—'instinctual'—and shared so it is not individual. Sharing refers to social sharing but there is no limitation as to the boundaries of this socially. No territorial or historical boundaries are implied as part of the definition."[5] This corresponds in part to Marshall McLuhan's theory of "the global village" introduced in his influential book, "Explorations in Communication'. The basic idea propounded here is that the ubiquity of the mass media, especially television, means that everybody in today's world is exposed to the same images almost simultaneously. In other words, it means that "even though most people remain rooted in a local or national culture and a local place, it is no longer possible for them to live in that place disconnected culturally from the world in which it is situated."[6] This, as the argument goes, has turned the whole world into a sort of "global village".

Initially, this shrinking of the world, as it were, was technology-driven—satellites, telecommunications, more and more efficient forms of travel, etc. However, the last three decades have seen the globalization of the world economy as never before—the world has indeed become one large marketplace. Moreover, in addition to the two aforementioned factors, crises, wars and catastrophes, both human and natural, have further accelerated huge migrations of population from one geographical location to another, thereby

[4] Bruce Lincoln, *Holy Terrors: Thinking About Religion after September 11* (Chicago: University of Chicago Press, 2003), 52, 56, 61.

[5] Nederveen Pietersee, *Globalisation and Culture: Global Melange*, 2nd edn (Langham MD: Rowman and Littlefield, 2009), 47–8.

[6] David Held, Anthony McGrew, David Goldblatt, and Jonathan Perraton, *Global Transformations: Politics, Economics and Culture* (Stanford: Stanford University Press, 1999), 369.

creating cross-cultural and religious pot-pourris as well as troubled and potentially volatile cross-cultural coexistence all over. To cite only a few examples: Hispanic, black and ethnic Asian groups in the US; similar groups in Europe and elsewhere: refugees in Kosovo, Bosnia, Serbia and so on.

Indeed as humanity races across the new millennium, an understanding and appreciation of different cultures has become a sine qua non of survival of humankind as we know it. This is because even though economic and political problems continue to loom large on the horizon, these cannot be segregated from the cultural dimension within which they operate. When applied to marketing, the point I want to emphasize is that there is no culture-free theory of marketing. When a promotional message is written, symbols recognizable and meaningful to the targeted market (the culture) must be used—or it is rejected. Understanding the subtleties of a multicultural and multinational business environment represents therefore one of the greatest challenges facing enterprises in the present era of globalization.

Having defined some of the broader cultural terms here, the following chapter will briefly examine their causal antecedents.

2

Prejudice and Stereotyping

Culture formation starts at the family level, is normally patriarchal in character and moves to group identity. Social interaction within the group strengthens this identity. Later, due to strengthening of group identity, there developed a differentiation of tasks and the need for leadership and order. This model expanded and over a period of time as the economic and social life became more complicated, we see the rudiments of a state appear, with its own set of beliefs and ideas, referred to loosely as its culture, better organized to maximize use of resources, wage war or defend its people from other states and cultures.

Anthropologically speaking, there is always a battle for domination. Group identity brings forward solidarity but can also lead to hostility with other groups. In the family, it is the father who ranks above all; in social life, it is the social class; at the State level, it is the ruling ideology or political class and at the international level, it is countries with the most economic and military clout. Over the centuries, the human desire to dominate one another has taken various forms of which religious conversion and economic empire-building were perhaps the most compelling. Religious differences, in particular, became ideologies or value systems through which a group of people could make themselves "right" and the others "wrong" thereby defining their own identity through their enemies, the non-believers or simply, the "Others". The concept of the "Other" is a recurring theme in modern thought (recall Jean Paul Sartre for example). Perception of the "Other", in fact, is not static. Culture is not simply a by-product of a family or confessional upbringing. It is deeply influenced by the dynamic of interacting with the "Other", as a result of which societal prejudices undergo changes[1]. Let us begin with a concrete example. A. Rose, an American historian, studied the reactions of white Americans to the Afro-American community over a period of time. Till the 1820s or thereabouts, as long as the Afro-American community meekly accepted its slave status and subjugation, they were seen to be "docile". With the first stirrings of disaffection and after the American Civil War of 1876, however, when slavery was abolished in the American South, the Afro-American community living there was seen to be no better than "animals", dangerous to the whites and, in particular, to their women[2].

Then there followed the history of the Jim Crowe laws, discrimination and segregation. It took the Civil Rights movement of the 1960s to place the Afro-American community in a more equal setting with its white counterpart.

Pretty much the same thing can be said about other communities. This can be illustrated by citing yet another survey carried out by B. Shrieke on the changing face of the Chinese community in the US.[3] The author points out that the Chinese, who went to work to build the US rail track, were initially viewed as—"hard-working", "docile" and "adaptable". But with the arrival of more Chinese to work at restaurants, laundries, Chinese medicine shops and other places, this attitude changed. Only a few years later, in 1867, they were perceived as "non-adaptable, secretive, filthy, servile, lying, vicious and possessing a criminal bent of mind." Likewise, many other migrants to the US such as the Japanese, Indians and Koreans

---

[1] "Cultural identities, unlike botanical species or animals, do not constitute any clearly delineated homogenous blocs. They are dynamic processes constantly traversed by the forces of assimilation and differenciation." Alex Mucchielli, *L'Identite* (Paris: Presses Universitaries de France, 1986), 33.

[2] Michaud Guy and Edmond Marc, "Vers une science des civilisations", *Editions complexes*, Bruxelles (1981), 135.

[3] Guy and Marc, "Vers une science des civilisations", 135.

were also similarly targeted at the turn of the 20th century by white workers who were afraid of cheap Asian labor.

And in our own times, Arabs were welcomed to the Detroit and Michigan areas to work in the booming automobile industry. After 9/11, however, there has been a veritable change in attitude. Likewise, when Indians first started migrating in the 1970s and 1980s, primarily to the US, they were usually engineers, doctors and academicians and well-respected although not quite integrated with the larger American community. But when these professionals were joined by others seeking better economic opportunities, they were considered to be part of the larger legal and illegal communities that flocked the West—and there was a corresponding change in attitude. Since then, there has been yet another shift, particularly for Indians and Chinese, first with the rise of the so-called knowledge industries and more recently because of the countries' growing power in the international system. A large number of the migrants have contributed to high-tech start-ups, for example, in the whole Silicon Valley phenomenon. Also, an increasing number have become venture capital bosses, bankers, managers of blue ribbon companies and so on. This, in turn, brings us to the factors that contribute, in some manner or other, to reinforcing negative prejudices: a downturn in the economy, for example. The conclusion here is that prejudice is dependent on a large number of factors; and when they are as close as possible to their hosts in terms of education, income, and living styles, immigrants are less prone to be seen as the threatening "other".

Having discussed prejudice, let us now look at another idea that is closely related to it—the stereotype. Stereotyping as cited by Enrico Fulchigoni[4] is a convenient way to explain prejudice. According to Samovar and Porter, stereotypes are "the perceptions and beliefs we hold about groups or individuals based on our previously formed opinions and attributes."[5] As an international branding expert, Wally Olins explains: "Most people know very little about nations other than their own. Where they know anything at all, their attitudes are

---

[4] Fulchigoni Enrico, *La civilisation de l'image* (Paris: Payot, 1972), 174.
[5] L.A. Samovar and R.E. Porter, *Communication between Cultures: A Reader*, 8th edn (Belmont, CA: Wadsworth, 1991), 280.

formed from myth, rumor and anecdote. These almost always lean towards grotesque caricature, which can be bruising to trade, tourism and inward investment."[6] The media often propagates such stereotypes. To take a few broad examples, the British are said to be conservative; the Germans lacking in humor; the French individualistic and Indians mystics with all that this conjures: poverty, ignorance and so on. What is being implied? Does it mean the British cannot progress? Or the French do not share? The view of Indians, clearly, is contradicted by India's contribution to the exact sciences, particularly in the field of mathematics.

Worse, stereotyping is often used to do away with the "Other." If the native Indians had to be done away with, they had to be first demonized. If the Africans had to be enslaved, they had to be first shown to be inferior. Stereotyping essentially promotes negative imagery to demean, so that what is done becomes excusable. These predatory impulses have resulted not only in genocide but also in ethnocide. The latter implies less physical elimination, instead the existing culture is sought to be undermined, the basis for foisting the theme of the "white man's burden".

Prejudice and stereotyping often get worse during hard economic times. After World War II, when labor was needed in Europe and Britain, they often turned to their erstwhile colonies. A large number of Pakistanis were imported into England to work in the textile mills. Algerians and Moroccans went to France; Germany had its share of Turkish "guest workers". There already existed, of course, a steady stream of migrants to the US. However, for countries such as France and England that had huge overseas empires, decolonization denied them resources from their erstwhile territorial holdings and when their economies saw a downturn, the attitudes toward their recent immigrants also hardened. The obvious conclusion here is that as long as migrant workers are needed—for example, after World War II, when so many young men and women were killed in Europe, and the economy was growing—multicultural relations are positive. But when the economy goes south, migrant workers are seen as belonging to the "Other" community, threatening the livelihood and even their hosts' way of life.

---

[6] Wally Olins, *On Brand* (London: Thames & Hudson Ltd, 2003), 150.

This is equally apparent in today's phase of globalization with what some scholars have described as the increasing "xenophobic culture of globalization". From the institutionalized racism of colonial times when racial beliefs—even eugenics—were not considered wrong, to the recent times where the effects of neo-Nazism are still felt;[7] what is most remarkable is the degree to which the issues raised over a hundred years ago are relevant even today. In this age of globalization, multiculturalism and religious resurgence, the same issues confront us albeit in new forms in our post-Cold War and post-9/11 world— for example, ethnic cleansing in the Balkans; genocide in Rwanda, and the resurgence of the far-right, anti-immigrant and neo-Nazi groups in Europe in the early 1990s followed a decade later by the 9/11 attacks, the global financial meltdown and the rise of ISIS. Yet, the point to consider is that even though cultures and religions show few signs of shedding some of their deepest differences and preju- dices, such attitudes are perhaps less acceptable today than even one hundred years ago.

In other words, modern States have made efforts to integrate immigrants into host societies implying a whole new way of dealing and interacting with them. European countries follow a policy of what they term multiculturalism, that is, immigrants are allowed to live within their own cultures as long as they do not assault the sensi- bility of the broader society they live in. This seems to have worked, at least for a while, but has often acted as a barrier to full integration. They continued to be seen as the "Others." This is not to suggest, for one moment, that this is a one-sided fault. Many immigrants due to their own cultural beliefs and practices, in fact, resisted integra- tion. In the US, the theory of the "melting pot" has become the stereotyped description by which the migrants have been assimilated into the larger American society. For the most part, the "melting" has taken place, particularly for those immigrants that came from Europe despite initial hesitation or bumps on the road if you will. It is significant, however, that certain communities such as the Afro- Americans who had been living in the country for two hundred years

---

[7] As explored in detail by Edward Said, in his books such as *Orientalism* (New York: Vintage Books, 1979) and *Culture & Imperialism* (New York: Vintage Books, 1993).

did not join the mainstream of American life until after the Civil Rights movement of the 1960s. We will see what happens in the future when an increasing number of immigrants start coming from more and more varied cultures.

While the relatively recent attempt of the "wider society"—in Western countries—to accept this onslaught of diversity has been called multiculturalism, in India the corresponding attempt goes under the name of secularism. It is important to note here that secularism in the European and Indian contexts has different connotations, the technicalities of which are beyond the purview of this book. Broadly though, secularism in India refers to the equal treatment of all religions by the State whereas in Europe, it is the separation of church and State. Sunil Khilnani compares the challenges that faced the fathers of Indian democracy with the simpler experiences of most other nations in the following words: "There were few models from either European or any other history that could be used to help focus India's assorted diversities into a political structure founded upon a democratic principle. The multiplicity of cultural and political voices in the society demanded recognition. No attempt was made to impose a single or uniform 'Indian' identity upon the new Indian nation."[8] In sum, India, as its first Premier, Pandit Jawaharlal Nehru, envisioned it "was a society neither of liberal individuals nor of exclusive communities or nationalities but of interconnected differences."[9]

Unity in Diversity

Indeed India, with its many religions, races, languages and political persuasions, has millennia of experience in radically different cultures living together. India was incessantly invaded by foreign powers and subjected to foreign rule for almost a thousand years. The outcome was the engendering of a broad and identifiable culture, which has been described variously. India's situation, in my view, is perhaps best described by Sunil Khilnani in his book, *The Idea of India*,[10] where

[8] Sunil Khilnani, *The Idea of India* (New Delhi: Penguin Books, 1998, 2004), 171–2.

[9] Khilnani, *The Idea of India*, 171–2.

[10] Khilnani, *The Idea of India*.

he suggests that we are like a "bowl of salad" where every ingredient is separate but distinctive and yet all contribute to its enriching. That also explains, in part, Pandit Nehru's famous observation of India's "Unity in Diversity". Interestingly, this is also the motto of the EU, a complex, heteregenous entity of linguistically, ethnically and culturally diverse states that came into existence on March 25, 1957.

In the Indian context, the dream of "an international unification of the separate existence of the peoples, a 'unity in diversity' that would draw them together" even while "preserving and securing their national life" was echoed more than a century ago, by Sri Aurobindo, the Indian nationalist leader turned philosopher and mystic.[11] In his major work of political thought, *The Ideal of Human Unity*.[12] Stressing commonalities as much as diversity he said:

> At present, the first great need of the psychological life of humanity is the growth towards a greater unity, but its need is that of a living unity not in the externals of civilization, in dress, manners, habits of life, details of political, social and economic order, not a uniformity ... but a free development everywhere with a constant friendly interchange, a close understanding, a feeling of our common humanity, its great common ideals and the truths towards which it is driving and a certain unity and correlation of effort in the united human advance.[13]

Let us recall Huntington's pithy formula: "In a multicivilisational world, the constructive course is to renounce universalism, accept diversity and seek commonalities".[14] We might call this convergent pluralism or unity in diversity that does not reject the notion that our common aspirations are greater than our varying cultural or ethnic aspirations. By acknowledging convergence and

---

[11] Sri Aurobindo, *Autobiographical Notes and Other Writings of Historical Interest* (Pondicherry: Sri Aurobindo Ashram, 2006), 475.

[12] The quoted passages occur in a chapter first published in March 1918. Sri Aurobindo, *The Ideal of Human Unity* (Pondicherry: Sri Aurobindo Ashram, 1998), 273.

[13] Aurobindo, *The Ideal of Human Unity.*

[14] Samuel P. Huntington, *The Clash of Civilizations and the Remaking of World Order* (New York: Touchstone, 1997), 318.

commonalities, it corrects the conservative tendency of pluralism to privilege the status quo of cultural differences. This is also one of the reasons why multiculturalism as a national policy after a period of enthusiastic experimentation has provoked a backlash in most of the countries where it has been tried. As British sociologist, Ali Rattani argues: "The idea of multiculturalism has succumbed too easily to an interpretation of ethnic cultures as having strictly definable boundaries, having unchanging essential components and lacking quite fundamental internal dissent." He and other scholars and activists now advocate moving on to what they term as "interculturalism" incorporating "a conception of connectedness, interaction and interweaving between the beliefs, practices and lifestyles of different (not separate) ethnic groups as part of national culture that are in constant flux."[15]

In the European context, in keeping with this trend in thinking, the British-Indian political philosopher Bhikhu Parekh advocates "a transformation and open-minded dialogue" among people of different cultures and religions as opposed to "a narrow and static view of multiculturalism" leading to "a compartmentalized social and cultural universe."[16]

This acceptance of diversity has become even more crucial in the age of globalization where we need to deal with a multitude of cultures. Prejudice and stereotyping are, in the end, essentially subjective. Fostering a global culture is to move progressively toward a global consciousness. This has happened repeatedly at the national level—I keep repeating as an example, the case of India's unity in diversity. This leads us to hope that even as we solve some of the contentious political issues, for example, the advent of a system of values, which would be recognized, the first stage of a globalized culture would come about easier. This could of course, and as predicted by Samuel Huntington, multiply and magnify cultural conflicts by providing "a basis for identity and commitment that transcends national boundaries and unites civilizations."[17] Yet, a greater unification of

---

[15] Ali Rattani, *Multiculturalism: A Very Short Introduction* (New York: Oxford University Press, 2011), 152.

[16] Bhikhu Parekh, *European Liberalism and the Muslim Question* (Amsterdam: Amsterdam University Press, 2008).

[17] Huntington, *The Clash of Civilizations*, 6.

humanity—what Sri Aurobindo describes as "a sound and harmonious world—with cultural system"—based on the unity of the human race founded on free groupings in consonance affinities,"[18] appears, against all odds, to have begun.

Sri Aurobindo's ideas, in this instance, are surprisingly similar to Huntington's in that he also foresaw a "civilization-based world order"[19] comprising "a European grouping, an Asiatic grouping, an American grouping, with two or three sub-groups in America, Latin and English-speaking, three in Asia, the Mongolian, Indian and West-Asian with the Moslem North Africa perhaps as a natural annexe to the third of these."[20] However, he was less inclined than Huntington to treat religions as intrinsically antagonistic and oppositional. Although he admitted that under certain circumstances, there could be a danger of "huge continental clashes,"[21] he was, nonetheless, less preoccupied with the risk of intercivilizational conflict and more with regional groupings emerging as a possible step toward realizing a diversified human unity. This does not mean that global diversity will vanish. Indeed it might even grow more with the resurgence of long-dominated cultures and societies, especially in Asia. At the same time, this fundamental sense of human unity will likely also become more compelling under the pressure of more and more human interactions. Though the UN, in this instance, was perhaps only an "imperfect initiative" the momentum unleashed by it leads us nonetheless to believe that "if the experience of history can be taken as a guide, it must inevitably increase until it conquers."

[18] Aurobindo, *Ideal of Human Unity*, 162, 243.
[19] Huntington, *The Clash of Civilisations*, 20.
[20] Aurobindo, *The Ideal of Human Unity*, 320.
[21] Aurobindo, *Autobiographical Notes and Other Writings of Historical Interest*, 475.

3

Toward Larger Unities

I have dwelt at some length here on the cultural aspects of globalization because it is one of its fundamental components. So fundamental, in fact, that the American writer, Samuel Huntington, thought the next Armageddon would be a *Clash of Civilizations*. The book admittedly paints a slightly depressing picture only to move forward to suggest that in a globalized world characterized by a growing rapprochement between nations and people, former prejudices and stereotyping, resulting from smaller unities, as I have termed them, are now giving way in the face of larger unities.

Let me explain further. Historically, we have moved along the path leading from tribes to kingdoms to empires and, finally, to the nation state. Initially, religion, empire and trade routes—for example, the Silk route and the Spice route, which enabled the exchange of goods and ideas between far-flung regions of Asia, Europe and sub-Saharan Africa over a millennium—brought people together. These were the very first elements of globalization. Arab traders brought Islam to the Indian subcontinent and Southeast Asia. India's association with British colonial rule gave us the English language, beginnings of industrialization and the modern institutions that govern India today. As long as everybody gained, people learned to live together despite differences.

But although trade, in the sense of exchange of goods and services between people has a long history, international trade, that is, the exchange of goods and services between nations emerged only with the rise of the modern nation State. Economically speaking, the integration of world markets became possible only with the advent of the telegraph in the second half of the nineteenth century. As Paul Hirst and Grahame Thompson point out: "If the theorists of globalization mean that we have an economy in which each part of the world is linked by markets sharing close to real-time information, then that began not in the 1970s but in the 1870s."[1] In fact, according to these scholars, in terms of certain factors such as the openness of national economies to trade and the scale of migration, between 1890 and 1914, during the latter part of what is known as the belle époque (or in America, the Gilded Age), trade and investment flows were higher and borders more open with levels of transnational migration higher than it is today. Thus as per the authors, the globalization thesis is overstated and the processes described by it, are not unprecedented.

According to yet other scholars, there, in fact, was a pre-modern phase of globalization. Indeed even long before Europe emerged from the Dark Ages, the human race was being slowly drawn together through exchanges that were not dominated by any one civilization. Beginning over 5,000 years ago, this phase encompasses most of history as a process of slowly and unevenly growing interconnectedness. This incipient "world system" stretched from Europe to China. It did not include the Americas and Australia and therefore was not a "global system" as sociologist Janet Abu-Lughod explains, but "it represented a substantially larger system than the world had previously known."[2] In its cultural aspect, this included peaceful transmissions such as the spread of Buddhism from India to China in the first millennium CE, which suggest that interactions among people of different cultures need not always be to the advantage of some and to the detriment of others. In the case of Southeast Asia,

[1] Paul Hirst and Thompson Grahame, "Globalization—A Necessary Myth", in *The Global Transformation Reader: An Introduction to the Globalisation Debate*, eds David Held and Anthony McGrew (Cambridge Polity Press, 2003), 101.

[2] Janet Abu-Lughod, *Before European Hegemony: The World System AD 1250–1350* (New York: Oxford University Press, 1989), 353.

for example, we still see the deep imprint of the long-standing and close interaction that took place with India for centuries, until these links were severed by the rise of European colonialism. Indian traders were as familiar a sight in ancient Greece and Rome as they were in Southeast Asia and China. This pre-modern phase of globalization is important to understand because its legacy is our multicultural world. Its relevance to us is that "it contained no single hegemonic power", so it "provides an important contrast to the world system that grew out of it: the one Europe reshaped to its own ends and dominated for so long."[3]

Whatever the theory of globalization, a decisive phase, in the long march of history, was undoubtedly the period of European expansion, beginning in the fifteenth century. Globalization, in so far as it is a product of Western expansion began, in fact, with Europeans finding sea routes to bypass the Arabs and lay their own hands on the riches of the East. In 1492 Christopher Columbus stumbled upon the "New World", with disastrous consequences for the indigenous populations of the Western Hemisphere. For about four hundred years, as Huntington puts it, and especially during the latter half of that period—"Western nations... conquered, colonized or decisively influenced every other civilization."[4] Yet the point I want to make here is that the post-modern phase of globalization may be evolving today, albeit in a different manner, toward a multicultural equilibrium such as the one that preceded the rise of the West.

Imperialism to Regional Integration

Clyde Prestowitz, the economist, distinguishes three waves or phases of globalization: (i) the European expansion and imperialism from around 1415–1914, which collapsed in the period of the two world wars and the Great Depression; (ii) a wave of American-led globalization from 1947 to 2000; and a third wave just begun, which he thinks is likely to shift wealth back to Asia. He sums up the situation at the outset of the first wave: "In 1415, China and the area we now call India produced about 75 percent of the global GDP. America was

[3] Abu-Lughod, *Before European Hegemony*, 4, 6.
[4] Samuel P. Huntington, *The Clash of Civilizations and the Remaking of World Order* (New York: Touchstone, 1997), 21.

still undiscovered and the countries of Europe were insignificant and backward. They were aware of the wealth of the East only because Arabs who controlled the overland trade routes deigned from time to time to let a few scraps fall from the table to the Western "infidel dogs."[5] In the five centuries after 1415, all this, however, was to be reversed with a vengeance.

The mid to late nineteenth century witnessed the consolidation of European imperial power in Asia and the Middle East, the subjugation of India and China, the colonization of Africa, the forced end to Japanese isolationism and the extension of the US power into Latin America and the Pacific. Indeed by the dawn of the twentieth century, the whole world had been reconfigured into a "single net of economic and strategic relations."[6] An integral aspect of this phenomenon that relates most directly to our topic is cultural globalization. The colonial powers—Britain and other European States—were among the most powerful agents of globalization of culture. In fact, many scholars point to sixteenth-century Europe as the original source of globalization, arguing that after all, Europeans established worldwide trade connections bringing their culture to different regions and peoples. J. Tomlinson, for instance, points out that the idea of "imperialism" contains the notions of a purposeful project with the intentions of spreading a social system from one center of power across the globe.[7] Yet, for all the exploitation and violence that accompanied the impact of the modern West upon the rest of the world, few would wish to undo the progressive changes that also occurred during the same period.

Another important fact is that the global flow of people, goods, and ideas was not just from the West to the East. Compared to other great Asian civilizations such as Ming China, the Ottoman Empire and the Moghuls, Europe, in fact, had no significant advantages in culture, mathematics, engineering and navigational technologies. Indeed, every one of the "high tech" fields of knowledge

---

[5] Clyde Prestowitz, *Three Billion New Capitalists: The Great Shift of Wealth and Power to the East* (New York: Basic Books, 2005), 8.

[6] A. Watson, *The Evolution of International Society* (London: Routledge, 1992), 265.

[7] J. Tomlinson, *Cultural Imperialism: A Critical Introduction* (Baltimore: John Hopkins University Press, 1991), 175.

in the world a millennium ago such as paper, printing, gunpowder, wheelbarrow, clock, kite and magnetic compass, was already well established in China and, at the same time, practically unknown elsewhere. It was globalization that spread them across the world including to Europe. Similarly, the decimal system, which emerged and became well entrenched in India between the second and the sixth centuries[8] and was also used extensively soon thereafter by Arab mathematicians, reached Europe mainly in the last quarter of the tenth century. Thus, some knowledge of Indian science and mathematics reached medieval Europe through the Muslims who also passed on the legacy of Greek science and made contributions of their own. But then, starting around 1500 CE, this whole scheme of things was dramatically overturned.

What caused the civilizational shift from the East to the West? According to Paul Kennedy, Professor of History at Yale University:

> Europe's greatest advantage was that it had fewer disadvantages than other civilizations... It was a combination of economic laissez-faire, political and military pluralism and intellectual liberty, which had been in constant interaction to produce the European Miracle. This mix of ingredients did not exist in Ming China or in the Muslim Empires of the Middle East and Asia. As a result, these societies seemed to stand still while Europe advanced.[9]

It is, however, the second half of the twentieth century and World War II in particular, that gave globalization a special impetus in terms of linkages, institutions and the spread of a global culture. Economic necessity after the horrendous loss of human lives in the two Wars also meant the meeting of alien cultures. Two major World Wars and hundreds of

---

[8] Although the earth's circumference was estimated by Erathosthenes of Alexandria in the third century BCE, it was the Indian mathematician and astronomer Aryabhata, who arrived at a more accurate calculation in the fifth century CE. Works by Aryabhata and other Indian scientists in the fifth century CE were later translated into Arabic and from Arabic into Latin.

[9] Paul Kennedy, *The Rise and Fall of the Great Powers—Economic Change and Military Conflict from 1500 to 2000* (London: Fondone Press, 1989).

smaller wars challenged thinkers to develop international institutions to prevent in the memorable sentence in the Preamble to the UN: "The Scourge of War." This was the start to supranational institutions.

In the second half of the twentieth century, we see the advent of such supranational institutions as the erstwhile League of Nations and now the UN, GATT and its successor, the WTO, Bretton Woods Institutions, the European Community, MERCOSUR, NAFTA, Asia-Pacific Economic Cooperation (APEC), ASEAN and our very own SAARC indicate a desire for greater cooperation and understanding among nations and peoples even if only for better economic gains. As Jean Monnet, one of the main architects of European Unity, observed, "Nothing is possible without men; nothing is lasting without institutions." And indeed, institutions have been at the heart of the EU since its inception. Led from the front by Robert Schumann of France and Konrad Adenauer of Germany, a war-devastated Europe came together on May 9, 1950 to pool its iron and steel resources as the first step toward a larger unity. The initial motivation rooted in the grim backdrop of the War, European leaders knew that their salvation lay on the path of economic integration. The other profound consequence of World War II was the transformation in the structure of world power. It marked the end of Europe's global hegemony and established the US and the Soviet Union as the two new global superpowers. As K. Waltz observes, "With only two powers capable of acting on a world scale, anything that happens anywhere is potentially of concern to both of them."[10] However, with the ever-hanging threat of the entire planet being wiped out as a result of a nuclear confrontation between the two superpowers, the idea of humanity as a "single global community" took root. Ironically and as observed by Sri Aurobindo, an "arrangement of the world that was worked out by economic forces, by political diplomacies, treaties and purchases and by military violence without regard to any moral principle, helped nonetheless at much cost of bloodshed, suffering, cruelty, oppression and revolt, to bring humanity more together."[11]

[10] K. Waltz, *The Theory of International Politics* (New York: Addison-Wesley, 1979), 171.

[11] Sri Aurobindo, *The Ideal of Human Unity* (Pondicherry: Sri Aurobindo Ashram, 1998), 158.

The European Union

Commonly regarded as the most successful model of regional integration, the EU or the European Economic Community as it was formerly known is best defined as a network of states involving the pooling of sovereignty.[12] It is a culmination of sorts of the dream envisaged, in 1849 by the French poet and novelist, Victor Hugo when he wrote:

> A day will come when all the nations of this continent, without losing their distinct qualities or their glorious individuality, will fuse together in a higher unity and form the European brotherhood. A day will come when the only battlefield will be the marketplace for competing ideas. A day will come when bullets and bombs will be replaced by votes.[13]

Needless to add, the EU has come a long way since its inception on March 25, 1957. Its powers, as we know, were gained by the "willing surrender" of aspects of sovereignty by individual member States—a "surrender" which helped strengthen European nation States in the face of the dominance of the US in the first three decades after World War II and the rise of the economic challenge of Asia Pacific.[14] The fact that almost all the States of Central and Eastern Europe that had earlier formed the Soviet Sphere of influence wanted to join the EU after the political change of 1989/90 is no doubt a significant pointer to the latter's success as a model of economic and regional integration.

However, very few people including Europeans themselves had little hope for the success of the European Community or the European Common Market as it was commonly called at the time of its inception. This was because of the problems related to integration and the level of national sovereignty that would have to be conceded to the community. After all, not only 1,000 years of economic separation had to be overcome, the European Common Market was also very uncommon, there were language differences, individual national

[12] R.O. Keohane and S. Hoffmann (eds), *The New European Community* (Oxford: Westview Press, 1990).

[13] Victor Hugo, *Opening Address to the Paris Peace Congress 1849 (21 August 1849)*, www. Ellopos net/politics/eu/hugo.html.

[14] W. Wallace, "Rescue or Retreat? The Nation State in Western Europe", *Political Studies* (1994): 52–75.

interests, political differences and centuries-old restrictions designed to protect local national markets. Germany, for example, protected its beer market from the rest of Europe with a purity law requiring beer sold in Germany to be brewed only from water, hops, malt and yeast. Italy protected its pasta market by requiring that pasta be made only from durum wheat. Skeptics, doubtful of whether such cultural, legal and social differences could ever be overcome, held little hope for a unified Europe. Their skepticism, however, proved wrong (incidentally, the European Court of Justice struck down both the beer and pasta regulations as trade violations).

Today, however, against the backdrop of one of the most serious financial challenges the EU has ever faced, many more appear to be gravitating toward the tribal notions of identity rather than the lofty principles of integration espoused in the hopeful period begun three decades ago with the fall of the Berlin Wall, and the dissolution of the Soviet Union. This has now led to ultra-right and xenophobic sentiments across the continent in what looks like an acknowledgment of the failures of the European Project. In the stunning Brexit referendum, British voters, on June 23, 2016, opted to leave the EU. In Germany, a poll found that 42 percent of Germans wanted a referendum on the EU membership.[15] In France, the unprecedented support extended to right-wing ideology appeared for a while to suggest that many voters there also wanted Europe to be a mosaic of States instead of an integrated commonwealth with a shared currency and open borders.[16] People want, in short, for Europe, to look more like it did before the EU's grand experiment; never mind that this experiment was designed to prevent the European nations from engaging in an endless cycle of wars. The weakening of US engagment with Europe, which Trump has already embarked upon, may only further reinforce these trends making it doubtful whether a cohesive Europe, would in the foreseeable future, play the role of an influential international actor, either in its own right or as part of a powerful trans-Atlantic partnership. For its supporters, however, the EU remains, despite its current challenges, a fascinating and avant-garde

---

[15] *Time*, December 19, 2016, p. 52.

[16] The fact that Le Pen did as well as she did despite not winning the elections suggests that the movement could revive.

example of multicultural integration in international relations that other countries and governments might also wish to emulate in order to make their own world more safe and prosperous. This view is reinforced by the fact that even though since 1945, there has always been at least one war somewhere in the world and one cannot therefore really speak of world peace, there has not been another World War. This has contributed to a faster growth of the international economy. The end of the Cold War has added to it.

Compared to the European instance, many other regions of the world, sadly, have not felt the need to fully incorporate rational economic arguments in their decision-making processes to push bilateral relations as cornerstones for regional cooperation. In East Asia, for example, there can be no integration without genuine reconciliation between Japan and China and China and Korea. The East Asia experience is replicated elsewhere with unresolved problems and deep suspicions, between, for example, Brazil and Argentina. The problems exist also in West Asia, and the Gulf, in several parts of Africa and in our very own subcontinental neighborhood where the upsurge of ethnic and religous conflict has become the single-most dominant political phenomenon of post-independent and post-Cold War South Asia. In this case, the departure of colonial rule from the Indian subcontinent and the traumatic events of two partitions (British-India into India and Pakistan in 1947 and the breakup of East from West Pakistan leading to the birth of Bangladesh in 1971) have only resulted in enduring conflicts between the two protagonists, that is to say, India and Pakistan, and a strong political unwillingness regarding greater regional cooperation. Subsequently, the developing regional political complex in South Asia that is the South Asian Association of Regional Cooperation (SAARC) grouping some of the poorest countries in the world, remains, despite its potential, the world's least economically integrated region as per the projections of the World Bank (Chapter 12 deals with this topic in more detail).

The Rise of the Multinational

The European model, as we know, soon expanded to other parts of the world. ASEAN, for instance, was created in 1967. Inaugurated in 1971, the South Pacific Forum (SPF) has since grown in strength as a regional organization in the Southwest Pacific-Oceania region. In the Middle East, the Gulf Cooperation Council (GCC) was created in 1981. In Latin America, several regional cooperation initiatives emerged including the MERCOSUR in 1991. In 1995, the Group of Three (G-3)—Colombia, Mexico and Venezuela—FTA was established. Trade negotiation between the USA, Canada and Mexico resulted in November 1993 in the NAFTA), creating from January 1, 1994 a free trade market of 360 million consumers. In South Asia, the organization to join the list of cooperative efforts among developing countries was the SAARC in 1985.[17]

The implications of this pro-market philosophical shift were so far-reaching that in an article published in *Forbes* magazine in 1998, international management expert, Peter Drucker, declared obsolete one of his core assumptions: "that national boundaries define the ecology of enterprise and management." He defined instead a new reality: "Management and national boundaries are no longer congruent. The scope of management can no longer be politically defined. National boundaries will continue to be important but as restraints on the practice of management not in defining the practice."[18] Indeed, in the case of multinationals, it is already passé.

Multinationals per se are of course not a new phenomenon. Fiat, General Motors (GM) and others were already multinational entities in the nineteenth century. What is new is their stunning growth. In the late 1960s, for example, there were only about 7,000 MNCs whereas in 1992, there were over 37,000 of them and they were responsible for 5.8 trillion dollars worth of sales—more than the value of all the world's trade exports put together.[19] Many transnational companies now effectively earn more than half

---

[17] A grouping of seven South Asian Countries, India, Bangladesh, Nepal, Bhutan, Sri Lanka, Pakistan, Maldives plus Afghanistan for trade ties and regional integration.

[18] Peter Drucker cited in Thomas D. Zweifel, *Managing the Global High Performance Team* (New York: Swiss Consulting Group Inc, 2012).

[19] *Newsweek*, June 26, 1995, 35, cited in Caroline Thomas, *Melvyn Reader, Development and Inequalities: Issues in World Politics* (London: Palgrave, 1997).

of their revenues outside of their own country. The "Japanese" Toyota, for example, is one of the larger employers in the US. It produces cars with American workers, American management and American parts. Should Toyota still be viewed as a Japanese firm? The American GM produces 40 percent of its cars beyond American shores. The company is as multinational as each of its cars. Whether GM is still an American firm is doubtful.[20] Similarly, about 75 percent of Coca Cola's operating income and two-thirds of operating revenue are generated outside of North America.[21] Foreign sales also account for more than 50 percent of the annual revenue of companies such as Hewlett Packard, IBM, Johnson and Johnson, Mobil, Motorola and Procter and Gamble.[22] The US companies that wish to achieve maximum growth potential must go "global" because 75 percent of the world market potential is outside of their home country.

Conversely, non-US companies such as Nestle, Lever, and Shell Oil earn a significant percentage of their revenues in the US. Even though the dollar value of the home market for Japanese companies is the second largest in the world (after the US), the market outside Japan is 85 percent of the world potential for many large Japanese companies such as Nissan and others. Similarly, for some of the world's biggest European firms, the competition is no longer just within the Community. Germany is the largest single country market in Europe but 94 percent of its world market potential is outside of the country.[23] The German SAP, for example, founded in 1972 is the world's largest business software company and the third largest software supplier overall. The company employs 52,000 people and serves more than 76,000 customers in over

---

[20] Benjamin Barber, *Jihad vs Mc World: How Globalism and Tribalism Are Reshaping the World* (New York: Ballantine Books, 1995), 30.

[21] Branislav Djorjevic, "The Importance of Global Marketing", *MEST Journal* 2, no. 1 (2014): 116–24.

[22] Alan M. Rugman, "Viewpoint: The Myth of Global Strategy", *International Marketing Review* 18, no. 6 (2001): 583–8.

[23] Warren J. Keegan, *Global Marketing Management*, 7th edn (India: Dorling Kindersley, 2002), 34.

120 countries.[24] Yet another case in point is India's software giant, Wipro Technologies, which derives more than 80 percent of its revenues from non-Indian customers.[25] Indeed, the proliferation of international organizations and supranational entities in recent years has led to the belief that the days of the nation State may well be numbered.

Yet, paradoxically, even as the primordiality of the nation State is increasingly being questioned by regional integration (from MERCOSUR in Latin America to NAFTA in North America to SAARC in South Asia and most importantly, the EU), the urge to create nations remains strong. This is evidenced by the fact that there are more nations in the world now than ever before. At the same time, the traditional perception of the nation State, as we shall see (Chapter 5), is now challenged with the advent of globalization.

[24] Barry Silverstein, "German Engineering Drives Global Brand Success", March 8, 2012, www.barrysilverstein.com/articles/brandchannel.pdf.

[25] Tobias C. Hochska and John Levingston, "Western Asian Strateigies", *Mc Kinsey Quarterly*, 2002.

4

What Is Globalization?

The Cold War, lasting roughly from 1945 to 1989, which fractured the world both physically and ideologically was replaced at the end of the twentieth century by another system: the current era of globalization that we are now in and which soon became the dominant international system.

Defined as "the crystallization of the entire world as a single place,"[1] the idea of "globalization" suggests interconnection and interdependency of all global areas as a result of economic and cultural practices, which do not, of themselves, aim at global integration but which nonetheless produce it.[2] Summarizing the different views about globalization among contemporary theorists, Held says that, first, globalization is characterized by homogenization of economy and culture. According to this school of thought, the modern trend of world integration is equated with the expansion of "Cultural Imperialism" on a broader scale where the world is increasingly becoming homogenized and Westernized, whereas others believe that the

[1] Roland Robertson, "Globalization and Societal Modernization: A Note of Japan and Japanese Religion: Sociological Analysis", in *Global Marketing and Advertising: Understanding Cultural Paradoxes*, 3rd edn, ed. Marieke de Mooj (California: Sage Publications, 2010), 6.

[2] J. Tomlinson, *Cultural Imperialism: A Critical Introduction* (Baltimore: Johns Hopkins University Press, 1991), 175.

impact of globalization is mixed. Second, there is significant increase in connectedness and sharing of cultures.[3]

Viewed in this way, globalization is the emergence of a networked world dominated by spectacular advances in ICT. This also corresponds to Anthony Giddens' definition of globalization as "the intensification of worldwide social relations, which link distant localities in such a way that local happenings are shaped by events occurring many miles away and vice versa."[4] Yet another well-known writer on globalization, Arjun Appadurai, argues that what is important in this context is what people imagine.[5] In other words, it is not so much the physical geography of their current location that is important but the geography that they construct and hold onto in their minds. In his view, the country and culture—the images, sounds, practices and languages that connect people living in different parts of the world—create a much stronger impact than mere physical geography.

Let us turn to the other formulation of globalization, that is, globalization as free market economics. This can be summed up in Friedman's words, as

> the inexorable integration of markets, nation-states and technologies to a degree never witnessed before, in a way that is enabling individuals, corporations, and nation states to reach around the world farther, faster, deeper and cheaper than ever before—the spread of free-market capitalism to virtually every country of the world.[6]

This neo-liberal view of globalization stresses the inclusive nature of an economic ideology that defines us all, whether we like it or not, as consumers. As Benjamin Barber observes in his book *Jihad vs McWorld*: "A consumer is a consumer is a consumer."[7] The

[3] D. Held (eds), *A Globalizing World: Culture, Economics, Politics* (London: Routledge, 2000), 18.

[4] Anthony Giddens, *The Consequences of Modernity* (Cambridge: Polity Press, 1990), 64.

[5] Arjun Appadurai, *Modernity at Large: Cultural Dimensions of Modernity* (London and Minnespolis: University of Minnesota Press, 1996).

[6] Lawrence M. Friedman, *The Horizontal Society* (New Haven: Yale University Press, 1999).

[7] Benjamin R. Barber, *Jihad Vs McWorld: Terrorism's Challenge to Democracy* (London: Corgi Books, 2003), 23.

cultural concomitant of this ideology, often characterized as the Americanization of the world, is equally inclusive since it is perceived to bring about, to a limited extent and in relatively superficial ways, the homogenization of humanity. The two above-delineated definitions of globalization are essentially complementary processes, although differing in their points of emphasis; one underpins the communicative aspect and the other, the economic dimension. But while the economic aspect of globalization has possibly attracted the most attention, some scholars have also commented on its psychological dimension. Writers such as Craik assert that by extending economic and political issues beyond their borders, globalization is also contributing to the growth of a global consciousness.

For the sociologist, Roland Robertson, globalization, as a concept, "refers both to the compression of the world and the intensification of consciousness of the world as a whole."[8] As the world has shrunk, our "consciousness" so to say, has expanded. Elaborating on this definition, political scientist, Manfred Steger observes that people's "awareness of the receding importance of geographical boundaries and distances fosters a keen sense of becoming part of a global whole. Reinforced on a daily basis, these persistent experiences of global interdependence gradually change people's individual and collective identities, and thus dramatically impact the way they act in the world."[9] For example, this has led individuals and societies everywhere to engage in the international arena on economic, political, and cultural issues that affect the entire planet. It has now been understood that our local environment is subject to global warming, ozone depletion and ecological disasters, with global fall-outs such as Chernobyl. The increasing global value placed on the preservation of the environment will no doubt have positive consequences in protecting the limited natural resources of this planet.

It is against this background that the book focuses, as stated previously, on the possibility of increasing multiculturalism brought about by the latest phase of globalization. Globalization, in this book's view,

[8] Roland Robertson, *Globalization: Social Theory and Global Culture* (London: Sage Publications, 1992), 8.

[9] Manfred B. Steger, *Globalization: A Very Short Introduction* (New York: Oxford University Press, 2003), 12.

is primarily an economic process aided as much by stunning advances in ICT as by the liberalization of economic policies in the developing world. This, most naturally, has also led to cultural flows across borders. "Whereas traditionally the values of nation states were the major influences on organizations based there, today business activities and the organizations that stimulate them are conduits for global culture more than they are recipients of national culture."[10] Yet the point I make here is that in promoting international or even regional commerce, we are moving not only toward an acceptance of diversity but also developing common multicultural ideas. We have learned to accept differences, often turning them to our advantage. For example, many supermarkets today have a separate section for halal products thereby increasing their clientele.

The West and the Rest

Though globalization, on the one hand, is perceived as an "opportunity for change,"[11] on the other, it is also provoking reactions in the opposite direction. For millions, globalization is not just characterized by systematic exclusion, marginalization and homogenization, it is also viewed widely as "having a fractious effect on local cultures by creating new global communities with common interests."[12] As Clark puts it:

> Globalization denotes movements in both the intensity and the extent of international interactions, in the former sense, globalization overlaps to some degree with related ideas of integration, interdependence, multilateralism, openness and interpenetration; in the latter, it points to the geographical spread of these tendencies and its cognate with globalism, spatial compression, universalization and homogeneity.[13]

[10] B. Parker, *Globalization and Business Practices: Managing across Boundaries* (London: Sage Publications, 1998), 226.

[11] D. French and M. Richards, *Television in Contemporary Asia* (New Delhi: Sage Publications, 2000), 18.

[12] French and Richards, *Television in Contemporary Asia*, 18.

[13] Ian Clark, *Globalization and Fragmentation, International Relations in the Twentieth Century* (Oxford: Oxford University Press, 1997), 1–2.

Or as Heising states: "When dominant cultures overtake and absorb marginal cultures in any part of the world, the danger of losing cultural integrity on the part of each culture is evident."[14] Or indeed as Tomlinson conceptualizes:

> The impact of globalization in the cultural sphere has, most generally been viewed in a pessimistic light. Typically, it has been associated with the destruction of cultural identities, victims of the accelerating encroachment of a homogenized, westernized consumer culture. This view [...] tends to interpret globalization as a seamless extension of—indeed, as euphemism for—Western cultural imperialism.[15]

Hence, even as the world is drawing together as a single society linked by common institutions and organizations, a shared culture and consciousness, globalization, for many, is Westernization by another name.

What do people mean when they talk about Westernization? As a matter of fact, a whole range of things, from the consumer culture of Western capitalism with its all too familiar icons (McDonald's, Coca Cola, Pizza Hut) to the spread of European languages (particularly English) to styles of dressing, eating, architecture and so on. Marshall McLuhan's famous concept of the "global village", which facilitated interactions between diverse cultures by transcending geographical boundaries, has assumed a dubious distinction with many scholars arguing that globalization, a product of American hegemony, is working in a fundamentally centripetal manner, forcing its ideology and lifestyle on other countries along with its products and services. Scholars such as Wunderlich and Warrier suggest that, historically, globalization is perceived to have originated from the economic and political domination of the USA, which is also spreading its values worldwide along with its products and

---

[14] D. Ray Heising, "The Meaning and Impact of Cultural Globalization", *China Media Research* 2, no. 3, 2006, http://www.chinamediaresearch.net/vol2no3/060312Jen_Hu_Chang_done.pdf.

[15] John Tomlinson, "Globalization and Cultural Identity", *The Global Transformations Reader: An Introduction to the Globalisation Debate*, 2nd edn, eds David Held and Anthony McGraw (Cambridge, UK: Polity Press, 2003), 269.

services.[16] In the words of Scholte, "globalization introduces a single world culture centered on consumerism, mass media, Americana and the English language."[17]

Elsewhere, Bhikhu Parekh writes: "The fact remains that Western culture today enjoys enormous economic and political power, prestige and respectability. Its interactions with other cultures occur under grossly unequal conditions and those at the receiving end often find it difficult to make autonomous choices."[18] Elaborating on this, Siu-Nam Lee observes that "communication imperialism is the process in which the ownership and control over the hardware and software of mass media as well as other major forms of communication in one country are singly or together subjugated to the domination of another country with deleterious effects on the indigenous values, norms and culture."[19] The broad implications are that diffused by the Western media, this process of domination of one culture by another, also known as Cultural Imperialism is a threat to the cultures of the peripheral Third World nations.

The argument does appear convincing when one looks at the obvious shifts in consumer lifestyles in emerging countries, in the way Coke, Pepsi and McDonald's have invaded their markets. The USA of course is responsible for some of the world's biggest and most successful global brands. From Apple to Ford, McDonald's, Coke and Nike, America-originated brands have set the standard for quality and consistency around the world. But while these American corporations seem innocuously enough to sell Nike shoes or Wrangler jeans (both manufactured ironically outside of the US), they are also perceived to sell the image of America as the land of "cool" (mis)leading consumers everywhere to demand the same American products,

[16] Jens-Uwe Wunderlich and Meera Warrier, *A Dictionary of Globalization* (London: Routledge, 2007).

[17] Jan Aart Scholte, *Globalization: A Critical Introduction* (New York: Palgrave Macmillan, 2000), 23.

[18] Bhiku Parekh, *Rethinking Multiculturalism: Cultural Diversity and Political Theory* (Houndmills, England: Macmillan, 2000), 164.

[19] Siu-Nam Lee, "Communication Imperialism and Dependency: A Conceptual Clarification", *International Communication Gazette* 41, no. 2 (1988): 74.

thereby reinforcing the fact that the concept of "Western Cultural Imperialism" operates at both the conscious and the unconscious level, providing images of what "good" life means and seeking to shape peoples' identities.[20]

While some States support the US because they consider it a benign, liberal power whose values and policies they also share and respect, many others resent its dominance, both economic and cultural. The champions of multiculturalism, for instance, maintain that "all countries are authentic in their own terms and neither the West at large nor the United States in particular, has the right to impose its beliefs and values onto others."[21] This is illustrated by the fact that some of the more popular products originating in the United States, that is, Coca Cola, McDonald's, Disney and others, are perceived to be so American that they are often universally attacked or boycotted as an integral part of anti-US propaganda. This suggests that in certain cases, global brands have difficulty in shedding their national images or country-of-origin perceptions.

The following case study is an attempt to understand the country of origin perception as reflected in international advertising.

[20] K. Negus, "The Production of Culture", in *Production of Culture/ Cultures of Production*, ed. P. Du Gay (London: Sage Publications/Open University, 1997).

[21] Keith Windschule, "The Ethnocentrism of Clifford Geertz", *New Criterion*, October 2002.

5

Country of Origin Perceptions

Defined as "the picture, the reputation, the stereotype that business-men and consumers attach to products of a specific country"—country of origin image is created by such variables "as representative products, national characteristics, economic and political background, history and traditions".[1] Historically speaking, this denotes an association with the place of origin perceived as a single place, which encapsulates the brand's origin, the place of design and the place of production. This sense of local origin as a "fixed" driver in consumer choice from food and beverages to fashion to early automotive brands and limited primarily to local products in the initial years when import and export were much less common, further led to differentiation by place or region, for example, wines grown in Champagne, Bordeaux and so on.

Following the end of World War II, even as American and European brands began to expand beyond their borders as also across the categories of goods and services, for many of them, their place of origin and heritage had continued to be a key part of their appeal. Indeed their name, identity, design and symbolism of logos became synonymous with their country or place of origin. With the advent of

[1] A. Nagashima, "A Comparison of Japanese and US Attitudes toward Foreign Products", *Journal of Marketing* 34 (1970): 68–74.

globalization, however, more and more manufacturers began moving production into countries where costs were lower. Defying conventional logic, one can today find Indian-designed software packages, Turkish washing machines and Brazilian-designed aircraft. Many brands borrow country-of-origin associations more as a marketing gimmick than any authentic reflection of culture or heritage. For example, the well-known ice-cream brand Haagen-Dazs was created as a fictional name of Scandinavian-Danish heritage and origin in order to trade on the perceived value of indulgency ice cream. In reality, however, the brand was a mass-produced premium priced ice-cream made in a factory in New York. Many other brands such as Neutrogena in pharmaceuticals or London Fog in clothing have also adopted a similar strategy through fictitious names and iconography. Similarly, although it is generally assumed that computer technology is derived from the US, one of Apple's largest plants is in fact in Cork, Ireland. Nobody, however, minds much if their personal computer (PC), is made in Ireland, Taiwan or Silicon Valley—as long as it works. Does this mean nation States are getting hollowed out in the era of globalization?

Empirical Evidence

According to the findings culled from more than 5,000 advertisements in France, Germany and India, it appears that the concept of nationhood has not disappeared despite LPG. As Holton puts it succinctly, "globalization, it seems, has not yet overrun the nation-State."[2]

Of course, some global brands will continue to be universally trusted because of their consistency in producing high-quality products, particularly in such areas as technology (examples are Sony, Nokia, IBM and Canon). The general trend, however, indicates that in the majority of instances, the most trusted brands everywhere are invariably local or originating in the same geographical region. These are national brands that are either old or include important national values in their advertising or both. For instance, in the shampoo category, the originally Austrian brand, Schwarzkopf, is the most trusted one in Austria and

[2] Robert J. Holton, *Globalization and the Nation-State* (New York: Palgrave McMillan, 1998), 6.

Germany. The French prefer their Renault and Citroen, the Germans their Mercedes and Volkswagen and the Czechs their Skoda. In the Indian case, the most trusted car brand is the homegrown Maruti, and in food and juices it is Parle. Russians, on the other hand, prefer fresh, homegrown food products but imported clothing and manufactured items. Emphasizing consumer demand for fresh, authentic and local produce, Sergei Platinin, director of a Russian company that markets fruit juices, says, "Before people used to want only to buy things that looked foreign. Now they want only Russian."[3]

What is particularly interesting in this case is the calculation on how much the customer would like the product to be linked to its country of origin. Usually this appears to be related to the feeling of nationalism that exists in the country in question at the particular time. An attempt made by BMW to launch its Series 7 line with a single advertisement campaign for Europe in the early 1990s, for example, resulted in the advertisement being withdrawn. Consumers outside of Germany reacted negatively because the car was shown with a German license plate.[4] Similarly, many other large multinationals, such as C&A and Marks & Spencers, had to withdraw from the European continent in the 1990s as a result of changing their different advertising campaigns for each country, where they operated, to uniform advertising for the whole of Europe. As the former EU Commission President Romano Prody once candidly put it, "National sovereignty is a concept set in stone in the 1648 peace treaty that established the nation State. It is the dominating thinking since the Westphalia Treaty. How can you change so many centuries of history in one shot?"[5]

The study indicates that in the case of certain products and services (for example, food and beverages, clothes and cars), national origins are seen to be the most important. Virtually all advertisements in the food and beverages category, for example, tended to

---

[3] Betsy McKay, "In Russia, West No Longer Means the Best: Consumers Shift to Home-grown Goods", *The Wall Street Journal* December 9 (1996): A9.

[4] "Chasing the Global Dream", *Marketing News*, December 2 (1996): 1, 2.

[5] Romano Prodi, "A Fitful Dream: European Unity Shaken by New Woes", by Sylvia Poggioli (http://www.npr.org/templates/story/story/story. php?storyId=128407020)

proclaim their country of origin as an intrinsic part of their marketing efforts: the Swedish Absolut Vodka is marketed everywhere as the "Absolut Country of Sweden;" and Long John sells the "Finest Scotch Whisky." Vecchia Romagna Brandt exports the Italian temperament—"Temperamento d'Italia. Vecchia Romagna. II Brandy." French wine-makers such as Vins de France, Moet & Chandon and Vins de Bordeaux also promote their French origins ("Appellation d'Origine" + French tricolor) by using some French, sometimes even in combination with German. For example, "Vins de France machen uns immer so schon frisch, leicht, rassig, kraftig. Und so ooh la la" (Vins de France); "Mit einem Cotes du Rhone zahl' Ich zur crème de la crème" (Cotes du Rhone); "Vive la différence." (Vins de Bordeaux). The Spanish wine-maker, Domecq, resorted to a series of well-known national symbols such as the Spanish Armada, Spanish lace and a Goya painting to market its wine named Carlos I. The Indian Darjeeling Tea is advertised in Germany as "mild, perfumed and typical of the Himalayan region where it is grown". The Indian Tata brand of bottled water goes everywhere by the name of Himalaya. The Swiss Gruyere cheese is advertised in France as "Le Gruyère Switzerland"—"Un fromage de caractère" ("A cheese with character") and accompanied by the Swiss flag.

Why are national origins so important in marketing food and beverages? Taking the example of France, one of the oldest wine-producing regions of Europe,[6] it is seen that the categorization of wines is a particularly complex, sophisticated and subtle process. This is because wines from each region have markedly different characteristics, which set them apart from one another. Bordeaux wines are quite unlike those from Burgundy: the grapes are different, the soil is different and even the shape of the bottles is different. The same applies to Champagne, which is produced in the area around

---

[6] The four largest wine-producing countries are France, Italy, Spain, and the United States. As of August 2015, China is ranked fifth worldwide; however, very little of China's wine production is exported. France is the single country most noted for wine production and virtually all of the world's most coveted wines are produced there (France produces between 7 and 8 billion bottles of wine annually, accounting for approximately 20 percent of total wine production worldwide).

Rheims called Champagne leading its producers to rally in its defense against similar products from other French regions and, more particularly, from other countries. In the case of Scotch whisky, it is said to derive its particular characteristics from the natural qualities of local water and soil. Irish whiskey (with an "e") is different from Scotch, and Bourbon is different again. In Germany, the process is just as intricate, with each region producing different bottles. Hock bottles, for example, are brown while Mosel bottles are green. Wine from Franconia comes in a special stubby-shaped bottle called bocksbeutel.[7] Commercially, these complexities are what make for the "real thing." As a French Corona Beer advertisement says— "Corona Extra: authentique, typique et Mexique" (Corona Extra: authentic, typical and Mexican).

Let us take a look at the automobile industry. Leading manufacturers such as Mercedes, BMW, Audi, Nissan, Volvo, Chrysler and Mitsubishi often use in their advertisement in France, a car with the local license plate. The reason is that France has relatively comparable cars and they want to appear as a local product to make the product more palatable. They do not to wish to be seen as competing with local manufacturers. This is the nationalism factor, which they do not want to arouse. Hence, Mercedes shows a French license plate, 727 2YL78. Audi retains the same visuals but changes the German license plate xH-ML 1444 to the French xx89 VA 02. Volvo presents itself as the "Le plus méditerrannéenne des Suédoises" (Most Mediterrannean of the Swedes). Similarly, for the German market, Volvo, Chrysler and Mitsubishi show a German license plate. Nissan emphasizes the fact that its cars are produced in Europe ("fabriquée en Europe"). Such approaches seem to emphasize a nationalistic tendency rather than a pan-European perspective.

In India, on the other hand, owning expensive cars is a status symbol. Customers wish to make the statement that they have bought a foreign car. Let us take the example of a German Mercedes. In this case, showing a German license plate with the car would enhance the status symbol factor. In the Indian case, interestingly, nationalism—which was in its heyday in pre-liberalization India (recall the 1970s slogan "Be Indian. Buy Indian")—continues,

---

[7] Wally Olins, *On Brand* (London: Thames & Hudson Ltd, 2003), 135.

even today, to be associated with national identity and national consciousness.[8] The predominant ideology conveyed is distilled by identifying the beliefs, values, images, festivals, customs, rituals and other symbols that members of the Indian society can identify with due to the learnt patterns of associations or codes.[9] For example, while the home-grown Bajaj bike advertisement says, "Motorcycles that echo the heartbeat of India", Hero Honda has made an effort to transform itself into a "national" company by developing campaigns around the theme of Indian nationalism: for example, "A billion hearts that beat as one". Yet another Hero Honda motorcycle advertisement reads, "Desh ki dhadkan". A few others such as Hyundai Motors have made all efforts to disguise their foreignness by selling their product against the backdrop of the iconic Red Fort and the Indian tricolor. All this, yet again, seems to suggest that the nationalism factor, despite globalization and the rise of MNCs, is still alive and kicking in most parts of the world.

Why is the nationalism factor so important in marketing cars? Historically speaking, consumers here also had little choice initially but to buy products or services from national companies. Hence, the independent and simultaneous growth of nationally identified brands like Mercedes in Germany, Ford in the US and Citroen in France. Designed traditionally for their own domestic markets, these automobile brands, still tend, by and large, to reflect national specificities or idiosyncrasies. American cars, for example, were built originally for a country where distances were vast and fuel cheap. They still come big and still take up plenty of road space and fuel. In general, it may be said that a large number of American consumers continue to look at cars as status symbols and want big and powerful vehicles—partly because of their high masculinity score and low uncertainty avoidance attributes.[10]

[8] Olins, *On Brand*.

[9] A. Berger, *Media Analysis Techniques*, 3rd edn (California, London, and New Delhi: Sage Publications, 2005), 30.

[10] Geert Hofstede, *Culture's Consequences: Comparing Values, Behaviors, Institutions and Organisations across Nations*, 2nd edn (Thousand Oaks, CA: Sage Publications, 2001).

Similarly, French cars (in fact, France, until the arrival of Henry Ford, was the leading automobile producer in the world) also stand for that country and its aspirations. Some of the cues known to resonate well with the French buyers in this instance are design, style and fashion. As de Mooij says, the French like to see more design, style and fashion in car advertisements[11]—they are often technologically highly sophisticated, very stylish and quite different from anything else around. In line with this trend, the Fiat produced Lancia Ypsilon car is marketed in France as "La Fashion Car", an epitome of French "elegance, seduction and temperament" (L'élegance, Séduction et Temperament), characteristics that Italians, like the French, also possess in ample abundance. It focuses on the well-known French fable of the Little Red Riding Hood (or "Le Petit Chaperon Rouge")—the advertisement visual shows the swanky red car flanked by a pack of wolves hungrily sniffing at it and in the background, the silhouette of a very seductive young woman, her face partially concealed by the trademark red hood. Similarly, the German brand Opel also took to this format to better sell in the French market—"Et pour etre la plus belle, la nouvelle Opel Calibra a pensé a tout" ("To make it the most beautiful, the new Opel Calibra has thought of everything").

Because Italians love style, most Italian cars are not only beautiful; they are also romantic, competitive and sporty. This is underlined by an Alfa Romeo advertisement for the French market that said, "Vous voulez partager notre passion pour cette marque légendaire toute empreinte de sportivité?" ("Would you like to share our passion for this legendary brand immersed in sportivity?"). Germany, on the other hand, is known to produce tough, well-engineered cars catering to discriminating customers. Italian and German consumers, in fact, are somewhat similar when it comes to buying cars because people in these nations traditionally look for fast acceleration and advanced technology and design. However, Germans also look for more verification, such as expertise. Germany, in addition, is a serious exporter—(let us recall that in 1914, shortly before World War I broke out, Germany had not only become the most powerful State

---

[11] M. de Mooij, "Mapping Cultural Values for Global Marketing and Advertising", in *International Advertising: Realities and Myths*, ed. J.P Jones (Thousand Oaks, CA: Sage Publications, 2000), 97.

in Europe but also one of the leading exporters in the world)—with one big eye always on the export markets. This often translates into a concerted effort to adapt to other market specificities (recall the French and German license plates for the French and Indian markets).

The fashion industry, on the other hand, is an interesting mix of global brands, national stereotyping and distinctive brand styles. Italy's fashion industry, for instance, is globally associated with such famous designers as Armani, Versace, Prada and Valentino. French fashion houses such as Dior, Chanel and Yves Saint Laurent, on the other hand, are associated with Haute Couture exclusivity. Certain American fashion products—products—Hilfiger, Gap, Levis, Nike, Ralph Lauren, Donna Karan, Marc Jacobs, and others—derive part of their brand power from being seen to be American, at least in origin. German brands, on the other hand, appear to be clearly disassociated from fashion (Jil Sander, and Hugo Boss)—from cosmetics and personal products (Lancaster and Nivea) by deliberately de-emphasizing their German origins. An interesting example is the German Comma, which adopted "Italian" product names (Cinque, Moda al dente, and others) to sell its high-end garments. This is in keeping with the general view that fashion products originating from France (Paris) or Italy (Milan) tend to sell better. As one marketing expert points out, "German" is synonymous with quality engineering "Italian" is synonymous with style and "French" is synonymous with "chic."[12] "British", on the other hand, is perceived as "cool". As Peter Schwarzenbauer, Chief Executive Officer (CEO), BMW-Mini and Rolls Royce, puts it, "We need to be more sensitive to Britishness, to do more to show Britishness to the outside world. People like it. It's cool."[13]

According to the data, Western products in India represent style, progress and advancement. Our frequent allusions to the West (139 times or 26 percent) are perhaps an indication of our identification with the open cultures of the West (see Table 5.1). In contrast, Indian

[12] Milbank Dana, "Made in America Becomes a Boast in Europe", *The Wall Street Journal* (January 19, 1994): B1.

[13] Peter Schwarzenbauer, CEO, BMW-Mini and Rolls Royce, "Germany's Answer to Mini Mid-Life Crisis", *Sunday Times*, cited in "Made In: The Value of Country of Origin for future brands", Future Brandfblog. futurebrand.com/www.futurebrand.com, March 25, 2014.

Table 5.1   References to "Other" Cultures

References to	France	%	Germany	%	India	%
Germany	8	3%	0	0%	24	5%
France	0	0%	15	3%	16	3%
Great Britain	32	11%	17	3%	19	4%
Spain	2	1%	19	3%	1	0%
Italy	8	3%	19	3%	8	2%
Switzerland	6	2%	38	7%	28	7%
Other European Countries	20	7%	39	7%	28	5%
Europe (EU)	21	7%	33	6%	8	2%
	97	34%	180	33%	108	21%
West					139	26%
India	4	1%	19	3%	–	–
India's South Asian neighbors	11	4%	11	2%	9	2%
China	2	1%	0	0%	6	1%
Other Asian Countries	27	10%	59	11%	36	7%
	44	16%	89	16%	51	10%
Arab Countries	13	5%	9	2%	14	3%
Africa	16	6%	34	6%	0	0%
Australia	1	0%	4	1%	0	0%
United States	40	14%	98	18%	66	13%
Other countries/ region	14	5%	17	3%	3	1%
	54	19%	115	21%	69	13%
Global Aspect	47	17%	52	10%	118	22%
Other	10	4%	60	11%	9	2%
Total:	282	100%	543	100%	525	100%

Source: Author.

advertising rarely mentions the neighboring countries (1–2 percent) or indeed even Asian countries. Indian advertising often makes a mention of advanced European countries such as Germany for high-tech products and France for fashion. There are niche products, for example, which are identified primarily with the French and sold in that language. In many such cases as perfumes since the smell cannot be described—many brands have made identical transfers in all three countries, for example, Chanel, Lancôme and Cacharel. A large number of garment advertisements alluded to traditional French elegance to sell. A Cardin advertisement, for instance, not only refers to such famous French style icons as Pierre Cardin, Brigitte Bardot, Jeanne Moreau and Catherine Deneuve—but also uses a smattering of fashionable French—Ooh la la. A Christian Bernard Watch advertisement shows the Eiffel Tower, the copy stating, "Paris sets the trend". A Louis Philippe advertisement visual depicts a large map of France highlighting some of the best-known wine-growing regions in that country. The text reads—"Louis Philippe in Chambrais. A fabric with a distinguished French lineage. A certain *je ne sais quoi* so typical of vintage France. And like good French wine, Chambrais is silky and smooth". Piaget markets its high-end watches with the French tagline—"Joallier en horlogerie depuis 1874" ("Genève"). Castrol Oils advertises its product as "the Champagne of engine oils". Royal Toothbrushes alludes to the French kiss—"What would happen to the French kiss without Royal?"

Interestingly, Indian advertising makes a large number of references to Germany but relatively fewer references to Britain. Germany is associated primarily with engineering brilliance, technological superiority and attention to detail—in short, uncompromising perfection. Illustrating this, the German Moderna Klober not only markets its chairs in India as "Chair-tech from Germany" but also uses entire phrases in German to better sell. The first advertisement states, "Im Grunde gibt es zwei Arten von Burostuhlen—Klober und nicht Klober; and a second one says, Einfuhlsam. Intelligent. Ansprechend. Nein, nicht der Mann. Der Stuhl". Clearly, it matters little whether the Indian consumer understands German or not—it suffices that he or she associates its use with uncompromising quality, perfection and superior product design. In the consumer mind, the halo effect of Mercedes, Siemens and brands like them created in the late nineteenth and early twentieth century by the best of German minds and known to focus on design, quality and service rather than on competitive pricing (for example, the Korean Air advertisement's emphasis on "Lebensqualitat non-stop") still lingers. In line with this trend, another advertisement selling engine oil (Liqui Moli) also uses the tagline "German engineering at work." Volkswagen cars are products of "superior German engineering." Audi's philosophy is all about pushing the boundaries of what is thought to be possible. To emphasize this, Audi even says it in German—Vorsprung durch Technik (Progress through Technology). Drawing on the fact that Germany also boasts of a superb motorway network, a Tata housing advertisement has retained the German term "Autobahn" to sell its own high standards in business ("German autobahn boasts the fastest, most dependable highways in the world. One Indian company sets these very standards in…").

Ironically, however, many products with German brand names are no longer designed and manufactured in Germany but outside of it. Also, not many know that Germany produces not just some of the world's finest automobiles but that German brand exports also have a long history of excellence regardless of industry segment.[14] In cosmetics, for instance, Nivea, whose name comes from the Latin for "snow white" has grown from its origins as a simple cream since 1911 into one of the most trusted skin care brands in the world. In clothing, Adidas is a global leader in sports footwear, apparel and accessories. In technology, SAP, founded in 1972, is the world's largest business software company and the third largest software supplier overall. Other well-known global German brands include Bayer (pharmaceuticals), Becks (Beer) Boss (clothing) and Braun (consumer products).[15]

This is supported by the findings of a study carried out in the 1990s on what "Made in means" by the branding consultancy Wolff Olins with the Financial Times. Over 1,000 senior executives from countries around the world were contacted and the results are quite fascinating. Although the executives claimed that national origins of products are very important, they displayed almost grotesque ignorance about the countries from which they said they bought products:

> For example, Germany was perceived primarily as a country that produces excellent cars and by extension other engineering products at high prices. Mercedes Benz, Audi and BMW overwhelm everything

---

[14] Barry Silverstein, "German Engineering Drives Global Brand Success", November 24, 2008, www.barrysilverstein.com/articles/brand-channel.pdf.

[15] Silverstein, "German Engineering Drives Global Brand Success".

else. German marketing skills were regarded as negligible and the emotional characteristics of its products not even worth mentioning. German products were seen to possess an attractive but narrow range of virtues. German achievements in banking, pharmaceuticals, electronics and other areas were largely ignored or unknown. So the picture that emerged was a simplistic caricature of the reality of German industry. Hence, even though Germany is the prolific producer of some of the world's finest products, consumers everywhere associate it primarily with world class cars. The marketing expertise of companies like BMW was ignored. The hi-tech triumphs of SAP were unknown. Major chemical companies like BASF and Bayer were not acknowledged. Deutsche Bank and other German financial institutions might just not have existed. German products with a high emotional or style content, such as Nivea, Jil Sander, Hugo Boss, Wella or for that matter Porsche didn't come into the picture. Because of traditional prejudices created over decades, huge chunks of German industry and commerce appear to derive absolutely no advantage from being perceived as German.[16]

Not surprisingly perhaps, Indian advertising contains the highest number of references to the US (66 times or 13 percent). The American influence is very diverse but perhaps most conspicuous in the fields of science, technology and popular culture. Broadly, the concepts about the US that emerge are: first, it is a land of democracy, liberty and freedom where every individual has an equal opportunity to achieve wealth, glory and power. The popular symbols regarding this are the Statue of Liberty, White House, Empire State Building, Legendary Harley Davidson motorbike, Harvard, Eton and so on. Second, it is the nation that leads in developing and utilizing smart technology, the popular symbols being the PC; Apple, Hewlett Packard, Intel, Microsoft; National Aeronautics and Space Administration (NASA); and smart bombs and bombers (what Philips and Jaguar have, respectively, referred to as "Stealth bombers", "B2 Bombers" and "Stealth Rangers"). Third is the popular culture which according to its detractors undermines and destroys everyone else's national culture. The popular symbols of this are McDonald's, Coke, Pepsi,

[16] Olins, *On Brand*, 143–5.

Rock and Roll, Hollywood and American showbiz. Popular references to Hollywood in Indian advertising include the movie Casablanca and actors Marilyn Monroe, Humphrey Bogart, Keanu Reeves, Tom Cruise, and Charlie Chaplin. American showbiz, on the other hand, is alluded to by Royal Toothbrushes that queried, tongue in cheek— "What would happen to American showbiz without Royal?"

Interestingly, the United States is both loved and hated worldwide. The global preponderance of the US-made label is perhaps a good indicator of the traditional love–hate relationship the world shares with the US and which has been described by Josef Joffe as "HHMMS"—"the Harvard and Hollywood McDonald's and Microsoft Syndrome."[17] Hence, despite its professed aversion to the perceived corrosive effects of "McDonalisation" (a popular term coined by the French sociologist, Georges Ritzer), the United States paradoxically remains the most frequently cited country in French advertising (40 times or 14 percent) followed by Great Britain (32 times or 11 percent). Most French advertisements also carry endorsements by well-known Hollywood actors, for example, Scarlett Johansson (Dolce Gabbana), Eva Mendes (Angel Eau de Toilette) and Leonardo diCaprio (TAG Heuer watches). In one instance, to sell its watch in the French market, Omega even uses a retro visual of President John F. Kennedy saying—"We choose to go to the moon." German advertisements also carry the highest number of references to the United States (98 times or 18 percent). However, Germany has also shown a predilection for Switzerland or more specifically, for its world-famous watches (38 times or 7 percent). France, on the other hand, appears to have a special fondness for all that represents British "cool" (32 times or 11 percent). All three countries, however, have made extensive references to the "global" aspect, with India showcasing the highest figures: India 118 times or 22 percent, France, 47 times or 17 percent, and Germany, 52 times or 10 percent.

Interestingly, both France and Germany have made relatively very few references to one another. French advertising contains only eight allusions to Germany (3 percent) but four allusions to India

[17] Josef Joffe, "Who's Afraid of Mr. Big?", *The National Interest*, no. 64 (2001): 45.

(1 percent) and eleven to South Asia (4 percent). German advertising, on the other hand, makes fifteen references to France (3 percent) but nineteen references to India (3 percent) and eleven to South Asia (2 percent). France has also made relatively fewer references to its erstwhile colonies. Africa, for example, is cited 16 times (or 6 percent). Contrast this to Germany, which has made 34 references (6 percent) to this continent in their advertising. This seems to suggest that the dynamics of world trade, as reflected in advertising, are now changing with investors looking more and more toward the emerging markets of India, China and others.

* * *

This chapter concludes with the observation that despite the idea of a "borderless world" propagated by the global media, the traditional relationship between the nation and brands has not become obsolete. On the contrary, in many cases, the nations and the brands associated with them, despite changing countries, continue to be deeply entrenched in the collective psyche of the country of origin. Volvo cars, for example, even though taken over from the Swedes—first, by the American Ford Motors and then by the Chinese—are still seen to embody sturdy Swedish values such as tough, safe, unshowy but self-confident. Whether produced in Brazil, India or China, Volvo will continue to project what customers think of as its Swedish heritage. Similarly, although the new BMW-controlled Rolls Royce or Tata Motors-owned Jaguar may no longer be made in Britain, their intrinsic "British" appeal remains. In other words, "where" a brand is seen to be from is, in fact, one of the most important drivers in influencing consumer purchase decision.

Certain countries, in particular, appear to resonate more strongly in consumer minds, but this may vary depending on the category. For example, the US figures as the strongest country overall. Germany, on the other hand, is strongly linked with the automotive category and technical expertise and it does not do so well in certain other categories such as fashion where France and Italy are lead players. Switzerland, even though it does not rank anywhere among the top countries overall, resonates with customers everywhere with certain core values such as "quality" (quality of life, quality of product and so on). This suggests that countries may differ in terms of relative strength when it comes to purchase decision. In other words, even though the country of origin of a brand may still be a significant factor in brand positioning strategies in certain category of products, often made unique by the nature of the soil or through association with traditional skills (for example, Scotch Whisky, Cuban cigars, and Burgundy wines), it may not be equally relevant when it comes to influencing consumer preference in all categories.

Companies also use stereotypes extensively to sell. This is because, as psychologists have emphasized, most people are "cognitive misers" relying on mental shortcuts to make decisions. They have broad but somehow vague stereotypes about specific countries and product categories that they judge "best." For example, English tea, French perfume, Chinese silk, Italian leather, Japanese electronics, Swiss watches and so on. Stereotypes trigger associations enabling consumers to make an instant decision. Unfortunately and as Olins explains, "Because nationally based brands tend to reinforce stereotypes, they often have the effect of exaggerating an already distorted picture. And this marginalizes vast swathes of a nation's products and services, which do not conform to these increasingly irrelevant stereotypes."[18]

Developing countries, in particular, are not only stereotyped but stereotyped on the basis of whether they are industrialized or in the process of industrializing. Indeed, as Christophe A. Bartlett and Sumantra Ghosal have pointed out, "Consider labels such as "Made in Brazil" and "Made in Thailand". Someday they may be symbols of high quality but today many consumers expect products from those countries to be inferior."[19] In contrast, industrialized countries have the highest quality image, and there is generally a bias against products from developing countries.[20] One might generalize that the more technical the product, the less positive is the perception if manufactured in a less developed or newly industrializing country.

[18]   Olins, *On Brand*, 160.

[19]   Christopher A. Bartlett and Sumantra Ghosal, "Going Global: Lessons from Later Movers", *Harvard Business Review* 78, no. 2 (2000): 133.

[20]   Gopalkrishnan Iyer and Jukti K. Kalita, "The Impact of Country of Origin and Country of Manufacture: Cues on Consumer Perceptions of Quality and Value", *Journal of Global Marketing* 113, no. 1 (1997): 7–28.

There is also the tendency to favor foreign-made products over those made domestically in less developed countries. A survey of consumers in the Czech Republic found that 72 percent of Japanese products were considered to be of the highest quality, German goods followed with 51 percent, Swiss goods with 48 percent, Czech goods with 32 percent and last was the US with 29 percent. Electronics manufacturers in South Korea have difficulty in convincing Russians that their products are as good as Japanese. Goods produced in Malaysia, Hong Kong or Thailand are more suspect still. Eastern Europe is considered adequate for clothing, but poor for food or durables. Turkey and China are at the bottom of the heap.[21] The MNCs, however, need to take into consideration in their marketing strategy the fact that a resurgent Asia today is much more than just an exotic continent. With the economic rise of countries such as India and China, there is now emerging a new form of Asian modernity that is true to its roots, but also looking to its future with confidence. This matters because brand-driven consumption is increasing exponentially worldwide with the explosion of new middle-class consumers in the BRICS markets.

The findings also reveal that location extends beyond the association with countries. The power of city brands was noted as being an equally powerful positioning aspect. In particular, the cities of London, New York, Paris and Milan are identified as being the strongest and most powerful city brands of origin, carrying with them associations of urban sophistication, style and design that help define and differentiate products. The city identifier built into brands like Rimmel (London), London Fog (London), DKNY (New York), Guerlain (Paris), Eau de Parfum (Paris) and Prada (Milan) is a prime example of how city of origin can be central to a brand story. The same kinds of association can also be harnessed at the regional level as demonstrated by brands like L'Occitane (Provence).

Lastly, as anti-globalization and anti-brand movements seek increasingly to diminish and limit the power of corporations, both countries and multinationals will be increasingly called to task to

---

[21] Mellow Craig, "Free-Spending Foibles", *Business Eastern Europe* (1997): 1.

manage their brands, in particular, the socio-environmental dimensions including reputation for expertise, ethical practices or sustainable ethics of the country in question. Whereas earlier, it might have been enough to "borrow" associations from a country for purely marketing purposes, consumers today are less ready to accept country of origin as a choice driver unless it is authenticated. In other words, although consumers have always made strong associations between brands and particular countries especially by category—for example, France for fashion, Germany for cars, and the USA for entertainment—and the data reinforce these connections—today the concept of "Made in" is getting more dependent on a combination of factors from heritage to design and physical manufacturing to leverage for competitive advantage in a world where we have unprecedented access to real-time information about the things we buy. This is in sharp contrast to the late twentieth-century strategy of supply chain and manufacturing capacity of the cheapest service of resources and labor to guarantee the highest margin—something that will become increasingly unacceptable to discerning consumers the world over.

Endorsing this viewpoint, Suresh Sundaram, Founder, Scentia Insights,[22] says: "A very important take away from this research is that origin, design and manufacture are considered equally important. But if we take Apple as an example, they try to make people forget where the product is manufactured and focus on where it is designed".

---

[22] Cited by Future Brand in a survey on "Made In: The Value of Country of Origin for Future Brands", available at www.futurebrand.com, accessed on March 25, 2014.

6

Globalization

Toward a Post-Modern Phase?

Colonialism, as seen previously, enabled Western cultures to impose their values on the conquered peoples of Asia, Africa and the Americas. The colonial era, of course, faded away in the twentieth century. The discourse of colonization, however, based upon the cultural superiority of the West that suggested that encounters between cultures are never on equal terms[1] has lingered, often providing the benchmark against which other cultures are supposed to measure their sense of worth.[2]

Is the world moving in a single direction toward homogeneity as a result of Western domination, economic and cultural? Is globalization really a euphemism for Americanization since European hegemony was promptly replaced at the end of World War II by American hegemony—the US emerging from the ravages of the war, together with the Soviet Union, as the most powerful economic and military nation in the world? Francis Fukuyama, for example, when asked the question replied,

---

[1] J. Tomlinson, *Cultural Imperialism: A Critical Introduction* (London: Pinter, 1991).

[2] Ian Clark, *Globalization and Fragmentation* (Oxford: Oxford University Press, 1997).

I think it is and that is why some people do not like it. I think it has to be Americanization because in some respect, America is the most advanced capitalist society in the world today and so its institutions represent the logical development of market forces. Therefore, if market forces are what drives globalization, then it is inevitable that Americanization will accompany globalization.[3]

Fukuyama, however, rejects the notion that globalization is leading to cultural homogeneity, asserting that it is only leading to homogenization of certain aspects of the economy and society.[4] Similarly, scholars such as Alden, Steenkamp, and Batra, who analysed the representation of global consumer culture in advertising, also view consumer culture as shared sets of consumption-related symbols (product, categories, brands, and consumption activities) that are meaningful to segment members and which flow primarily from the US.[5]

The US, no doubt since the collapse of the Soviet Union in 1990, enjoyed a unipolar interlude during which time it was a truly global hegemonic power. Other countries had to acquiesce to it, either by choice or compulsion. It is this period which may now be coming to an end. The US remains, of course, against any metric of economic and military might, a pre-eminent power and the chief source of technological innovation. But it is no longer a hegemonic power. Its relative power has declined as other powers, chiefly China, has accumulated significant economic and military capabilities. This is paralleled by the fragmentation of Europe—a key pillar of Western ascendancy.

The following case studies illustrate the fact that what we are now experiencing is, in the words of Nederveen Pieterse, a process whereby non-Western cultures are also impacting the West[6]—a process that he describes as one of "accelerated globalization" and "cultural mixing in which introvert cultures are gradually receding

[3] Economic Globalization and Culture: A Discourse.ml.com/wom/forum/global and htm.

[4] Economic Globalization and Culture: A Discourse.ml.com/wom/forum/global and htm.

[5] D.L. Alden, I.B.E.M. Steenkamp, and R. Batra, "Brand Positioning through Advertising in Asia, North America and Europe: The Role of Global Consumer Culture", *Journal of Marketing* 63, no. 1 (1999): 75–87.

[6] Tomlinson, *Cultural Imperialism*, 62.

and translocal cultures made up of diverse elements are coming to the foreground.[7] My own view here is that in the contemporary world that we live in, no society can remain isolated and, consequently, it is interdependence between nations rather than the process of homogenization envisaged by globalization that has emerged to the surface today.

Global or Local?

A key question in global marketing and advertising is the choice between "going global" or "going local." In marketing theory, this concept was first used by Theodore Levitt who generated a storm of controversy in 1983 when he wrote in the *Harvard Business Review* that companies must learn to operate as if the world were one large market ignoring superficial regional and national differences and selling the same products in the same way throughout the world. As he put it famously in his article titled "Globalization of Markets", "The globalization of markets is at hand. The multinational operates with resolute constancy ... it sells the same way everywhere."

Proponents of this one-size-fits-all approach to global advertising believe that, in the era of the "global village", tastes and preferences are converging, rendering tailored advertising obsolete. This argument suggests, "Most human wants and desires are similar if presented within recognizable experience situations. People everywhere want value, quality and the latest technology made available and affordable; everyone everywhere wants to be loved and respected, and we all get hungry."[8] Keeping this in mind, many MNCs have adopted a world branding strategy. For example, Levi's has adopted a world branding for its jeans because the company recognizes that tastes in music, fashion and technology among the young are becoming increasingly similar. Teenagers wearing Levi's jeans are seen to portray common values irrespective of the part of the world in which they find themselves. As the creator of the Diesel, a designer jeans brand,

---

[7] Tomlinson, *Cultural Imperialism*, 62.

[8] Dean M. Peebles, "Executive Insights Don't Write off Global Advertising", *International Marketing Review* 6, no. 1 (1989): 73.

Renzo Rosso explains, "A group of teenagers randomly chosen from different parts of the world will share many of the same tastes."[9]

Which factors must companies take into account when advertising globally? Should product or brand names be changed? When should visuals or copy be customized? How often do companies opt for identical transfers? While some scholars have argued that the emergence of a global market is indicative of an increasingly homogenous market, others hold that globalization actually increases heterogeneity through an increased effort to preserve local cultures.[10] Still others point to the "glocalisation" of worldwide consumption attitudes through a strategy of "think global, act local."[11]

To address the question of whether uniform strategies ought to be used in advertising across cultures, a comparative study of Western and non-Western advertising is in order. A select sample of consumer products has therefore been chosen from the original corpus of advertisements, ranging from luxury cars and perfumes to low-end, mass-produced consumer goods such as personal and household products, and food and drink to demonstrate the international advertising strategies of major companies in France, Germany and India.

Let us first consider a quintessential luxury item—perfume. The advertisements by parfumiers such as Cacharel, Giorgio Armani, Chanel, Lancôme, and Guy Laroche have been studied. By and large, these companies use the same advertisements across France, Germany and India. Lancôme, for instance, has retained its original French copy "Le parfum des instants précieux" (The perfume of precious instants) and visual (a white female model) in its Indian advertisements also; Paloma Picasso has retained its French copy "Paloma Picassso crée Minotaure" (Paloma Picasso creates Minotaure) and visual for both the French and German markets. Any changes are minimal, and usually in deference to local sensitivities. Cacharel, for example, advertises its Eden perfume in France using a frontal view of a nude young woman, accompanied by the slogan, "Le parfum

[9] Alice Rawsthorn, "A Hipster on Jean Therapy", *Financial Times*, August 20, 1998, 8.

[10] For example, Theodore Levitt, "The Globalization of Markets", *Harvard Business Review* (1983).

[11] For example, Jackson 2004, Kotler 1986, Quelch 1985.

défendu." The Indian version of the advertisement is translated into English ("The Forbidden Fragrance") and the visual shaded to obscure the model's nudity.

High-end garment companies likewise tend to use the same advertisements across markets. Benetton, for example, uses its United Colors of Benetton branding all over the world. But while in France and Germany, Benetton retained the English term "AIDS" (acquired immune deficiency syndrome) instead of the French SIDA (syndrome immuno-déficitaire acquis) in its advertisement in India, this was replaced with the fashion capitals of the world, namely, Paris, New York and Milan.

Watch companies, primarily Swiss, also use globalized advertisement copy—"Omega Is a Sign of Excellence"; Tissot is "Swiss Quality"; Rado "A Different World"; Rolex is "Officially Certified Swiss Chronometer"; and Hermès "Water-Resistant Swiss." Piaget has retained the original French text "Joallier en horlogerie depuis 1874—Genève" for its Indian market also.

In the case of computers, the visuals remain the same, though understandably, the technical specifications are translated. However, some terms such as "Intel Inside" or "Pentium Processor" are retained everywhere. This suggests that certain product types (for example, high-tech goods) are more likely to be positioned globally.

In the technical product category, the Philips slogan is the same in both India and Germany: Germany, Philips invents/Philips invents for you; and India, "Philips—we Invent for you."

Telecommunications companies, however, take a more mixed approach. Nokia and Alcatel use their English slogans, "Connecting People" and "Your Reliable Partners in Communications", respectively worldwide. In deference to the local culture, however, Nokia carries local translations such as Menu (France); Speicher (Germany) and Menu (India). In a developing country like India, Nokia not only emphasizes the fact that it is the "world leader in cellular phones" but also that its mobile phones are user-friendly. In one case, Motorola uses the phrase "Tu me manques" in France, with a literal English translation—"I Miss You"—appearing in its German advertisements. Yet, it uses the French "Je t'aime" ("I love you") in both France and Germany, as the phrase is nearly universally understood throughout Europe. Siemens sells cell phones in Germany using the phrase "You can count up to ten, can't you?" In a developing country with high rates of illiteracy such as India, though, such an advertisement could be misconstructed as offensive. Hence, Siemens advertises in India as a "global player" ("Connecting to the "Global Village"). In keeping with its global yet local approach, Siemens shows not just the Statue of Liberty and the Tower Bridge of London but also the Taj Mahal. The Indian Tata Telecom advertisement, on the other hand, showed visuals of the White House and Buckingham Palace.

Travel companies also use a mix of standardized and customized advertising. Delta uses the same advertisements across France, Germany and India. Korean Air uses the slogan "Les routes de la sérénité" in France but has adapted to "Lebensqualität non-stop" for the German market since the German consumer is known to have a special resonance with "quality of life". Singapore Airlines advertises in India as "Surprising Singapore"; and in Germany, the same English advertisement is slightly modified—"The Most Surprising Tropical Island on Earth". The visual remains unchanged. Yet another advertisement also targeting the Indian market says "Incentive Isle Singapore: "Where the world comes together"; and in France, the same concept is retained—"Singapore—Tout le monde s'y retrouve" ("Singapore—where the world comes together"). A German Cathay Pacific advertisement invites its passengers to a meal of spaghetti and tomato sauce on its flight to Hong Kong. In India, the same advertisement, however, is slightly modified to show rice noodles and Chinese calligraphy instead. The text remains unchanged—"the best way to the big noodle".

In the case of automobiles, BMW advertises in Germany as "Freude am Fahren" ("Craze for Driving"), extolling the national craze for speed in a country with no speed restrictions on its highways. In nationalist France, on the other hand, BMW has made a special effort to integrate into the local culture by showing a one-page visual of the famous Mona Lisa painting (horizontally positioned to resemble a car), Versailles gardens and so on. In India where social status is all-important, BMW uses this specifically—"Setting the Pace in Automotive Status." Of particular interest is the fact that while BMW, Mercedes and Audi usually depict their products with French license plates in French advertisements, their Indian advertisements show German license plates—subtly emphasizing their foreign origin and subsequent "snob value".

Consumer electronics companies, however, appear to be the most likely to advertise differently across cultures. Leading companies continue to use global slogans, but they also produce domestic advertisements appealing to local tastes. For instance, Sony in India uses a Hindi slogan (*"Zindagi ke khubsoorat lamhe. Ek baar phir!"*) while depicting a local wedding in the background—a bow to the Indian habit of videotaping all our major ceremonies for posterity. In France, on the other hand, it is the Eiffel Tower.

How can the differences apparent in this broad survey be explained? Apparently, internationally recognized luxury brands tend to stick to their global slogans, as the brand names, to use a cliché, "sell themselves". All three international languages—English, French and German—are used widely, but English appears to dominate because so many brand names originated in the English-speaking world. Niche products, such as fashion and style items, are identified in French and sold using that language across markets.

Advertisers do, however, pay attention to the sensibilities of their target consumers, as evident with the Siemens and Cacharel advertisements. Although Cacharel's advertisements depicting a nude model made the same basic appeal in France and India, the shading of the model in the Indian version suggests a subtle bow to cultural pressures.

The MNCs often wish to transform themselves into "national" companies in the minds of their target audiences and their advertisers thus develop campaigns around particular themes suited to the local market (for example, the Sony Handicam advertisement, *"Zindagi ke khubsoorat lamhe. Ek baar phir,"* for which local experts were consulted). Sometimes, advertisers use local symbols but leave the copy untouched—for example, an advertisement will show an Indian girl instead of a Western one. Similarly, companies may maintain the same symbols in their marketing materials but change the text to fit the local language and tastes.

One interesting detail that runs against popular belief is that a large number of American multinationals, such as Coca Cola, Nike and McDonald's, do localize their advertisements. As these companies sell mass-produced consumer items and aim to reach the greatest possible number of people, they must necessarily make local appeals. Even their products undergo occasional changes (for example, McAloo Tikki burger must be sold only in India). These companies are more likely to copy the themes of their advertising in Europe but put it into local context; visually the most obvious will be Indians instead of Caucasians. On the other hand, expensive luxury items such as cars, haute couture and electronics use uniform advertisement campaigns because their products appeal to an elite class of consumers that is more likely to speak a foreign language or be familiar with the product itself.

Advertisers also take into account the level to which they expect customers to identify with a product's country of origin. As noted earlier, German carmakers like Audi tend to depict their vehicles with French license plates when selling in France. French companies already sell comparable cars and hence, Audi wants its cars to appear local to make them more palatable and to avoid being seen as competing with local manufacturers. In India, on the other hand, a customer buying a Mercedes typically hopes to make a statement by purchasing a foreign car. Depicting its vehicles with German license plates in its Indian advertisements thus makes Mercedes more attractive to local high-end consumers.

The findings indicate subtle differences between advertising content across the three countries examined. In India, advertising language tends to take a longer, narrative form. Since new foreign products must be introduced to consumers and as advertising is relatively cheaper, advertisements are more descriptive and occupy longer time slots. German consumers, on the other hand, want facts—advertisements in the German media compress essential data about products in order to convince and persuade the customer. In France, however, advertisements emphasize a product's aesthetic qualities. They tend to be quirky and visually appealing. The French also tend to exclude English-speaking original advertising, even through legal means. In contrast, the Germans tend to tamper less with the original English when selling the product.

Lastly, it appears that although different industries may face different degrees of convergence of consumer demand, the trend is especially strong in certain industries or categories. The least culturally bound products or services like cigarettes, alcohol, industrial products and services, hi-tech products (computers, compact disc players, television), fashion, perfumes and jewellery are easier to market internationally than culturally bound products like food or drink. This is because in high-tech industries the products and services never existed until technology brought them to consumers. Indeed, consumers in different parts of the world were taught to use these products or services and therefore had very few culture-specific preferences. As a result, the convergence of consumer demand in these industries is especially strong. In contrast, in industries where there has been a long-standing demand—such as skincare or food—the convergence of consumer demand is relatively weaker.

The study suggests that companies selling products across cultures must exercise caution when considering whether to standardize or to localize advertising. Ignoring local sensibilities can cause offense and create the opposite of the desired effect. This does not mean, however, that advertisements must always be tailored to local contexts for maximum impact; in fact, maintaining the original "foreign" advertising can even be an asset. These examples hold out a simple lesson for branding strategies of tomorrow. Things have changed. All companies seeking to expand globally need to ask the question whether their products are culturally, socially and linguistically appropriate for the targeted market. As one writer has observed, "the debate on whether there is cultural homogenization remains open ... there are no surveys that people are becoming alike."[12]

Homogeneity or Hybridity?

This case study argues that the "Cultural Imperialism" thesis is not only particularly complex and multilayered but that in the present era of globalization, the traditional relationship of the "West with the rest" may substantially be changing in nature due to the famous shift of the heart of the global economy from the Trans-Atlantic to the Asia-Pacific. Indeed as the book argues, the Western cultural domination theory is now severely challenged with the world cultures

[12] For example, Kanso 1991, Robertson 1995, Terpstra and Sarathy 2000.

moving toward what Nederveen Pieterse has referred to as "cultural hybridization"—"the hybridization is the making of global culture a global mélange"[13].

According to the data, culled through an analysis of about more than 5,000 advertising samples, 30 of the 92 companies that advertised for the same product in France, Germany and India, have refrained from reiterating the same product advertisement. Of the 63 foreign companies operating in France, only 38 have not adapted to local circumstances. In Germany, of the 65 foreign companies present, only 26 have not adapted. In India, of the 36 companies operating in the country, only 11 have chosen to retain the same advertisement without modification. According to the survey, while most French companies tend, by and large, to retain the same product name as also the French language—in Germany, nine of the 21 American companies found have not used English in their advertising and only two have retained the English product name. Among the companies to use English in Germany, only three are British while 17 others are from non-Anglophone countries. Of the 16 German companies present in Germany, seven have resorted to English to sell. Of these, only two—the German Bose ("Better Sound through Research") and Hugo Boss ("Men at Work")—have retained their universal English slogan in France also.

Interestingly, the American Chrysler and Motorola have resorted to French to sell in Germany (for example, as mentioned earlier, the Motorola advertisement "je t'aime" and the Chrysler Voyager advertisement "Grand Café des Arts"). A number of Swiss watchmakers—Rado, Tissot, Rolex, Hermes, Longines, Raymond Weil and Vuarnet—on the other hand, have used their global English slogans everywhere. The Japanese Sony and Pioneer have used Italian sounding product names—"Scala" and "Impresso"—to position their products globally. Many automobile manufacturers have turned to using names for their cars that are either recognizable in many languages or invented and not found in any one of them—for example, Mondeo (Ford), Pajero (Mitsubishi), and Laguna (Renault). For their

[13] "A Survey of the 20th Century: Semi-integrated World", *The Economist*, September 11, 1999, 541–2.

Indian market, Piaget and Moderna Klober have used entire phrases in French and German to better sell. Clearly, it matters little whether the Indian consumer understands French or German—it suffices that he or she associates their use with French chic and German uncompromising quality and superior product design. Conversely, a few Indian companies have also resorted to French and German terminology to sell in the home market—for example, 'Voilà" (MindWare Software), "Airbus Industrie" (Tata Industries) and "Autobahn" (Tata Industries).

Paradoxically, however, even though the effects of globalization are felt everywhere, not every country is eager to give in to what they perceive as the corrosive effects of globalization. Hence, even though both France and Germany have used English relatively extensively in their advertising, Germany seems to accept English more easily than France as the language of international commerce. In France, for example, only five out of the 12 non-English speaking companies had used English. Of the three British companies found in that country, only one (Jaguar) had effectuated a translation of the English slogan ("Don't Dream it. Drive it") even while retaining it for the German market. Of the 20 American companies found, 12 had translated their slogan into French. The American Rank Xerox Company is one of the few companies to retain its English slogan in both France and Germany—"The Document Company."

One of the reasons why the overall figures for English are lower in the case of France—163 as compared to 634 for Germany (see Table 6.1)—is because France over the years has equipped itself with a veritable arsenal of decrees and directives against what it terms as "Franglais" or the intrusion of English into French (for example, le weekend, le parking or le marketing). With more than 420 linguistic combinations now theoretically possible, France is plagued by the very real fear that soon everybody will simply give up and speak English.[14] Advertisements containing English terms, with a few exceptions, are therefore outlawed (by the 1994 Toubon law) unless accompanied by a translation. For the German market, on the other hand, there are no such restrictions. As a result, the large majority of manufacturers

---

[14] Nederveen Pieterse, *Globalization and Culture: Global Melange* (Lanham MD: Rowman and Littlefield Publishers, 2003), 53.

Table 6.1   Foreign Language Inputs

	France		Germany		India	
English	163	79%	634	78%	–	–
French	–	–	77	10%	12	35%
German	2	1%	–	–	5	15%
Hindi	3	1%	–	–	–	–
Spanish	4	2%	24	3%	2	6%
Italian	13	6%	28	3%	–	–
Arabic	3	1%	–	–	7	21%
Other	19	9%	45	6%	8	24%
Total	207	100%	808	100%	34	100%

Source: Author.

have used some form of English in that country. As with the French language (weekend, parking and so on), German vocabulary also has absorbed its own share of foreign terms such as "swingt", "rendez-vous", "clever" and so on. Many companies also increasingly prefer the popular mixture of English and German otherwise known as Denglish. Audi, for example, promises you "Die Power."

In contrast to French advertising, which has only two German language inputs (Heineken and Citroen advertisements) German advertising contained 77 French language inputs. For example, "Baroque à la maison" (title-Ligne Roset); "Bourgeois. D'accord. Petit jamais" (title—Ligne Roset); "Restaurant chez…Café" (Davidoff Classic and Light Cigarettes); "Je t'aime" (Motorola) and "Grand Café des Arts" (Chrysler). Interestingly, some companies also combined French with German and English: for example, "Zelda. Die belle époque lebt" (title—Cor). "VINS DE FRANCE machen uns immer so schon frisch. Leicht. Rassig Kraftig. Und so OH LA LA" (Vins de France); "Mit einem Côtes du Rhône zahle Ich zur crème de la crème" (Vins de France); "Rendez-vous mit einer Konigin (Cunard Travels); and "Die Black Linie steht fur Noblesse und Eleganz" (Volkswagen). In India, where English is the norm, what is particularly interesting is that Indian advertising contained 12 French terms and five German terms (see Table 6.1).

This study concludes with the observation that the Western Imperialism thesis, while recognizing the trends toward Americanization, does not give adequate recognition to the various modes of resistance. It seems to assume that people passively fall prey to increasing Americanization and Westernization. For example, it ignores the way the French government has sought to restrict the import of words of non-French origin through the implementation of such laws as the 1994 Toubon Loi (law).

Similarly, the thesis, although useful in highlighting the exchanges in the economic domain, may not necessarily recognize all the complexities in certain other areas of cultural exchanges such as food, drink and entertainment where Western cultural products have to negotiate the complex local histories and traditions. Many international companies underestimate the strength of local products in the markets they enter. And they overestimate the value of their own reputations. Perhaps one of the causes of McDonald's success in foreign markets is that in addition to maintaining a strong brand image and consistent service standards around the world, its product offer has a local touch. In the Indian case, for example, McDonald's has brought about tremendous product innovations to suit the Indian palate. As the Indian market is 40 percent vegetarian, with an aversion to beef and pork among meat-eaters but with the general Indian fondness for spice with everything, McDonald's has come up with the McAloo Tikki potato burger, Mac Curry Pan (cottage cheese), the all-mutton McMaharajah, and sauces like McMasala and McImli to satisfy the Indian taste for spice. McDonald's has also introduced wraps, keeping in view India's penchant for chapattis. However, when it comes to other things, McDonald's has strict standardized specificities for its technology, product, client service, hygiene and operational systems.[15] As the McDonald's example in India shows, economic development is encouraging a new form of hybridization.

Similarly, Coke and Pepsi are sweeter in India than elsewhere. Both companies use well-known Indian actors such as Hrithik Roshan and Shah Rukh Khan to sell their products thereby associating what is fashionable in America with what is also fashionable in India. Yet others have sought to transform themselves into "national" companies

[15] Bureau of the Census, Statistical Abstract of the United States, 2000, Table 1373, US Department of Commerce, Economics and Statistics Administration, Washington DC, 2011.

by developing campaigns around the theme of Indian nationalism. Hyundai Motors, for example, made all efforts to disguise its foreignness by selling its product against the backdrop of the Red Fort and Indian tricolor. All this seems to suggest that globalization and localization, as far as they refer to culture, are interpretative processes. As Featherstone puts it, "no society ever receives cultural products from the outside passively, without engagement. They are usually modified and molded by the recipients to suit their local needs, values and aspirations".[16] Or as noted by Tomlinson:

> But what does this distribution of uniform cultural goods actually signify, other than the power of some capitalist firms to command wide markets for their products around the world? Well, if we assume that the sheer global presence of these goods is in itself a sign of a convergence towards a single capitalist culture, we are probably utilizing a rather impoverished concept of culture—one that reduces a "culture" merely to its material goods.[17]

In other words, there are no "global" or "foreign" meanings without "local" reference points, and vice versa; culture itself exists only when it is viewed relative to another culture. As Braudel puts it famously, "civilizations continuously borrow from their neighbors even if they 'reinterpret' and assimilate what they have adopted...."[18]

* * *

Recapitulation

Two points of relevance emerge: the first is that globalization can be "a tandem operation of local/global dynamics leading to a cultural mixing or global mélange of cultures.[19] This view is

[16] *The Economist*, November 22, 1997.
[17] Mike Featherstone, *Consumer Culture and Post Modernism*, 2nd edn (London: Sage Publications, 2007).
[18] Tomlinson, *Cultural Imperialism*, 62.
[19] Fernand Braudel, *A History of Civilisations*, trans. by Richard Mayne (New York: Penguin Books, 1999), 22, 29, 30.

endorsed by scholars such as Nederveen Pieterse, for example, who suggest that what is taking place today is a global culture of hybridization, a process of braiding rather than simply diffusion from developed to developing countries.[20] It is also reiterated by Roland Robertson who describes globalization as a dialectical movement in which the global is enriched by local specificities—to which it gives a universal reach—and in which the local is, for its part, also enriched by the influences stemming from the global."[21] Second, it would seem that with the emergence of the BRICS markets, the world cultural experiences are moving, not in a singular direction of uniformity as suggested but rather as a two-way process that also includes the impact of non-Western cultures on the West.

In 1983, Theodore Levitt, in fact, both overestimated and underestimated globalization. He did not anticipate that some markets would react against Western globalization. He also underestimated the power of globalization to transform entire nations to actually embrace elements of global capitalism as has been happening in the former Soviet Union, China, India and other parts of the world. More than twenty years later, this was put across more succinctly by Thomas Friedman, author of *The World Is Flat: A Brief History of the Twenty-First Century*. In his book, Friedman argues that a number of important events such as the birth of the Internet coincided to "flatten" the competitive landscape worldwide by increasing globalization and reducing the power of the states. Friedman's list of "flatness" includes the fall of the Berlin Wall, the rise of Netscape and the dot.com boom that led to a trillion dollar investment in fiber-optic cable; the emergence of communication software platforms and open source code enabling global collaboration and the rise of outsourcing, offshoring, supply chain and in-sourcing. According to Friedman, these flatteners converged around the year 2000 creating a "flat

---

[20] Pieterse, *Globalization and Culture*, 45.

[21] R. Robertson, "Problematic Globalization Theory 2000, Major Problematic", in G. Ritzer and B. Smart (eds), *Handbook of Social Theory* (London: Sage Publications, 2000), 102.

world, a global web-enabled platform for multiple forms of sharing knowledge and work, irrespective of time, distance, geography and increasingly language."[22] Friedman further observed that at the very moment this platform emerged, three huge economies materialized—those of China, India and the former Soviet Union and "the three billion people who were out of the game, walked into the playing field."[23]

What follows from this is not simply the point that the Imperialism thesis underestimates the cultural resilience and dynamism of non-Western cultures, their capacity to indigenize Western imports, but also that in the modern world, the earlier trend of cultural influence from the West to the periphery is now increasingly being contested. In India, for instance, pride in Indianness appears to have increased hand in hand with globalization. In line with this trend, the former fascination with all things "Western" is now gradually giving way to the sentiment that "desi" is just as "cool." In fashion, music and food, this often translates as a fusion of the East and West (for example, tandoori pizza, Bhangra and global desi for a range of fashionable East–West outfits).

The point I seek to make here is that if indeed a global culture is emerging, it will be, as Nederveen Pieterse puts it, essentially a hybrid, "cut and mix" culture.[24] As such, this perspective does not give prominence to globalization as a homogenizing force, nor does it believe in localization as a process opposed to globalization. Rather hybridization advocates an emphasis on processes of mediation that it views as central to cultural globalization. This position acknowledges that cultures have been in contact for a long time through empire, trade and religion. Therefore, a degree of hybridization of all cultures can safely be assumed. Cultural globalization, as Lie puts it, builds on existing theories and ideas of dependence, Westernization, Cultural Imperialism, cultural

[22] T.L. Friedman, *The World Is Flat: A Brief History of the Twenty-First Century* (Fairar, Strauss and Giroux, 2005), 50.

[23] Friedman, *The World Is Flat*, 205.

[24] Nederveen Pieterse, "Globalization as Hybridization", in *Global Modernities*, eds M. Featherstone, S. Lash, and R. Robertson (London: Sage Publications, 1995).

synchronization and the "global village".[25] Consequently, globalization, in my view, is more likely to be associated with multiculturalism rather than with Westernization. Indeed, evidence of this is now reflected in many diverse fields, for example, movies, art, literature, fashion, music and dance as also, increasingly, in the cutthroat world of advertising.

The following case study is an attempt to calibrate the growing impact of multiculturalism as reflected in advertising across two diverse continents and three different countries under globalization.

7

Impact of Multiculturalism

The initial task of this case study was to look at the percentage of multicultural advertisements in France, Germany and India to find out how far we have moved forward toward the goals previously mentioned, that is to say, toward, commonly understood symbols, visuals, and texts in international advertising. The data collection method, as stated before, takes into account 13 criteria or parameters (see Table 7.1) and is quite rigorous.

According to the data (see Table 7.2), France with an active base of 344 companies had a total of 1,112 advertisements. Germany, with a larger economy, had a base of 501 companies, with 2,557 advertisements. Surprisingly, nearly 400 Indian companies had actively advertised. They had a total of 1,174 advertisements. The large number of Indian companies can be explained by the fact that newer companies want to develop a brand image, get their products known and increase their market share. France had a total of 1,112 advertisements (including duplicates), Germany 2,557 and India, 1,174. In terms of original or non-duplicate advertisements, however, France had a total of 683 advertisements. Germany, 1,453 advertisements and India, 898 advertisements.

For the purposes of the multicultural analysis, only the original advertisements were taken into account to avoid duplication (see Table 7.2). For example, even though the perfume category in France

Table 7.1   Multicultural Elements

Criteria	France		Germany		India	
Textual Elements						
Title	86	19%	301	29%	126	23%
Slogan	28	6%	199	15%	46	8%
Product Name	119	26%	329	26%	51	9%
Other (Text)	49	11%	106	8%	52	10%
Visual Elements						
Person	39	8%	80	5%	57	10%
Animal	14	3%	48	4%	14	3%
Landscape	23	5%	48	4%	6	1%
Object	21	5%	35	3%	48	9%
Symbol	28	6%	47	4%	24	4%
Text in Image	28	6%	50	4%	8	1%
Other (Image)	15	3%	21	2%	76	14%
General Composition	11	2%	20	2%	38	7%
Total	461	100%	1284	100%	546	100%

Source: Author.

had a total of 87 advertisements (7.8 percent), only the originals were taken into consideration. This amounted to 38 advertisements (5.6 percent). All original advertisements were further analysed in terms of "strong" or "weak" elements (for example, "company name" is considered as "weak" element since it is unmodified in all three countries). France, in this case, had 279 "strong" multicultural advertisements (41 percent) and 112 "weak" ones (16 percent), which amounted to a total of 391 multicultural advertisements (57 percent) in that country. Germany, on the other hand, had a higher figure of 793 "strong" multicultural advertisements (55 percent) and 157 "weak" ones (10 percent), which amounted to a total of 950 multicultural advertisements (65 percent). India also had a relatively high volume of 362 "strong" multicultural advertisements (40 percent) and 99 weak ones (11 percent), which amounted to a total of 461 advertisements (51 percent) (Table 7.2).

Table 7.2　Total Multicultural Advertising

Each country group is divided into **Advertisements Originals** (Strong, %), **Advertisements multicultural** (Strong %, Weak %) and **Total** (Strong %, Weak %).

Categories/Subcategories	France — Ad. Originals	France — Ad. multicultural	France — Total	Germany — Ad. Originals	Germany — Ad. multicultural	Germany — Total	India — Ad. Originals	India — Ad. multicultural	India — Total
0 Perfume	38　5.6%	17　6.1% · 4　3.6%	21　45%　11%	18　1.2%	17　2.1% · 1　0.6%	18　94%　6% · 6　0.7%	6　1.7%	0　0.0%	6　0.00　0%
i) Cosmetics	8　1.2%	3　1.1% · 0　0.0%	3　38%　0%	6　0.4%	4　0.5% · 0　0%	4　67%　0% · 8　0.9%	4　1.1%	0　0.0%	4　50.00　0%
ii) Fashion									
Clothes	38	16 · 2	18	86	58 · 18	76	64	53 · –	53
Fabric	2	1 · –	1	1	1 · –	1	24	10 · –	10
Shoes	3	3 · –	3	11	9 · –	9	20	4 · 8	12
Accessories	13	2 · 1	5	9	8 · 1	9	8	5 · –	5
Sum Totals	56　8.2%	22　7.9% · 3　2.7%	25　39%　5%	107　7.4%	76　9.6% · 19　12.1%	95　71%　18% · 116　12.9%	72　19.9%	8　8.1%	80　62%　7%
iv) Watches	35　5.1%	17　6.1% · 4　3.6%	21　49%　11%	50　3.4%	37　4.7% · 2　1.3%	39　74%　4% · 19　2.1%	10　2.8%	2　2.0%	12　53%　11%
v) Press	6　0.9%	1　0.4% · 3　2.7%	4　17%　50%	9　0.6%	5　0.6% · 0　0%	5　56%　0% · 3　0.3%	0　0.0%	0	0　0%　0%
vi) Gastronomy									
Alcohol	42	22 · 6	28	104	50 · 5	55	24	12 · 5	17
Tobacco/Cigarettes	–	– · –	0	35	30 · –	30	18	9 · –	9
Food/Drink/Restaurants	11	4 · –	4	30	8 · 10	18	7	1 · 1	2
Sum Totals	53　7.8%	26　9.3% · 6　5.4%	32　49%　11%	169　11.6%	88　11.1% · 15　10%	103　52%　9% · 49　5.5%	22　6.1%	6　6.1%	28　45%　12%
vii) Leisure and Travel									
Airlines	29	25 · 3	28	42	39 · 2	41	20	15 · 2	17
Countries and Regions (foreign)	7	7 · –	7	37	37 · –	37	8	8 · –	8
Countries and Regions (nat.)	2	– · –	0	–	– · –	0	31	3 · –	3
Travel Agencies	8	8 · –	8	6	3 · –	3	1	1 · –	1
Hotels	17	7 · –	7	12	1 · –	1	16	4 · 1	5
Sum Totals	63　9.2%	47　16.8% · 3　2.7%	50　75%　5%	97　6.7%	80　10.1% · 2　1.3%	82　83%　2% · 76　8.5%	31　8.6%	3　3.0%	34　41%　4%
viii) Automobiles									
Bicycl./Motocycl.	1	1 · –	1	1	1 · –	1	6	– · 5	5
Cars	58	30 · 14	44	130	75 · 24	99	18	10 · 2	12
Heavy Vehicles	3	2 · 1	3	8	3 · –	3	1	– · –	0
Vehicle rental	1	1 · –	1	9	9 · –	9	10	2 · 1	3
Vehicle accessories	3	– · –	0	9	5 · 1	6	31	11 · 4	15
Sum Totals	66　9.7%	34　12.2% · 15　13.4%	49　52%　23%	157　10.8%	93　11.7% · 25　15.9%	118　59%　16% · 66　7.3%	23　6.0%	10　10.1%	33　35.00　15%
ix) Computers	37　5.4%	31　11.1% · 5　4.5%	36　84%　14%	73　5.0%	61　7.7% · 12　8%	73　84%　16% · 20　2.2%	6　1.7%	6　6.1%	12　50.00　30%
x) Telecommunication	36　5.3%	9　3.2% · 2　1.8%	11　25%　6%	68　4.7%	58　480.0% · 8　5%	46　56%　12% · 30　3.3%	12　3.3%	13　13.1%	25　40.00　43%
xi) Technical Products									
Audio-Video	18	10 · 7	17	28	21 · 6	27	45	21 · 10	31
Cameras	5	– · 5	5	25	11 · 14	25	3	1 · 2	3
Photocopying machines	3	– · 3	3	18	11 · 6	17	6	3 · –	3
Sum Totals	26　3.8%	10　3.6% · 15　13.4%	25　38%　58%	71　4.9%	43　5.4% · 26　16.6%	69　61%　37% · 54　6.0%	25　6.9%	12　12.1%	37　46%　22%
xii) Housing/Furniture									
Furniture	30	3 · 7	10	70	37 · 14	51	20	11 · –	11
Household articles	10	2 · 2	4	32	16 · 2	18	26	4 · 7	11
Housing Construction	8	– · 1	1	46	7 · 2	9	35	13 · 11	24
Housing Finance	1	– · 1	1	18	1 · –	1	4	– · 1	1
Sum Totals	49　7.2%	6　2.2% · 10　8.9%	16　12%　20%	166　11.4%	61　7.7% · 18　11.5%	79　37%　11% · 85　9.5%	28　7.7%	19　19.2%	47　33%　22%
xiii) Industry and Commerce	12	5 · –	5	2	1 · –	1	52	21 · –	21
Multi-diversified industries	–	– · –	0	17	9 · –	9	13	2 · 3	5
Chemicals Industry Sector	–	– · –	0	3	– · –	0	20	10 · –	10
Steel/Metallurgy Sector	10	3 · 3	6	9	2 · –	2	30	12 · 5	17
Mechanical/Electrical Sector	18	3 · 11	14	36	15 · 10	25	18	8 · 2	10
Diverse Industry Sector	–	– · –	0	–	– · –	0	29	13 · –	13
Textiles Sector	–	– · –	0	–	– · –	0	29	13 · –	13
Agricultural Sector	–	– · –	0	2	– · –	0	10	1 · –	1
Fairs	2	– · 1	1	7	3 · –	3	7	3 · –	3
Public Sector	9	9 · –	9	18	8 · –	8	6	4 · –	1
Other	4	4 · –	4	9	2 · 2	4	16	4 · –	4
Sum Totals	55　8.1%	24　8.6% · 15　13.4%	39　44%　27%	103　7.1%	40　5.0% · 12　7.6%	52　39%　12% · 201　22.4%	75　20.7%	10　10.1%	85　37%　5%
xiv) Finance and Insurance									
Banks/Credit Cards	37	5 · 2	7	75	34 · 8	42	53	15 · 8	23
Insurance	8	1 · –	1	81	17 · 2	19	12	– · –	0
Sum Totals	65　6.6%	6　2.2% · 2　1.8%	8　13%　4%	156　10.7%	51　6.4% · 10　6.4%	61　33%　6% · 65　7.2%	15　4.1%	8　8.1%	23　23.00　12%
xv) Health	7　1.0%	2　0.7% · 1　0.9%	3　29%　14.0%	25　1.7%	10　1.3% · 3　1.9%	13　40%　12.0% · 16　1.8%	8　2.2%	1　1.0%	9　50%　6%
xvi) NGOs	5　0.7%	4　1.4% · 0　0.0%	4　80%　0%	16　1.1%	6　0.8% · 0　0.0%	6　38%　0% · 1　0.1%	0　0.35%	0	0　0.0%　0%
xvii) Energy	5　0.7%	0　0.0% · 0　0.0%	0　0%　0%	26　1.8%	5　0.6% · 0　0.0%	5　19%　0% · 24　2.7%	8　2.2%	0　0.0%	8　33%　0%

xviii) Media	54	8.5%	11	3.9%	24	21.4%	35	19%	41.0%	98	6.7%	57	7.2%	4	2.5%	61	58%	4%	38	4.2%	8	2.2%	0	0.0%	8	21%	0%
ix) Diverse Delivery Services	5	1	–	1	14	10	–	10	9	4	1	5
Cultural Activities	20	6	–	6	8	6	–	6	1	1	–	1
Lottery	2	–	–	0	9	2	–	2	6	3	–	3
Other	8	2	–	2	7	3	–	3	5	–	2.2%	1	1.0%	0
Sum Totals	35	5.1%	9	3.2%	0	0.0%	9	26%	0%	38	2.6%	21	2.6%	0	0.0%	21	55%	0%	21	2.3%	8	2.2%	1	1.0%	9	38%	5%
Totals	68	100%	279	100%	112	100%	391	41%	61%	1458	100%	793	100%	157	100%	950	55%	10%	898	100%	362	100%	99	100%	461	40%	11%
Weightage of Multiculturalism		41%		16%		57%					55%		10%			65%				40%		11%		51%
		Strong		Weak		Strong-Weak					Strong		Weak			Strong-Weak				Strong		Weak		Strong-Weak

Source: Author.

The initial view, looking at this body of advertisements, indicated that where there were international sales or prospects of international sales, multicultural advertising was resorted to. However, when the product was meant only for the local market, there was much less of multicultural advertising. For instance, in the case of perfumes, French advertising in this category contained only 56 percent of multicultural elements. In contrast, Germany and India showed 100 percent. For the fashion category also, French advertising contained only 44 percent of multicultural elements, while the corresponding German and Indian figures stood at 89 percent and 69 percent respectively. However, for some of the other categories, such as "Food and beverages" or "automobiles," for instance, there was less disparity in the figures between the three countries.

Not surprisingly perhaps, customers were targeted somewhat differently. However, what was increasingly apparent is that advertisers use multicultural images and texts that appeal globally. For example, the Taj Mahal, Eiffel Tower, or pyramids of Egypt are recognizable internationally as symbols of beauty and excellence that their products are supposed to reflect; or take landscapes that conjure beauty; or product names (such as Shalimar, Samskara and Jaipur used by international parfumiers such as Guerlain and Boucheron) that immediately bring about feelings of exotica. Another remarkable conclusion was the almost similar degree of openness to the foreign element in all the three countries, denoting a high level of acceptance of multicultural products. In figures, 57 percent of advertising in France made use of multiculturalism to sell. The figure in Germany at 65 percent was even higher. A large number of Indian companies, 51 percent, also made use of multicultural advertertisements (see Table 7.2).

However, one needs to add an important rider here. While all three countries have made extensive use of multicultural advertisements, some groups of products did not see this. The French perfume industry for example, advertised exclusively in France. This is understandable since the overwhelming number of perfumes sold in France were French. A large number of Indian products also did not take recourse to multicultural advertising since these products were sold in India only, although, of course, they used English overwhelmingly.

Empirical Evidence

1. Perfume

This product category contained five identical transfers: (i) France + Germany: Eternity for men eau de toilette (Calvin Klein); (ii) France + Germany: Chanel No 5; (iii) France + Germany: Egoiste Platinum (Chanel); France + India: Tresor (Lancôme); France + India: Drakkar Noir (Guy Laroche). The fact that four out of six French advertisements in Germany were identical transfers seems to indicate an opening for French products in that country.

Germany, interestingly, had the highest number of multicultural advertisements in this instance—17 strong advertisements and one weak advertisement in a total of 18 original advertisements, which amounted to 100 percent multicultural advertisements. Twelve companies had advertised in this category. Thirteen of the 17 advertisements found in this country made no references to Germany. There were, however, 15 references to France. Examples include: "Azarro pour homme" (Azarro), "Eau de toilette" (Calvin Klein), "Paloma Picasso cree Minotaure" (Paloma Picasso) "Parfum de peau" (Montana); and "Ungaro pour l'homme" (Ungaro). There were altogether 14 references to the English language, mostly product names, slogans, or titles. For example, "Obsession for man" (Calvin Klein), "Night flight to the stars" (Joop); "The new fragrance for men" (Aramis), "Eternity for men" (Calvin Klein); "Heaven" (Chopard), "Universo—the ecstasy of the unknown" (Les Parfums de Coty); "Escape" (Calvin Klein), and "Like a desert rain" (Panama Jack). Some product names reinforced Italy: "Azarro"; "Universo", "Gio", and "Ungaro". Others such as "Havana" (Aramis) emphasize a Latino ambience through its visual of a hacienda and a colored man.

France, in contrast, had fewer multicultural advertisements—17 of 38 original advertisements were strong multicultural advertisements (four were weak advertisements). This amounted to 21 (17+4) multicultural advertisements (56 percent). Altogether 17 companies had advertised. This category also contained the largest number of English words (nine times). Some of the most interesting product names were found here: for instance, Shalimar (Guerlain) Jaipur (Boucheron), and Samsara (Guerlain). These product names were utilized to reinforce the exoticism of India along with a visual of the Taj Mahal.

In India, all six advertisements used multiculturalism to sell. Five companies had advertised in all. Cacharel, as mentioned earlier, advertised its Eden perfume in France with the frontal view of a young woman with the slogan "Le Parfum Défendu". In India, this was translated as "The Forbidden Fragrance" and the same advertisement was slightly shaded to make the nudity of the French advertisement less obvious. For its Trésor perfume advertisement, the French Lancôme made an identical transfer of image and text ("Le Parfum des Instants Précieux"). Guy Laroche also made an identical transfer of its Drakkar Noir advertisement, the visual showing the naked upper torso of a Caucasian male. Yet another company, Baccarose, also used the theme of virility (naked male torso) to market its "Copper for men" deodorant ("Before you get close, get Copper"). A Ralph Lauren advertisement evoked the popular game of polo through its product name, "Polo," and the visual of a polo player. Yet another advertisement evoked Africa through its visual of the African savannah (title—"Living without boundaries") and the product name of "Safari." Premium Toileteries, on the other hand, showed a couple kissing thereby indicating a certain infiltration of Western stereotypes.

2. Cosmetics and Toiletries

In France, this product category carried three "strong" multicultural advertisements (zero weak advertisements) in a total of eight original advertisements (38 percent). Five companies in all had advertised. Examples include English product name "Kiss-Kiss" lipstick (Guerlain). In Germany, there were four strong multicultural advertisements (zero weak advertisements) in a total of six original advertisements (67 percent). Six companies had advertised. For example, "Basic Homme" (Vichy Laboratoires). In India, there were four strong multicultural advertisements (zero weak advertisements) in a total of eight original advertisements (50 percent). Six companies had advertised. Examples include Lancôme that carried the same visual of model Isabella Rossini. The French text "La France a son mot à dire sur la beauté", however, was translated for the Indian market as "France has a word for beauty".

3. Travel and Leisure

In this product category, German advertising contained a total of 80 strong multicultural advertisements (two weak advertisements) in a total of 97 original advertisements. This amounted to 82 (80+2) multicultural advertisements (84 percent). Altogether 34 companies had advertised. France contained a total of 47 strong multicultural advertisements (three weak advertisements) in a total of 63 original advertisements. This amounted to 50 (47+3) multicultural advertisements (80 percent). Altogether 39 companies had advertised. Indian advertising contained a total of 31 strong multicultural advertisements (three weak advertisements) in a total 76 original advertisements. This amounted to 34 (31+3) multicultural advertisements (45 percent). Altogether 28 companies had advertised in this category.

Let us now come to the various sub-categories.

Airlines

This sub-category in France contained 25 strong multicultural advertisements (three weak advertisements) in a total of 29 original advertisements. Seventeen companies had advertised. In Germany, it contained 39 strong multicultural advertisements (two weak ones) in a total of 42 original advertisements. Altogether, 14 companies had advertised. In India, this subcategory contained altogether 15 strong multicultural advertisements (two weak advertisements) in a total of 20 original advertisements. Nine companies had advertised.

In Germany, 19 out of 42 airlines operating in that country were German; in France, three out of 29 were French and in India, three out of 20 were Indian. Most airlines resorted to English to sell: nine times in France as opposed to 41 times in Germany. In English speaking India, the foreign languages used were Arabic (four times) and French (one time). The majority of airlines in Germany also retained their universal English titles/slogans. For example, "You will love the way we fly" (Delta Air Lines)." One airline can make a difference" (Continental Airlines), and "The American Way of life" (American Airlines). Interestingly, the majority of German carriers, including Lufthansa, also used English to sell. For example, "Happy Days, Happy Weeks" and "Lufthansa Airline" (instead of the German term "Fluglinie"). Some, such as Interot Airways and Condor, resorted to Denglish—"Art Directors". Milchtrinker und Vielflieger, "Modebewusste, Italienfreaks und Vielflieger:" (Interot Airways); and "Clever fliegen, Starten und landen in Augsburg"/"Holiday ohne Ice"/"Die besten trips seit' 68" (Condor). Many Asian airlines also interspersed German with the occasional English word. For example, "Lebensqualitat non-stop" (Korean Air); "Kuala Lumpur 747–400. Jeden Dienstag, Non Stop" (Malaysia Airlines).

Visually speaking, the majority of airlines advertising in Germany have made some form of reference to it. For example, Deutsche BA showed the German flag; and Singapore Airlines and British Airways showed the Black Forest and Brandenburger Tor. Aer Lingus, on the other hand, made references to the home country of Ireland through such famous literary names as Joyce, Yeats, Beckett, Shaw and so on ("Hier konnen Sie mit Joyce, Yeats, Beckett, Shaw, Behan und Guiness vertaut machen"). The US was undoubtedly the most popular travel destination in Germany followed by Asia. This was supported by the fact that there were altogether 10 references to Asia in German advertising, that is, 10 advertisements inserted by five airlines, out of which four were Asian—Cathay Pacific, Singapore Airlines, Korean Air and Malaysian Airlines.

In France for the same sub-category, 10 out of 29 French adver-tisements (inserted by 14 foreign airlines) also referred to the US, with the majority of the images showing such universal stereotypes as the Empire State Building (Continental Airlines); American Flag; Manhattan Skyline, and Niagara Falls (US Air). An interesting exam-ple was the American Airlines slogan "America (i)n sur toute la ligne" in France. In Germany, this appeared as "The American way of life". In the German case, some airlines such as Air Liberte, made visual references both to the home country (French flag + bottle of chilled champagne) and country of destination (Big Ben). As with Germany once again, the second most popular travel destination in France was also Asia. References to Asia included altogether 10 advertisements inserted by five airlines out of which four were Asian. Most of them were the same as in Germany—Cathay Pacific (The Heart of Asia), Singapore Airlines (Surprising Singapore), and Malaysian Airlines ("Discover Malaysia"). Visuals included Thai currency (Thai Airways); the Chinese symbols of yin and yang (Korean Air); Niagara Falls (Air Canada); dolphins (Delta Air Lines); American flag (Delta Air Lines); Asians (Malaysia Airlines); and French flag (Air France/ Air Inter).

Indian advertising contained altogether 32 examples of multi-cultural advertising. Apart from Air Mauritius and Jet Airways, all other airlines found were the same as in Europe, that is, Air Canada, Delta, Emirates, Gulf Air, Cathay Pacific, Malaysia Airlines, and Singapore Airlines. Most of them, once again, emphasized the global or regional aspect in their advertising: "The Heart of Asia" (Cathay Pacific); and "The First Global Airline from South East Asia" (Malaysia Airlines). The "global" aspect was underlined four times: for example, by Malaysia Airlines, which showed a globe— "Malayasia Airlines now flies to six continents. The first global airline South-East Asia's;" and by Cathay Pacific, which indicated its base, Hong Kong as the "world's best city for business." A Gulf Air advertisement said, "Introducing New York—We're spreading the international smile". What is interesting is that Gulf Air reiterated the same stereotypes for both its Indian and European markets, that is, American Flag, Statue of Liberty and so on. Air Canada used the French term "*en route*" ("This week, 148 lucky people will relax at home *en route* to London").

What is the most interesting here is the emphasis on the "global" or "regional" aspect—four advertisements inserted by three airlines—Delta, Singapore Airlines and Swiss Air—emphasized their "global excellence"; the British Airways slogan said—"The world's favorite airline"; Lufthansa presented itself as the airline with the largest worldwide network ("Weltweit grosstes Strecknnetz"); and Malaysia Airline said it was the first global airline of South-east Asia." The concept of "global integration" was reiterated by the American

United Airlines slogan, "Come fly the Airline that is uniting the world". Cathay Pacific emphasized that it is "The Heart of Asia." Interestingly, the concept of European integration, appeared in two British Airlines advertisements for the German market—"Diamond Euro Class"/"Die neue Club Europa".

Hotels

This subcategory in France contained seven strong multicultural advertisements (zero weak ones) in a total of 17 original advertisements. Altogether 10 companies had advertised. Seven out of 10 advertisements (inserted by six out of 10 companies) contained 19 multicultural elements. For example, a Sofitel Hotel advertisement used the English term "weekend" without the mandatory translation. Euro Disney advertised for Disneyland Paris with Mickey Mouse. Two other advertisements, also in English—"For the World's Finest (Fly Buy Dubai) and "From your heart" (Abu Dhabi Airport Duty Free)—showed Arabic writing. This is perhaps not so surprising when one considers the fact that France has a strong Arab population. The term "weekend," of course, is now quasi French—it is integrated into the French language with such other popular terms as "football", "volley", "goal", "meeting", "faire un sitting", le "parking", un "sketch", and un "gag", usually without the mandatory translation. In contrast, the English term "airbag" is always accompanied by the equivalent French translation, "coussin gonflable de protéction".

In India for the same sub-category, in addition to five Indian hotel advertisements, four other advertisements inserted by three foreign companies were found that advertised with the same visual in all three countries. This subcategory contained four strong multicultural advertisements (one weak advertisement) in a total of 16 original advertisements. Eight companies had advertised in all. In India, a high PDI society,[1] terms such as "luxury" and "status" have

---

[1] Geert Hofstede, *Culture's Consequences: Comparing Values, Behaviours, Institutions and Organizations across Nations*, 2nd edn (Thousand Oaks, CA: Sage Publications, 2001).

a very positive value or power of sell and are therefore reiterated: For example—"Five Star luxury holidays"; luxuriously appointed rooms"; "Nepal's premier five star deluxe hotel"; "...grandeur, luxury and elegance" (Hotel Yak & Yeti); "It's a whole new experience in luxury" (Hyatt Regency, Delhi)..."most luxurious beach"; ...all in 5 star luxury (The Retreat, Mumbai). "A million bulbs, each a shining tribute to your own status" (Hotel Hyatt); "Introducing modern luxury" (Westin Hotels and Resorts); and "No one can beat the Ashok for its grandeur and old-world charm—a delightful combination that spells luxury"/"the Ashok—one of the finest luxury hotels in Southern India"; (Ashok Elite Hotels, Delhi, Bengaluru, Kovalam).

Countries and Regions (Foreign)

This sub-category in France contained seven strong multicultural advertisements (zero weak advertisements) in a total of seven original advertisements. Five companies had advertised. In Germany, this sub-category contained 37 strong multicultural advertisements (zero weak advertisements) in a total of 37 original advertisements. Fourteen companies had advertised. Indian advertising in this instance contained eight strong multicultural advertisements (zero weak advertisements) in a total of eight original advertisements. Three companies had advertised.

According to the data, Germany contained the highest volume of multicultural advertisements—37 advertisements inserted by 14 different companies containing 103 multicultural elements. Of these 16 resorted to a foreign language to sell (in all, five foreign languages were used). Examples included: "India" (advertisement slogan for India); "A world of its own" (advertisement slogan for Indonesia); 'Portuguese blues" (advertisement slogan for Portugal); and "Espana" (advertisement slogan for Spain). The widespread use of English, once again, emphasized the fact that this language has wider acceptance in Germany.

Most travel advertisements resorted to national stereotypes along with traditional tourism, that is, sun, sand and sea, to sell. An advertisement marketing Israel for example, emphasized the fact that its "Kibbuz" cannot be described only experienced ("Unseren Kibbuz kann man nich erklaren, den muss man erleben"). The visual depicted a camel, a sun-kissed beach dotted with lush palm trees. A second advertisement pointed out that it is only in Israel that one could gorge on a falafel at 3 am and visit the flea market at noon ("Falafel um 3.00 Uhr und mittags auf den Flohmarkt. So einen Urlaub kann Ich nur in Israel"); India, on the other hand, was described as a land of "boundless vitality and culture", "its waters as smooth as silk where even the fish swim in saris" ("In Indien ist das Wasser wie Seide und sogar die Fische tragen Saris"). The visual showed a tiger, fishermen, a river, fish and sari-clad Indian women.

The more interesting advertisements, however, emphasized art, culture, history, food, architecture and other unique characteristics through sophisticated imagery. For example, a French travel advertisement promoting Belgium showed the image of the Flemish artist, Peter Paul Rubens, the text inviting the reader to "spend a weekend with this seductive bearded guy of excellent family background" ("Et si vous passiez votre prochain weekend avec ce séduisant barbu d'excellente famille?"). Elsewhere a German advertisement marketing Spain showed images of Post-Impressionist and Renaissance painters, Vincent van Gogh and Albrecht Durer ("Alte Meister und junge Wilde treffen sich auf dem Paseo del Arte"). These advertisements, of course, are targeted at upper-class consumers, as they are more open to the kinds of symbols that are significant to their status and self-expressive aims,[2] and not to mention the foreign language that is also often retained (that is, "Paseo del Arte").

Interestingly, advertisements in all three countries used universal archetypes such as human passion and desire for adventure to incite the reader to visit the suggested exotic locations. For example, "passion...one week in Israel" ("passions...une semaine en Israel"); and "passion...one week in Cote d'Ivoire" ("passions...une semaine en Cote d'Ivoire"). Both French and German advertising also widely used the concept of "a different world" ("Wie Klange aus einer anderen Welt") (As ringing bells from another world) or "supernatural world" ("monde du surnaturel"). A French advertisement marketing Hong Kong, for example, not only described it as the "most unique place on

[2] Sidney J. Levy, "Social Class and Consumer Behavior", in *On Knowing the Consumer*, ed. Joseph W. Newman (New York: John Wiley, 1966), 146–60.

earth" ("Hong Kong—un monde unique au monde"), but also one "where the supernatural is married to wisdom" ("Il existe un monde ou le surnaturel se marie avec la sagesse"). All advertisements marketing Hong Kong used certain characteristics typical of Chinese advertising such as an indirect approach, respect for the elderly, magic, prosperity, social status and tradition to sell. For example, a German tourism advertisement marketing Hong Kong used the visual of Chinese wise men and the concept of "good fortune" and "longevity"—"certain colors are associated with good fortune and longevity" ("Welche Farben haben Gluck und langes Leben"). The same visual was retained for the French market also, but the text was slightly modified to suggest "a world where lights shine bright with thousand colors" ("Il existe un monde ou les lumières brillent de mille couleurs").

The term "color", in particular, appeared to have a certain resonance with consumers of both the countries. Another tourism advertisement also reiterated this concept to sell Spain in Germany—"the most colorful of our islands is found at the end of the world" ("Unsere farbigste Insel liegt am Ende der Welt"); and yet another one suggested that a trip to India would add color to one's life: ("Bringen Sie Farbe in Ihr Leben—auf nach Indien"). (Bring colour into your lives—travel to India). We have previously seen the importance of smell in perfume advertisements. A German advertisement specifically used this appeal to market Hong Kong as a "fragrant harbor" ("Kreuzten Piraten vor dem duftenden Hafen"). (Pirates circling around the fragrant harbor). Yet another one promoting Mexico sought to tempt its readers through its "hot and fiery Guacamole" ("Wollen Sie eine feurig-scharfe Guacamole probieren?").

However, once again, it was really the proliferation of the "supranational" elements that best subscribes to our thesis of a growing trend toward regional and global integration, that is, a larger unity. Some of the examples illustrating this were: a French travel advertisement for Turkey describing its incredible diversity as a part of multicultural Europe ("La Turquie quand l'Europe devient plurielle"); (Turkey when Europe becomes multicultural); two French and German advertisements that highlighted the integration of Austria in the European Community—"Welcome to Europe" ("Bienvenue a l'Europe/"Servus Europa"); a German advertisement for Indonesia that invited the reader to visit "a land of "more than 300 diverse cultures where one will be culturally pampered" ("In einem Land mit uber 300 verschieden Kulturen wird man Sie kultiviert verwohnen"), and an Indian advertisement for South Africa that said—"South Africa. A world in one country"; and yet another one promoting Singapore, that said, "Incentive Isle Singapore: "Where the world comes together." Interestingly, the same advertisement in France was very similar—"Singapore—Tout le monde s'y retrouve" ("Singapore—where the world comes together").

Travel Agencies

In France, this subcategory had eight strong multicultural advertisements (zero weak advertisements) in a total of eight advertisements. Five companies had advertised. Germany contained three strong multicultural advertisements (zero weak advertisements) in a total of six original advertisements. Three companies had advertised in this case. The Indian subcategory displayed one strong multicultural advertisement (zero weak advertisements) of a total of one advertisements. One company had advertised.

In France, also, the majority of travel advertisements resorted to traditional tourism, that is, sun, sand and sea to sell. For example, "sunshine…one week in New Caledonia" ("plein soleil…une semaine en Nouvelle Caledonie"). Most advertisements were targeted at the globe-trotting men and women for whom the world is rapidly becoming a "world without frontiers". TMR, for example, invited the reader to ring in the New Year in New York, the visual showing once more, such familiar stereotypes as the Empire State Building, and the Statue of Liberty.

In Germany, a Cunard Travels advertisement used German in combination with French—"Rendez-vous mit einer Konigin"—to sell a trip to the UK. The visual appropriately showed Buckingham Palace and the Queen. Some other German tour operators such as LTU Reisen attempted to strike a balance between Nature and Culture ("genau das richtige Verhaltnis zwischen Kultur und Natur") (Just the right relationship between Culture and Nature) through their proposed voyage to Mexico combining "sunbathing", "coral reefing" ("Sonnenbaden"/ "nach Korallen tauchen") with a visit to the Mayas ("Mayas besuchen"). Exotica was an integral part of a dream holiday package—for example, a German tour operator, LTU Tjaereborg, used the terminology "Arabian nights" ("Marchenurlaub aus 1001 Nacht") (1001 Tales from Arabian Nights) and the visual of nomads and camels to market Morocco and Tunisia. LTU Meier's Weltreisen marketed Bali and Sumatra through its advertisement text—"temples like sea sands" ("Tempel wie Sand aus Meer") and the visual of exotic female temple dancers.

In India, for the same subcategory, a Travel Agency, Sita World Travel, displayed the logos of 28 different international airlines. The advertisement title said "Frequent travelers have always had the choice of the world at any of our own 24 one stop locations". Interestingly, references to our South Asian neighbors, however, included Bangladesh only—"Visit Bangladesh" (Bangladesh Parijatan Corporation).

High-End Fashion

In this principal product category, French advertising contained altogether 22 strong multicultural advertisements (three weak advertisements) in a total of 56 original advertisements. This amounted to 25 (22+3) multicultural advertisements (45 percent). Altogether 34 companies had advertised. German advertising contained 76 strong multicultural advertisements (19 weak advertisements) in a total of 107 original advertisements. This amounted to 95 (76+19) multicultural advertisements (89 percent). Altogether 45 companies had advertised. Indian advertising contained 72 strong multicultural advertisements (eight weak advertisements) in a total of 116 original advertisements. This amounted to 80 (72+8) multicultural advertisements (69 percent). Altogether 40 companies had advertised.

In France, both text and image contained more or less an equivalent number of multicultural elements (text: 11 advertisements; image: seven advertisements; text + image: four advertisements); German advertising, however, had more text than image (text: four advertisements; image: eight advertisements; text+ image: 22 advertisements) since they tended to describe the product; in a developing country like India, on the other hand, image, understandably, had priority: (image: 20 advertisements; text + image: 23 advertisements; text: 14 advertisements).

Let us examine the diverse sub-categories.

Clothing

In France, this sub-category contained 16 strong multicultural advertisements (two weak advertisements) in a total of 38 original advertisements. Altogether 22 companies had advertised in this instance. Germany had a total of 58 "strong" multicultural advertisements (and 18 weak advertisements) in a total of 86 original advertisements. Thirty-two companies had advertised. In India, this sub-category contained 53 strong multicultural advertisements (zero weak advertisements) in a total of 64 original advertisements. Twenty-five companies had advertised.

In France, the multicultural elements were composed primarily of English titles/slogans and were almost always accompanied by the mandatory French translation: "Men at work"/Hommes au travail (Hugo Boss). Benetton, however, retained both its universal slogan "United Colors of Benetton" and the English term "AIDS," *sans* translation.

In Germany, English was used much more extensively. Examples included "Successful Living" (slogan—Diesel); "The Chance to be different" (Title—Knock out); "They're a big hit with the girls around here" (text in image—Mustang); "Giving out parking tickets is great fun, wearing jeans is even better" (text in image—Mustang); "Fits the man" (slogan—Marlboro Classics); "Art of Fashion" (slogan—Rosner); "Realizing the meaning of life" (title—S.Oliver); "Looking for a new challenge" (title—S.Oliver); "Commanding Officer" (title – Comma); "Taking the day off with your girl" (title—S.Oliver); "Men at work" (slogan—Boss); (title—Boss); "On the road again. Off the road again" (title—Timberland);"Dressed for attraction. Dressed for action" (title—Timberland) and "Design for function" (slogan—Offermann); Sometimes English was used in combination with German. For example, "Wir mussen uns hier ab mit old German traditions and that's der Dank" (text in image— Mustang); "etwas oversized" (title—Bueckle); "Hallo wir sind Land's End aus America" (title—Land's End); "New York, New York" (title—Joop); and "Erstens Eton. Zweitens Harvard' (title—Tony Gard); Italy was represented by "Moda al Dente" (slogan Cinque); Lacoste retained its French copy, "Salut! Le Style. Liberté. Egalité. Fraternité." (Salut, The Style, Liberty, Equality, Fraternity). Visuals comprised penguin (Bueckle); crocodile (Lacoste); desert (Eduard Dressler and Panama Jack), Buddha statue (Ticoline), map of Italy (Lamy), American flag (Comma), Marilyn Monroe (Bueckle), American cowboy (Marlboro), Grand Canyon (Eduard Dressler) and canals of Venice (Loro Piana).

Indian advertising contained a large number of references to France. Companies often highlighted the "distinguished" French origin of their product—even resorting to some French in an effort to better sell. For example, "Ooh la la" (Cardin); "Voila" (Cardin); and "… je ne sais quoi" (Louis Philippe). A Cardin advertisement referred to the popular French style icons of the 1960s, 1970s and 1980's—Brigitte Bardot, Catherine Deneuve and Jeanne Moreau ("Contrary to popular belief, it wasn't Brigitte Bardot, Catherine Deneuve or Jeanne Moreau who drove French men to madness and frenzy. It was a man"). The advertisement visual depicted a young Indian woman seated at the hairdressers' reading the French *"Elle"* magazine for women. Yet another Cardin advertisement drew on France's well-known culinary expertise—"Come to think of it, French dressing has the same effect on women as on French salads".

To sell its product line named Monte Carlo, one Indian garment manufacturer—OWM, showed an Indian couple dressed in the company's clothing studying a menu (Menu du Jour) in a French Bistro that read—"Bistro Romain 55F; Quiche aux Poireaux, Oeuf dur Provencal"... Italian chic was just as popular with the Indian consumer. Drawing on this, Oswal Knit marketed its clothing line as "Gadoni of Italy." To sell its range of formal shirts, Vimal referred to Julius Caesar—"How an adventurous Kashmir goat kid fuelled Caesar's warm passions." Others such as C.D. and Newman emphasized "Italian Fit" and "Fine Italian Designer Wear"; and Allen Solly referred to its British origins—"Shirts born in Nottingham, England and raised in New England". As for the US, only two companies, Raymond and Arrow have referred to it. While Arrow marketed itself as "America's shirtmakers since 1851", Raymond named its shirts, "Park Avenue". Raymond also resorted to Darwin's theory of the fittest o sell its trousers—"Darwin's theory of survival of the fittest is now a range of trousers"; The Zodiac range of shirts was marketed as "The soul of Europe"; The Lee Cooper Jeans slogan said "The original European jeans since 1908." In visuals, Digjam showed a Dalmatian; and Grasim Gwalior, a Greek statue.

Shoes:

In France were found three strong multicultural advertisements (zero weak advertisements) in a total of three original advertisements. Only two companies had advertised. In Germany were found altogether nine strong multicultural advertisements (zero weak advertisements) in a total of 11 original advertisements. Altogether six companies had advertised. The Indian sub-category comprised four "strong"(eight weak) multicultural advertisements in a total of 20 original advertisements. Five companies had advertised.

As for multicultural content, the British JP Tod's retained its English slogan in both France and Germany—"Hand-made entirely by expert shoe-makers" In India, Bata products were marketed under the names of "The Irish Classic" and "The Alpine Beauty". Lakhani alluded to Picasso: "Picasso was a painter. The six color sole in our new shoe might make you think otherwise".

Accessories:

In France, two strong multicultural advertisements (one weak advertisement) were found in a total of 13 original advertisements. Altogether, nine companies had advertised. In Germany eight strong multicultural advertisements (and one weak advertisement) were found in a total of nine original advertisements. Altogether six companies had advertised. The Indian sub-category contained five multicultural advertisements (zero weak advertisements) in a total of eight original advertisements. Altogether three companies had advertised.

French examples included Armani reading glasses marketed under the Italian sounding product name of "Occhiali;" and Joop, which advertised almost exclusively in English—"Joop Luggage"; Joop Leather; Joop Jewellery" Companies marketing in Germany, on the other hand, used Denglish extensively in an effort to be more "hip" or "cool"—'Light Brille aus Danemark (Ticoline); and "keine Extras, keine Gags" (Ticoline). (Light glasses from Denmark, No extras. No gags). Visuals included an ostrich and a flamingo (Louis

Vuitton). In the Indian case, the VIP luggage range evoked classical Greece, and the first traveler in history, Ulysses, through its product name—"Odyssey".

Watches

In this product category, French advertising contained altogether 17 strong multicultural advertisements (four weak advertisements) in a total of 35 original advertisements. This amounted to 21 (17+4) multicultural advertisements (60 percent). Altogether 19 companies had advertised. German advertising contained 37 strong multicultural advertisements (two weak advertisements) in a total of 50 original ads. This amounted to 39 (37+2) multicultural advertisements (78 percent). Altogether 14 companies had advertised. Indian advertising contained 10 strong multicultural advertisements (2 weak advertisements) in a total of 19 original advertisements. This amounted to 12 (10+2) multicultural advertisements (64 percent). Altogether 9 companies had advertised.

Interestingly, in France, practically all the companies retained their univeral English slogans and this despite having originated in French-speaking Geneva. For example, Hermès—"Water-resistant Swiss"; Rado Switzerland—"A different world"; Breitling—"Instruments for Professionals" and Raymond Weil (Geneva)—"Precision Movements".

In Germany also, practically all the major brands, primarily Swiss again, used English to advertise their product. In many instances, the product names were a mixed bag of French and English. For example, Tissot advertised its product as "Ballade" and "Swiss Quality Time". The Chopard models were named "Tonneau" and "Happy Sport". Maurice Lacroix advertised its product as "Les Mécaniques. Of Switzerland." (The Mechanics of Switzerland). Rolex marketed its product as "label de qualité (label of quality). Officially Certified Chronometer. Swiss'.

In India, Piaget retained the original French slogan in an effort to better sell its high-end watches—"Joaillier en horlogerie depuis 1874 Genève". Christian Bernard advertised with the tagline, "Paris sets the trend" and a visual of the Eiffel Tower.

Pens

In this product category, French advertising contained one strong multicultural advertisement (three weak advertisements) in a total of six original advertisements. This amounted to four (1+3) multicultural advertisements (67 percent). Altogether three companies had advertised. German advertising contained five strong multicultural advertisements (zero weak advertisements) in a total of nine original advertisements, which amounted to 56 percent. Altogether three companies had advertised. The Indian subcategory contained no multicultural advertisements in a total of three original advertisements. Altogether three companies had advertised.

Examples in Germany included the company Lamy, which evoked Italy through its product names "Milano" and "Venezia" even while retaining the English title of "Oldtimer." Montblanc also resorted to English—"The Art of Writing" (slogan). Elysee, on the other hand, advertised in French—"Vernissage" (title).

Technical Products

This product category in France contained a total of 10 strong multicultural advertisements (15 weak advertisements) in a total of 26 original advertisements. This amounted to 25 (10+15) multicultural advertisements (96 percent). Altogether 15 companies had advertised. German advertising contained 43 strong multicultural advertisements (26 weak advertisements) in a total of 71 original advertisements. This amounted to 69 (43+26) multicultural advertisements (98 percent). Altogether 24 companies had advertised. Indian advertising contained a total of 25 strong multicultural advertisements (12 weak advertisements) in a total of 54 original advertisements. This amounted to 37 multicultural advertisements (68 percent).

Let us examine the various subcategories.

Audio-Video:

This subcategory in France contained 10 strong multicultural advertisements (seven weak advertisements) in a total of 18 original advertisements. Altogether, 11 companies had advertised.

In Germany, this subcategory contained 21 strong multicultural advertisements (six weak advertisements) in a total of 28 original advertisements. Thirteen companies had advertised. In India, this subcategory contained 21 strong multicultural advertisements (10 weak advertisements) in a total of 45 original advertisements. Fifteen companies had advertised.

This sub-category contained the highest number of multicultural advertisements in all three countries. Examples in Germany include the Grundig title in English: "Grundig Video-recorder with show-view and text-programme". The Japanese Pioneer marketed its product with the same slogan in all three countries—"The art of entertainment". The German Bose also reiterated its English slogan everywhere—"Better sound through research". The Mitsubishi slogan and title is also the same in all three markets—"Electronic Visual Systems" and "No limits". The Samsung, Nokia and Philips slogans worldwide are—"Technology that works for life"/"Connecting People" and Philips invents for you". Interestingly, most German advertisements emphasized "design" as a tool for enticement thereby highlighting its resonance with the German consumer—"Verlieben Sie sich in das Design" (Fall in Love with Design); "Design fur die Sinne" (Design for the senses); and "Design darf verfuhren" (Design is permitted to tempt).

In France, Carrefour televisions were marketed as "Television First Line." The Japanese Sony advertised its product as "Scala", after the famous Opera House in Milan of the same name (visual included). Other visuals included: crocodile (Grunding), Rembrandt painting; (Mistsubishi); Mona Lisa painting (Alkyos).

Interestingly, in India, where English was not taken into account as a foreign language in the database, 21 of 45 advertisements found had resorted to multiculturalism, thereby indicating greater variety of content. The advertisements were characterized primarily by references to Japan, which suggests that the world market is dominated by it. For example, "A TV from Japan" (Akai), "The upright and honorable means of procuring a TV from Japan" (Sega); and "Get the power of the Japanese generator" (Novino Gold Battery); References to the UK included a Philips advertisement—"In the Queen's English, that's visibly sharper pictures." Interestingly, Philips also compared its television remote (Matchline Television) to American "stealth bombers"—"It's easy to see it as a stealth bomber"/"Less controls than a stealth bomber with a wider angle view". Onida, on the other hand, touted its "global" ambitions—"One Indian brand is thirsting for global competition." Yet another Onida advertisement alluded to American rock and roll—"Can't stand hard rock around the clock." Sony used Hindi to sell—"Zindagi ke khubsoorat lamhe. Ek baar phir!" Visuals included populars stereotypes such as the Statue of Liberty and Manhattan skyline (Onida); and Caucasians (Philips/BPL).

Cameras:

In France, this subcategory contained no strong multicultural advertisements and five weak advertisements in a total of five original advertisements. Two companies had advertised. The German subcategory had a total of 11 strong multicultural advertisements (14 weak advertisements) in a total of 25 original advertisements. Six companies had advertised. In India, this subcategory had a total of one strong multicultural advertisement (two weak advertisements) in a total of three original advertisements. Three companies had advertised.

In Germany, all of the 25 original advertisements contained some form of multiculturalism, mostly English copy, to sell. For example, the German Contax title said, "The Classic Evolution"; and the Japanese Canon said, "My camera." Toshiba used the English slogan—"In touch with tomorrow;" and the American Kodak used the image of a lion.

Xerox/Other:

In France, this subcategory had no strong multicultural advertisements (three weak advertisements) in a total of three original advertisements. Two companies had advertised. In Germany, it contained 11 strong multicultural advertisements (six weak advertisements) in a total of 18 original advertisements. Five companies had advertised. The Indian subcategory contained three strong multicultural advertisements (zero weak advertisements) in a total of six original advertisements. Three companies had advertised.

Most of the multicultural advertising content found in India comprised (foreign) company names, with the majority being Japanese. Of the 60 companies found, 26 were Japanese, five were American and the rest were French, German and Indian. The preponderance of Japanese names suggested that Japan is the market leader. Some examples were particularly interesting. To sell its fax machines (Panafax), Godrej, for instance, carried citations by famous European military strategists such as Clemenceau, Clausewitz and Napoleon Bonaparte—"War is too important to be left to Generals (Clemenceau), "the greatest number of troops should be brought into action at the decisive point" (Clausewitz); and "God is on the side of big battalions" (Napoloen Bonaparte). One of the reasons for the Indian fascination with such military jargon could be because the country has gone to war several times with its neighbors over disputed territories and therefore has a certain opening for such sophisticated terms (recall the Philips and Jaguar references to Stealth bombers and B2 Bombers respectively).

Housing /Furniture

The housing category comprised a large number of original advertisements: France had 49 of a total of 68 original advertisements (7.2 percent), Germany—166 of a total of 240 original advertisements (11.4 percent), and India—85 of a total of 129 original advertisements (9.5 percent). The multicultural content, however, was relatively less—due perhaps to the conservative nature of this category.

In France, only six out of 49 original advertisements used strong multicultural elements (10 weak advertisements). This amounted to 16 (6+10) multicultural advertisements (32 percent). 24 companies had advertised.

In Germany, 61 out of 166 original advertisements were strong multicultural advertisements (18 weak advertisements). This amounted to 79 (61+18) multicultural advertisements (48 percent). Altogether 66 companies had advertised.

In India, 28 out of 85 original advertisements were strong multicultural advertisements (19 weak advertisements). This amounted to 47 (28+19) multicultural advertisements (55 percent). Altogether 43 companies had advertised. Examples included the German LBS Bausparkasse title in Denglish—"Oldie but Goldie. Modernisiert mit uns." (Gets modern with us). A Tata Housing advertisement used the German term "autobahn" to sell—"German autobahn boasts the fastest, most dependable highways in the world. One Indian company sets these very standards in..."

Coming to the furniture category—in France, this category contained altogether 3 strong multicultural advertisements (seven weak advertisements) in a total of 30 original advertisements. Eleven companies had advertised in this case. Examples included both English and a combination of English and French otherwise known as "Franglais". "Le Confort, c'est tellement Stressless!" (Stressless) (Comfort, it is so stressless).

In Germany, this category contained the highest volume of multicultural advertisements, that is, 37 strong multicultural advertisements (14 weak advertisements) in a total of 70 original advertisements. Twenty-five companies had advertised. Here also, the majority of companies (five out of nine companies) preferred to use English or its combination with German to sell. Interestingly, three companies also used French, in combination with German to sell. Some examples were: "The human touch" (slogan-Leolux); "Design tells about life, our wishes..." (title-Leolux); "The art of fine seating" (Jori); "Clever einrichten" (Ikea); "Feel at home in the office" (Werndl); "High Leitz im Buro" (Leitz); "Komfortable Royal" (Auping); "Creation" (Rolf Benz); 'Laut is out" (Buderus); (Clever decoration... Hight Leitz in Office. Comfortable Royal). "Test the best" (B&W); "Baroque a la maison" (title-Ligne Roset); "Bourgeois. D'accord. Petit jamais" (title—Ligne Roset); "Zelda. In France. Die belle époque lebt" (title-Cor); Visuals included a polar bear (ADK Kachelofenbau); a penguin (Hoechst); an Orang Outan (France Telecom); and a polar bear (Flow Tex).

The Indian category comprised a total of 11 strong multicultural advertisements (zero weak advertisements) in a total of 20 original advertisements. Twelve companies had advertised. Indian advertising in this case, presented some of the most interesting examples. For instance, a German firm, Moderna Klober, used entire phrases in German to sell: *"Im Grunde, gibt es zwei Arten von Burostuhlen. Klober und nicht-Klober"/"Einfuhlsam. Intelligent. Ansprechend. Nein, nicht der Mann. Der Stuhl".* Jaguar not only named its bathtubs "Stealth Rangers" but also used the title of "B2 Bombers"—"The sleek lines. Space age engineering; A unique shape. The ultimate shape; the ultimate thrill. Is it a single Lever Mixer or a B-2 Bomber?"/"Invisible to enemy sensors and radar, B2 Bomber can penetrate sophisticated air defenses" An Indian ceramic company, Madhusudhan Ceramics modified the popular song "Que sera sera" to "Say Cera Cera" to market its bathroom fittings named CERA. The advertisement also displayed a framed picture of Hollywood actor Tom Cruise in the bathroom. Yet another advertisement by Kitply for wood-polishing referred to Egyptian mummies—"They tried to mummify me," Bosch used a Sumo wrestler and Godrej used Batman to plug their washing machines.

It was particularly interesting to note that Indian companies had a tendency toward self-glorification. This could be due to the fact that India, as we know, is a high power distance country.[3] Examples included "India's first. World's finest" (Modiguard); "internationally acclaimed" (Nuwud Ltd); "the world's most advanced washing system" (Godrej); and "the world's No. 1 in Air Conditioning" (Carrier). One of the very few allusions to our South Asian neighbors came from Polar, which marketed its fans to neighboring Bangladesh with the tagline—"Two of India's hottest looking models have migrated to Bangladesh".

Household Articles:

France had two strong multicultural advertisements (two weak advertisements) in a total of 10 original advertisements. Six companies had advertised. This included an advertisement by Porcelain Franklin that showed the Liberation of Paris.

In Germany, this subcategory contained 16 strong multicultural advertisements (two weak advertisements) in a total of 32 original advertisements. Fifteen companies had advertised. The German Zwilling used the translation of its brand name (Zwilling in English translates as "Twin") to describe its kitchen knives as "Twin PROfection". The German Arzberg preferred the English term "Cult" over the German "Kult". Fissler marketed its products as "Country Line". The visuals included dolphins and flamingos (AEG).

[3] Hofstede, *Culture's Consequences.*

The Indian subcategory contained 11 strong multicultural advertisements (zero weak advertisements) in a total of 20 original advertisements. Thirteen companies had advertised. Examples included Opal Glass Tableware, which evoked French chic through its product name—"La Opala"; and the Kenwood title in French— "l'image d'une voiture McLaren".

Commerce and Industry

This product category in France contained a total of 24 strong multicultural advertisements (15 weak advertisements) in a total of 55 original advertisements. This amounted to 39 (24+15) multicultural advertisements (71 percent). Altogether 21 companies had advertised.

German advertising contained a total of 40 strong multicultural advertisements (12 weak advertisements) in a total of 103 original advertisements. This amounted to 52 (40+12) multicultural advertisements (49 percent). Altogether 34 companies had advertised.

Indian advertising contained the highest figures in terms of multicultural content—75 strong multicultural advertisements (10 weak advertisements) in a total of 201 original advertisements. This amounted to 85 (75+10) multicultural advertisements (42 percent). A larger number of companies (97) had also advertised here rather than in France or Germany.

In France, examples of multiculturalism included references to the emerging BRIC markets of China and Russia. References to the European Community, interestingly, were confined to just two advertisements by the German Nordrhein: "L'Evenement Europeen" and "Bienvenue au carrefour de l'avenir europeen"; The Export Promotion Bureau (EPB)—Government of Pakistan, used the English slogan— "Made for the world. Made in Pakistan"; The Italian Cap-gemini Sogeti advertised as "Made in Italy". Visuals include a map of Europe and the European flag.

In export-oriented Germany, most advertisements, once again, resorted widely to English or Denglish to sell: for example, "Works for you" (Hoechst); 'Der erste People Mover "fliegt" von Terminal zu... (AEG); (The first People Mover flies from Terminal to...). "High-Tech Mit Keramik" (Kyocera); "Computers, Communication, Microelectronics" (Fujitsu); "Post-it" (3M Innovation); "Basis fur Business" (Messe Dusseldorf); "Basic Functional Japanese" (Nordrhein Westfalen); and "Information Engineering, Business Process/Engineering, Transition Engineering" and "Good Morning Germany" (IEF). Visuals included the Tower Bridge of London (Raab Karcher); penguin (Hoechst); orang outan (AEG); world map (BMW AG); polar bear (Flow Tex); and European Flag (Nordrhein-Westfalen).

Indian advertising in the immediate post-liberalization era is characterized primarily by gung-ho optimism in practically all the subsectors. Since the Indian economy was closed in the past, it was rather slow in opening up to other countries. With the liberalization of the economy, however, there was an opportunity to reverse all that. And it is happening to a large extent with India's so-called champion companies, that is, Tata, Birlas, Wipro, Infosys, and others, aggressively integrating India into the global economy. It is perhaps not surprising then that the large majority of companies emphasized the "global" aspect in ther advertising. As Leela Fernandes puts it, "In the era of globalization, Indian advertisers were quick to realize that the "local and global" were not diametrically opposite but were "mutually constitutive imaginary moments in every attempt to make sense of the world."[4] Companies highlighting this included: the Indian Modern Textile Group which advertised as, "Made in India, worn all over the world"; Welspun Textiles that said, "At home both in the Domestic and Global markets". "Thinking the global way" (Lloyds); "You are a citizen of the global village now" (IDBI); "Globalization. India signs GATT and accepts the challenge to meet international quality standards" (Arihant Group); "MSS is taking the business of India truly global" (MSS); "What do you think partner? Are we ready for the world?" (IDBI); and "Our golden key to global markets" (Indo Rama); The visuals included: cover of "Time" magazine; foreign currency + globe; Caucasians; international flags; the Great Wall of China; pagoda + dragon; MAD comic strip; the White House; Eiffel Tower; Big Ben, the Statue of Liberty, American cowboys, Roman Colosseum, BMW, Volkswagen, and Toyota emblems and so on …

---

[4] L. Fernandes, "Nationalising 'the Global': Media Images: Cultural Politics and the Middle Class in India", *Media, Culture and Society* 22 no. 5, (2000): 611–28.

What are the Overall Conclusions?

First, I would like to believe there is a growing acceptance and understanding of common multicultural symbols and texts, a direct consequence of globalization. The data shows that people in these three countries, in spite of coming from somewhat different cultures, respond almost similarly to corporate advertisement strategies. This reflects common aspirational goals of a slowly, but surely growing groups of consumers. Thus a general conclusion can be made that the aspirational goals and values, if you will, in such diverse countries as France, Germany and India are converging to an extent under globalization, as indicated by the evidence. And that at a certain level of development, it is possible to communicate in a common cultural manner.

Second, the findings indicate that there is remarkable similarity in the symbols and texts used in each country. This suggests a high degree of openness in understanding and acceptance of universal symbols of culture. As globalization increases and markets become international, the trend is toward commonly understood multicultural symbols, visuals, and texts. Indeed, this commonality of understanding shows the growth of a culture that is common to all the three countries.

Third, this does not mean there are no interesting differences. German advertisements use a wider range of symbols and texts than the French. This is not surprising as Germany is the country with the highest merchandise exports in the world and therefore, it also tends naturally to have a high content of multicultural elements in advertising. The French, on the other hand, tend to exclude the US and English-biased inputs, even through legal means. They even translate the English equivalent into French. In contrast, Germany tends to tamper less with the original English when selling the product. What is interesting, however, is that the highest number of advertisements using the orginal language, be it English, French or German is found in India. The use of English is not surprising because most advertisements in India address a class of consumers that speaks English at some level or the other. This, once again, only reaffirms the assimilative nature of Indian civilization. Our association with the West dates back to three hundred years. Today, the use of the English language and the institutions that govern India reflect that association.

Fourth, the remarkable conclusion here is the almost similar degree of openness to the foreign element in all three countries. Following liberalization of its economy, India appears to be as open as any European country to multicultural influences. The interesting part is that Indian companies tend to use more multicultural advertisements than their European counterparts, this is perhaps an indication of a traditional opening to other cultures and ideas, particularly Western as indicated by the data. Our problem, however, is not globalization, but the pace at which we can manage it. Sometimes, our advertisements tell us that we may be lagging behind in our understanding of our threshold levels. For example, an Indian garment company, Oswal Garments, has in an advertisement, an Indian couple sitting in a restaurant in Monte Carlo with the French "Menu Du Jour" in full view -"Quiche aux Poireaux", "Oeuf dur Provencal"; Cardin shows a young Indian woman reading the French "Elle" magazine at the hairdressers; Godrej uses the image of Batman to plug washing machines while Egyptian mummies figure in an advertisement for Kitply.

Fifth, a product in spite of being global has usually originated in a particular country and often continues to be associated with that country. France, for example, is synonymous with Eiffel Tower; Germany with the automobile industry, Spain with bull-fighting; and India with Taj Mahal. The country-of-origin effect can be further extended—there are some symbols that not only identify countries but also evoke a particular way of looking at it. The Taj Mahal or an Indian temple sculpture, for instance, would not only suggest India but also hint at its "exotic" nature.

PART II

8

From the Margins to the Center
The Global South

The end of colonization, by far the most far-reaching political development of the mid-twentieth century, ushered in the transition to an age of more equal relations among civilizations. Decolonization overturned the expansionist logic that linked modernization to Westernization. It meant that the irresistible trend of globalization was no longer tied to this logic but could now take a different course. As sociologist Martin Albrow points out:

> We need to entertain the idea that globalization, far from being the last stage of a long process of development, is the arrest of what was taken for granted, a transformation arising out of a combination of different forces, which unexpectedly changes the direction of history. It could be the transition to a new era rather than the apogee of the old.[1,2]

From a Western perspective, this meant, as Albrow notes, exchange with "rival civilizations, such as India and China, which operated

---

[1] Martin Albrow, *The Global Age: State and Society beyond Modernity* (Stanford: Stanford University Press, 1996), 101.
[2] Albrow, *The Global Age*, 35.

in different conceptual frames.... is now a factor in the transformation that makes the Global Age."[3]

Historically speaking, although there was a steady shift in the concentration of capabilities from the West to the East since the end of World War II, it took a decisive turn when the smaller early industrializing nations of Asia—Japan, South Korea, Taiwan and Singapore—were joined by the continental sized states of China and India. In the last two decades, incomes of 80 percent of the population in the West have stagnated while per capita income in China has quadrupled, and in India, it has more than doubled. Indeed, with their combined populations of about 2.6 billion (40 percent of world population), and GDP annual growth rate of nearly 9 percent (China) and 7 percent (India) over the past one decade, they represent a major and sharply rising influence in the global economy.

Both China and India, functioning under different "models" of development—China with a centralized "state-directed" political system, though rapidly incorporating the private system—and India, under a "mixed", that is State-market driven democratic structure— are, in fact, "re-emerging" powers. Their return to center stage after several centuries of imperial domination presages, according to economic historian Angus Maddison, the reincarnation of an earlier era in Asian geopolitics when both countries, together, accounted for over 50 percent of the world GDP (in 1600, China had 28 percent, and India had 23 percent). But this had declined due to the long years of colonization.

Today, however, both countries have risen up once again to count increasingly more in the strategic calculus of nations—their parallel revival exemplifying Asia's dramatic resurgence in the global system when the rise of Asian economic powers represents (metaphorically if not politically speaking), the whole shift in the center of gravity of global economic power from the trans-Atlantic to the Asia Pacific.

---

[3] Daniel Burstein and Anne de Kezer, *Big Dragon China's Future: What it Means for Businesses, the Economy and the Global Order* (New York: Simon & Schuster, 1999), 97.

Describing this shift in his book, *The Future of Power* Harvard Professor Joseph Nye states:

> Now what we are seeing in this century is, what I would call, the recovery of Asia to normal proportions, roughly half the world's population and half the world's product—and that really starts with Japan, it goes on to Korea, to Southeast Asian countries like Singapore and Malaysia. Now we are very much focused on [China] with its ten percent growth rates. Though I don't think they are going to stay at ten percent. And increasingly, we will be focused on India, which is now growing at eight and nine percent growth. But what the net effect of this will be, essentially, is a shift of the power of the world economy, from West to East.[4]

China, especially, has achieved great success in its economic development since it adopted reform policies a decade ahead of India. India, on the other hand, came to public notice when a report published by Goldman Sachs in 2001 startled the world by hyphenating India with China as the two economic locomotives of the twenty-first century. "In US dollar terms, China could overtake Germany in the next four years, Japan by 2015 and the US by 2039. India's economy could be larger than all but the US and China in 30 years."[5] A follow-up study published in 2007, titled "India's Rising Growth Potential" concluded that the Indian economy can "sustain growth rates of 8 percent until 2020, significantly higher than the 5.7 percent that we projected in our original BRICs paper…"[6]

Indeed and as predicted, China's GDP soon overtook that of the UK. China became the world's fourth-largest economy in 2005, passed Germany as the third largest in 2007, and in 2010, it overstepped Japan as the second largest, after only the US.[7] India, on the other hand, and as predicted by the IMF, overtook Japan in PPP terms in 2012 to become

---

[4] Joseph Nye, "Transcript: The Future of Power", Chatham House, London, May 10, 2011, 2 (www.chathamhouse.org.uk).

[5] Tushar Poddar and Eva Yi, "India's Rising Growth Potential", BRICs and Beyond, Goldman Sachs Global Economics Group, 22 January 2007, p. 11.

[6] Poddar and Yi, "India's Rising Potential", 11.

[7] Martin Jacques, *When China Rules the World: The Rise of the Middle Kingdom and the End of the Western World* (London: Allen Lane, 2009), 192.

the world's third largest economy. With nearly 23 percent of the global population, a study by McKinsey Global Institute (MGI) suggests that if India continues with its recent growth, average household incomes will triple over the next two decades and it will become the world's fifth largest consumer economy by 2025, up from 12th position now.

With the huge GDP coming from India and China, not to speak of ASEAN and Japan, Asia is no doubt likely to regain its pre-eminence, accounting for more than 60 to 70 percent of the world GDP by 2050 if not sooner.

China's rise, in this case, matters not only because of its economic size but also because of its unique political structure. India, on the other hand, as a large nation rising in the East, based on political and economic liberty is proof that open societies, free trade and multiplying connections to the global economy can represent pathways to lasting economic prosperity and success. As pointed out by economists Peter Lindent and Jeffrey Williamson, "Even though no one study can establish that openness to trade has unambiguously helped the representation of Third World economy, the preponderance of evidence supports this conclusion."[8] This is further corroborated by a Pricewaterhouse Coopers Report that predicts that by 2040, the E7 (that is, emerging countries of China, India, Indonesia, Brazil, Russia, Mexico and Turkey) will be twice the economic size of G7, the seven major advanced countries.[9] The important lesson to draw here is that globalization need not be against the interest of developing countries.

Civilizations and Post-Cold War Conflicts

It is within this framework that certain post-Cold War writers such as Francis Fukuyama, for example, propounded his theory of the "end of history", which unabashedly proclaims the global triumph of liberalism and free-market capitalism.[10]

[8] David Dollar and Aart Kraay, "Growth Is Good for the Poor", *Foreign Affairs* 81, no. 1, January/February 2002.

[9] Rakesh Sood, "Stability in the Time of Change", *The Hindu*, March 10, 2017.

[10] F. Fukuyama, *The End of History and the Last Man* (New York: Free Press/Maxwell Macmillan), 1992.

The same frame of reference, however, is also alluded to in Samuel Huntington's post-Cold War—Clash of Civilization—thesis wherein he argues that culture would become a fundamental source of conflict in the future. As the world becomes more interconnected, some cultures, Huntington projects, such as the heavily religious Islamic civilization, will be the most resistant to the spread of Western values, institutions and ideas regarding democracy and liberalization. In his view, "The New World Order" will be formed along nine cultural blocs—Western, Sinic, Orthodox, Islamic, Latin American, Hindi, Buddhist, Japanese and possibly African. Huntington postulates that relations between the West, the engine of globalization and the other eight will be confrontational with the continuation of Westernization and could pose a grave threat to world peace". He writes that, "What is universalism to the West is imperialism to the rest"—and—"non-Western societies wish to free themselves from Western economic, military and cultural domination."[11]

This trend is also susceptible to an upsurge of ethnicity and religious revivalism in some parts of the world.[12] But while Fukuyama agrees with Huntington that cultural differences will loom larger in the future "as all societies will have to...deal not only with internal problems but with the outside world" he differs from Huntington in that he states that these differences may not necessarily be a source of conflict. He considers cultures as "distinctive and functional", but at the same time, he also views them as a process that has now moved beyond national boundaries and "into the realms of the global economy" where they are a potential source of rich cross-cultural fertilization.[13] What makes Fukuyama's analysis more interesting perhaps is that it is less culturally deterministic.

In the same vein, Benjamin Barber also argues that globalization twists the world in two ways. On the one hand, it is bending the world toward markets, guided by the ideology of globalism. This is

[11] Samuel Huntingdon, *The Clash of Civilizations and the Remaking of World Order* (UK Ltd: Simon & Schuster, 1996), 22.

[12] Jan Nederveen Pieterse, "Globalization as Hybridization", in *Global Modernities*, eds, M. Featherstone S. Lash, and R. Robertson (Thousand Oaks, CA: Sage Publications, 1995), 45–65.

[13] F. Fukuyama, *The Social Virtues and the Creation of Prosperity* (London: Hamish Hamilton, 1995), 5.

McWorld, an America-centric, media-driven version of global capital-ism. On the other hand, and even as it is bending the world toward McWorld, globalization is also magnifying ethnic, religious and racial divisions leading to Jihad, a threat to democracy everywhere.[14]

Indeed, today, we are being increasingly challenged in the realm of ideas by other forces. Fukuyama's claim that "liberal democracy remains the only coherent political aspiration" is challenged by at least two differing world-views; one that comes from the Muslim world, which states that globalization, in the main, is an expansion of Western ideas that threaten, through superior force and propaganda, the Islamic way of life. While this may reflect the uneven distribution of power in the common mind, radical Islam sees Muslim societies as being slowly destroyed by the import of what they term as the cor-rupt influences of the West. India is in a special position to appreciate this. The other comes from those who espouse the so-called Asian values, which suggest that there are alternative paths to success. The rise of China, for instance, is seen as underlining the strong influence of Confucian values.

But all this is not new. Already in 1958, writing on cultural divergences and convergences, the Italian writer, Stefano Bakonyi[15] had pointed out that the vigorous expansion on the part of Western cultures had carried Western emotional values and concepts to the far corners of the globe and had made them a common depository also of non-Western cultural communities. At the same time, he had also warned that this process would lead to a counter-expansion of non-Western values, in particular those of the potent sleeping coun-tries of India and China. Indeed the push toward globalization of markets that had begun with the creation of free trade areas (the EU, NAFTA, Central European Free Trade Agreement (CEFTA) and so on) and the worldwide decrease in trade barriers (GATT), had led first to the emergence of the "East Asian Tigers" and soon thereafter, to that of China and India in what is now commonly referred to as the "Asian century".

---

[14] Benjamin Barber, "Jihad Vs McWorld", *New York Times*, 1994.

[15] Stefano Bakonyi, "Divergence and Convergence in Culture and Communication", *Journal of Communication* 8, no. 1, (1958): 24–30.

As the twenty-first century progresses, China, India and other economies will continue to grow while the US share of the world economy will likely drop. In fact, the idea of what the world will be like in 2050 shows it to be a very different place with the US economy being overtaken by China—and with India not that far behind. Does this mean that India, China and the United States, as the three most powerful nations in the world, will inevitably fall into what is often termed as the Thucydides trap, named after the ancient Greek historian, who observed a dangerous dynamic between a rising Athens and a ruling Sparta? According to Thucydides, it was the rise of Athens and the fear that this instilled in Sparta that made war inevitable. In other words, rising powers tend to feel a growing sense of entitlement and demand greater influence and respect. Established powers, faced with such challengers, on the other hand, tend to become fearful, insecure and defensive. In such an environment, misunderstandings are magnified, empathy becomes elusive and third party actions that would otherwise be inconsequential or manageable, are liable to trigger wars that the primary players never wanted to fight in the first instance.

In the case of the United States and China, Thucididean risks are further compounded by civilizational incompatibility, which makes it more difficult to achieve rapprochement. Hence, even while many took comfort in the belief that as China grew richer and stronger, it would follow in the footsteps of Germany, Japan and other countries that have undergone profound transformation to emerge as advanced liberal democracies, some scholars such as Samuel Huntington, disagreed. In his essay, "The Clash of Civilizations", published in 1993, the political scientist had argued that far from dissolving into a global liberal world, cultural fault lines would become a defining feature for the post-Cold war world. Huntington's argument is remembered today, primarily for its prescience in spotlighting the divide between "Western and Islamic Civilizations"—a rift that was revealed most vividly by the 9/11 attacks and their aftermath. But Huntington saw the gulf between the US-led West and Chinese civilizations just as deep, enduring and consequential.

Prior to the 2007–08 global financial and economic crisis, China had generally yielded to the unilateral American assertion of power, enacted market-oriented economic reforms, and joined established international institutions. Its rapid recovery from the crisis, however, has led it to promote its own interests more aggressively than before. Despite the continuing gap in security capabilities vis-à-vis the US, China has shown a willingness to assert its power against the countries of the region, through unilateral occupation of the offshore islands it claims in the South Sea as its own, challenging the right of the US navy to operate in the disputed waters, constructing large artificial islands, building military installations and harassing fishing boats from countries that also claim islands in the US area. This has trapped China and the United States in a rivalry that could easily turn violent. In the coming years, any number of flash points could produce a crisis in the US-Chinese relations including further territorial disputes over the South China Sea and tensions over North Korea's burgeoning nuclear program. Since it will take at least another decade or more for China's military capabilities to fully match those of the United States, China no doubt, will be cautious about any lethal use of force against the Americans. But in the event it feels that long-term trend lines are no longer moving in its favor and that it is losing its bargaining power, it could also initiate a limited military conflict to attempt to reverse this trend.

In a certain sense, this was perhaps a foregone conclusion. Once the momentarily triumphant civilization, that of the West, began losing its dominating momentum, the revival and self-assertion of those that had been suppressed was inevitable. Today, there is every reason to believe that revitalized Asian and other nations, however, they may evolve through the interactions of a globalized world, will likely preserve the continuity of their basic cultural identities. As the West becomes one civilization like any other in a multicultural world, what can no longer be sustained is the attempt to claim a unique and privileged status for values supposedly emanating from the West. However, as Pankaj Mishra points out, the Western mind has not yet entirely adjusted to this new reality:

> For most people in Europe and America, the history of the twentieth century is still largely dominated by the two world wars and the long nuclear stand-off with Soviet Communism. But it is now clear that the central event of the last century for the majority of the world's

populations, was the intellectual and political awakening of Asia and its emergence from the ruins of both Asian and European empires.[16]

The course that globalization is likely to take in the future remains, of course, a subject of lively debate. But as the expansionism of the modern West collides with the revival of non-Western cultures, some scholars expect to see a radical change of direction—in the words of the sociologist Martin Albrow, the "final reversal of the process begun by Columbus."[17] The following chapters deal with this topic in more detail.

[16] Pankaj Mishra, *From the Ruins of Empire: The Intellectuals Who Remade Asia* (New York: Farrar, Straus and Giroux, 2012), 8.

[17] Albrow, *The Global Age*, 100.

9

Emerging Markets and Their Potential
Post-liberalization India

The initial task of this case study was to look at the total volume of advertisements in France, Germany and India, in the immediate post-liberalization era, to see how India fares as compared to the two more advanced European nations in terms of its market potential.

The study shows that in the post-liberalization era, Indian companies had advertised quite liberally. Surprisingly, nearly 400 Indian companies had actively advertised. They had a total of 1,174 advertisements (Table 9.1). The large number of Indian companies, in this instance, can be explained by the fact that newer companies look to advertising to develop their brand image, get their products known and increase their market share. However, except for a few (for example, Tata Group, Mahindra Group, Aditya Birla Group, Wipro and Infosys), Indian companies are not yet internationally known. They must first learn the language of intercultural communication if they wish to succeed in getting their message across to the global community.

For the purpose of the analysis here, the totality of advertisements in a category, that is both originals and duplicates, has been taken into account. This amounted to 1,112 advertisements for France, 2.557 advertisements for Germany and 1,174 advertisements for India.

Table 9.1   Total Advertising Volume

	Product Category / Sub-Category	Companies France		Germany		India		Original Advertisements France		Germany		India		Advertisements(Total) France		Germany		India	
i)	Perfume	17	4.9%	12	2.4%	5	1.3%	38	5.6%	18	1.2%	6	0.7%	87	7.8%	56	2.2%	8	0.7%
ii)	Cosmetic	5	1.5%	6	1.2%	6	1.5%	8	1.2%	6	0.4%	8	0.9%	16	1.4%	18	0.7%	8	0.7%
iii)	**Fashion**																		
	Clothes	22		32		25		38		86		64		49		112		92	
	Fabric	1		1		7		2		1		24		3		2		25	
	Shoes	2		6		5		3		11		20		4		20		24	
	Accessories	9		6		3		13		9		8		15		14		12	
	Sum Total:	34	9.9%	45	9.0%	40	10.1%	56	8.2%	107	7.4%	116	12.9%	71	6.4%	148	5.8%	153	13.0%
iv)	Watches	19	5.5%	14	2.8%	9	2.3%	35	5.1%	50	3.4%	19	2.1%	51	4.6%	77	3.0%	26	2.2%
v)	Pens	3	0.9%	3	0.6%	3	0.8%	6	0.9%	9	0.6%	3	0.3%	19	1.7%	15	0.6%	9	0.8%
vi)	**Gastronomy**																		
	Alcohol	22		38		9		42		104		24		70		239		32	
	Tobacco/Cigarettes	–		11		8		–		35		18		–		59		35	
	Food/Drink./Restaurants	6		15		4		11		30		7		13		51		11	
	Sum Total:	28	8.1%	64	12.8%	21	5.3%	53	7.8%	169	11.6%	49	5.5%	83	7.5%	349	13.6%	78	6.6%
vii)	**Leisure and Travel**																		
	Airlines	17		14		9		29		42		20		58		92		31	
	Countries and Regions(foreign)	5		14		3		7		37		8		9		61		8	
	Countries and Regions (national)	2		–		7		2		–		31		2		–		31	
	Travel Agencies	5		3		1		8		6		1		11		6		1	
	Hotels	10		3		8		17		12		16		26		18		20	
	Sum Total:	39	11.3%	34	6.8%	28	7.0%	63	9.2%	97	6.7%	76	8.5%	106	9.5%	177	6.9%	91	7.8%
viii)	**Automobiles**																		
	Bicycles/Motorcycles	1		1		3		1		1		6		1		1		13	
	Cars	15		25		5		58		130		18		100		263		23	
	Heavy Vehicles	3		2		1		3		8		1		13		10		1	
	Vehicle Rental	1		3		6		1		9		10		2		15		11	
	Vehicle Accessories	2		5		15		3		9		31		3		29		45	
	Sum Total:	22	6.4%	36	7.2%	30	7.5%	66	9.7%	157	10.8%	66	7.3%	119	10.7%	318	12.4%	93	7.9%
ix)	Computers	19	5.5%	23	4.6%	10	2.5%	37	5.4%	73	5.0%	20	2.2%	60	5.4%	141	5.5%	23	2.0%
x)	Telecommunication	15	4.4%	21	4.2%	11	2.8%	36	5.3%	68	4.7%	30	3.3%	72	6.5%	132	5.2%	43	3.7%
xi)	**Technical Products**																		
	Audio-Video	11		13		15		18		28		45		28		72		66	
	Cameras	2		6		3		5		25		3		8		35		9	
	Photocopying machines /Other	2		5		3		3	%	18		6		6		34		11	
	Sum Total:	15	4.4%	24	4.8%	21	5.3%	26	3.8%	71	4.9%	54	6.0%	42	3.8%	141	5.5%	86	7.3%
xii)	**Housing/Furniture**																		
	Furniture	11		25		12		30		70		20		42		77		30	
	Household Articles	6		15		13		10		32		26		12		66		50	
	Housing Construction	6		21		14		8		46		35		13		70		44	
	Housing Finance	1		5		4		1		18		4		1		27		5	
	Sum Total:	24	7.0%	66	13.2%	43	10.8%	49	7.2%	166	11.4%	85	9.5%	68	6.1%	240	9.4%	129	11.0%
xiii)	**Commerce and Industry**																		
	Multi-diversified industries	3		1		17		12		2		52		17		2		64	
	Chemicals Industry Sector	–		5		6		–		17		13		–		25		13	
	Steel/ Metallurgy Sector	–		3		8		–		3		20		–		10		20	
	Mechanical/Electrical Industry	3		2		18		10		9		30		10		13		31	
	Diversified Sector	5		10		16		18		36		18		20		63		20	
	Textiles Sector	–		–		11		–		–		29		–		–		38	
	Agricultural Sector	–		2		6		–		2		10		–		5		10	
	Fairs	2		3		4		2		7		7		3		8		7	
	Public Sector	6		3		2		9		18		6		10		28		6	
	Other	2		5		9		4		9		16		6		16		18	
	Sum Total:	21	6.1%	34	6.8%	97	24.4%	55	8.1%	103	7.1%	201	22.4%	66	5.9%	170	6.6%	227	19.3%
xiv)	**Finance and Insurance**																		
	Banks/Credit cards etc	16		22		24		37		75		53		55		140		67	
	Insurance	5		21		4		8		81		12		17		133		12	
	Sum Total:	21	6.1%	43	8.6%	28	7.0%	45	6.6%	156	10.7%	65	7.2%	72	6.5%	273	10.7%	79	6.7%
xv)	Health	6	1.7%	16	3.2%	9	2.3%	7	1.0%	25	1.7%	16	1.8%	19	1.7%	49	1.9%	24	2.0%
xvi)	NGOs	5	1.5%	8	1.6%	1	0.3%	5	0.7%	16	1.1%	1	0.1%	8	0.7%	18	0.7%	2	0.2%
xvii)	Energy	3	0.9%	5	1.0%	12	3.0%	5	0.7%	26	1.8%	24	2.7%	13	1.2%	49	1.9%	27	2.3%
xviii)	Media	21	6.1%	26	5.2%	13	3.3%	58	8.5%	98	6.7%	38	4.2%	87	7.8%	126	4.9%	46	3.9%
xix)	**Diverse**																		
	Delivery Service	2		3		4		5		14		9		10		22		10	
	Cultural Activities	16		8		1		20		8		1		26		9		1	
	Lottery	2		3		4		2		9		6		2		13		6	
	Other	7		7		2		8		7		5		15		16		5	
	Sum Total:	27	7.8%	21	4.2%	11	2.8%	35	5.1%	38	2.6%	21	2.3%	53	4.8%	60	2.3%	22	1.9%
	Total:	344	100%	501	100%	398	100%	683	100%	1453	100%	898	100%	1112	100%	2557	100%	1174	100%

Source: Author.

According to the data (Table 9.1), in the perfume category, France, which is internationally known for its perfumes, contains the highest volume of advertisements, that is, 87 advertisements (7.8 percent) while Germany has 56 advertisements (2.2 percent) and India has eight advertisements (0.7 percent). Similarly, in the cosmetics category, France, internationally renowned for its beauty products, with 1.4 percent, once again, is the undisputed market leader as compared to Germany (0.7 percent) and India (0.7 percent). The categories on "Watches" and "Pens" also carry more weight in France (4.6 percent and 1.7 percent respectively) than Germany (3 percent and 0.6 percent respectively) and India (2.2 percent and 0.8 percent respectively). This is not surprising since France has an internationally established market reputation in this case also.

What surprises, however, is the high-end garment category in the Indian case. The overall figures indicate that India, with a total of 153 advertisements (13,0 percent), leads in comparison to France, with 71 advertisements (6.4 percent) and Germany, 148 advertisements (5.8 percent). It is only upon closer inspection of the textile sub-category that an explanation is found. This subcategory in India contains 25 advertisements, whereas Germany and France have two and three advertisements respectively. This is due primarily to sociocultural reasons. Indians generally buy fabric en masse to get them hand-stitched by local tailors particularly during the festive seasons. In Europe, on the contrary, it is the *prêt a porter* that dominates.

India also has the highest advertising volume of 7.3 percent in the technical product category followed by Germany with 5.5 percent and France with 3.8 percent. What is particularly interesting is that in the audio-video sub-category, India has 66 advertisements, which is more than the double of France (28 advertisements) and almost the equivalent of Germany (72 advertisements).

Let us consider the food and beverages category next. Germany with 349 advertisements (13.6 percent) leads in this category in comparison to France with—83 advertisements (7.5 percent) and India with—78 advertisements (6.6 percent). The difference is induced primarily by the "Alcohol" sub-category. Germany, with 239 advertisements in this subcategory, is clearly a "heavyweight"; France, in contrast, has only 70 advertisements, and India, with 32 advertisements, ranks even lower. Apparently, France, internationally known for its Champagne, Bordeaux and other equally delectable wines, cannot beat Germany when it comes to consumption of beer ("Bierbauch" is the quintessential German term for the beer induced pot-belly).

Both European countries, however, have a much higher volume of advertisements for bottled water/juices as compared to India. According to de Mooij, consumption of bottled water and juice correlates with high uncertainty unavoidance, so high uncertainty avoidance cultures drink more of these products.[1] It also appears that high uncertainty avoidance cultures have a passive attitude to health in that they focus on purity in food and drink and using more medication; low uncertainty avoidance cultures, on the other hand, exhibit a more active attitude toward health by focusing on fitness and sports.[2] Both France and Germany, as we know, score high on avoidance of uncertainty. Germans, with the lowest score in power distance but higher scores in uncertainty avoidance, will look for products that are natural and offer claims supported with scientific information. French consumers, even though they score the highest on power distance, are also just as strong on uncertainty avoidance. This combination suggests that they will look for uncontaminated and scientifically tested products and in these cases, advertisements for personal care items would focus on purity or highlight scientific attribute.[3] Not surprisingly perhaps, in the food and beverages category in France, several advertisements for bottled water have been found, which showed the brand in a nature setting and emphasized its purity attribute. Vittel, for example, advertises with the tagline "There is something in this water. We can never thank Nature enough" ("Vittel. Il ya quelque chose dans cette eau. On ne remerciera jamais assez la nature").

[1] Marieke de Mooij, *Global Marketing and Advertising: Understanding Cultural Paradoxes* (Thousand Oaks, CA: Sage Publications, 2010).

[2] Marieke de Mooij and Geert Hofstede, "Convergence and Divergence in Consumer Behavior: Implications for International Retailing", *Journal of Retailing*; de Mooij, *Global Marketing and Advertising*.

[3] Marieke de Mooij, *Consumer Behavior and Culture: Consequences For Global Marketing And Advertising*, 2nd edn (Thousand Oaks, CA: Sage Publications, 2011).

To highlight certain important socio-cultural differences between the three countries, let us take a look at the tobacco subcategory. While the French sub-category has nil advertising (due to legal restrictions imposed by the 1991 Evin Law), Germany and India, in contrast, have 59 and 35 advertisements respectively. Clearly, even though direct advertising of cigarettes is gradually being banned in the First World, it is still a force to reckon with in many European countries. In fact, faced with anti-smoking laws and campaigns, a number of tobacco companies in Germany such as HB appear defiant—"Ich rauche gern" ("I enjoy smoking") and "Thank you for smoking". Interestingly, some of them even espoused the cause of multiculturalism. Drum Cigarettes for example, advertises as "No racism". A Peter Stuyvesant advertisement says, "Come together"/"Love is a circle".

In the "automobile" category, not surprisingly perhaps, Germany, with 318 advertisements (12.4 percent) is the leader. France and India, in contrast, have only 119 (10.7 percent) and 93 (7.9 percent) advertisements respectively. The difference is induced principally by the cars subcategory where Germany, known the world over for its automobile industry, leads with 263 advertisements as compared to France, which has 100, and India, which has a mere 23. In the case of India, however, this is made up elsewhere, namely in the bicycles/motorcycles subcategory, which, has been included here due to their overwhelming usage by the majority of Indian households. France and Germany, with only one advertisement each have practically no weightage in this subcategory, whereas India, in contrast, has a total of 13 advertisements. The differences are socio-economical. Until very recently, not many Indians could afford to buy even a single car. The fact that this survey found a total of 23 advertisements for both imported and indigenous cars indicates that these advertisements in magazines such as *India Today* are targeted at a privileged section of the society.

The paucity of advertisements for bicycles/motorcycles in Europe, on the other hand, indicates that their usage is restricted primarily to students, sports fanatics as also environmentalists and busy executives. The Harley Davidson motorbike advertisement promising "freedom on the road," for example, is positioned to appeal to the executive-type customer in the upper-income bracket who is prepared to pay an exorbitant price for owning an American Classic. These customers, in fact, are not just buying a motorcycle but the associated dream of escaping their busy schedule. In contrast, in a developing country like India, particularly rural India, they constitute the favorite mode of transport for the vast majority of the population,

In the finance and insurance category, while India (79 advertisements or 6.7 percent) and France (72 advertisements or 6.5 percent) have more or less the same ranking, Germany with 273 advertisements (10.7 percent), is without doubt the market leader. The disparity is induced primarily by the insurance sub-category where both France and India contained very little advertising—17 and 12 advertisements respectively. Gemany, on the other hand, has 133 advertisements. It appears that the Germans tend to insure themselves against all potential calamities. This is because as de Mooij explains, German consumers have a weaker uncertainty avoidance ranking than the French so they require more rationality in making purchases[4]. As a result, advertising copy in Germany often needs to reassure buyers by providing them with warranties and money-back guarantees.[5]

Now let us take a look at the leisure and travel category. Tourism, of course, is one of the most obvious forms of economic and cultural globalization. It is not only a significant earner of a country's foreign currency but it also exposes people, from various countries and social strata, to other cultures. It would appear that falling prices and increasing ease of international travel are now pushing more and more people of all social classes to travel, particularly in the West. France has the highest figures in this instance—106 advertisements out of a total of 1,112 advertisements (9.5 percent). Germany and India have 177 (6.9 percent) and 91 (7.8 percent) respectively. The data indicates that in the case of the West, the roots of travel as a relatively widespread mass phenomenon do not

---

[4] Marieke de Mooij, "Mapping Cultural Values for Global Marketing and Advertising", in *International Advertising: Realities and Myths*, ed. J.P. Jones (Thousand Oaks, CA: Sage Publications, 2000), 80.

[5] Gerard J. Tellis, *Effective Advertising: How, When, and Why Advertising Works* (Sage Publications, 2003); S. Yeniurt and J.D. Towsend, "Does Culture Explain Acceptance of New Products in a Country?: An Empirical Investigation", *International Marketing Review* 20, no. 4 (2003).

lie in international but domestic and regional travel. India, on the other hand, has relatively fewer travel advertisements but a large number of luxury hotel advertisements targeting the elite, which emphasize its potential to become a world class travel destination in the future.

The Indian industry and commerce category contains a much larger corpus of advertisements than France or Germany—227 advertisements (19.3 percent) as compared to only 66 advertisements (5.9 percent) for France and 170 advertisements (6.6 percent) for Germany. For purely business studies, my methodology would highlight the demand trends. For example, the data would indicate an urge toward modernization in India, as well as the exponential growth in the market for computers and cell phones. It would also indicate that since saturation points have not been reached, it is a market that global companies should enter.

Some sectors in particular, such as textiles, which is South Asia's traditional area of strength and steel and metallurgy (which were found to be doing well in India but not so well in the European case) hold out special promise for export growth in the future. The trend suggests that some of the traditional industries, such as cotton and jute, textile industries, mining and tea manufacture, which were at their peak in the pre-liberalization era, are now gradually being sidelined in favor of a range of other industries such as steel, chemicals, cement, automobiles, and consumer electronics. These had grown over different time periods and are likely to further grow as developed markets get more and more saturated. The trend further indicates that as international competition rapidly opens up new opportunities, developing countries will be increasingly targeted by foreign companies seeking low-cost manufacturing bases. India, in this instance, presents the attractive opportunity of an emerging market with a huge skilled but cheap workforce that also speaks English in most cases as the language of the business world.

In terms of intra-regional trade, however, the paucity of advertisements seem to suggest limited economic interdependence between the SAARC member countries. Although Indian firms are aggressively seeking to integrate with global markets, they do not seem to be as eager to expand their regional market. One reason for this could be that India's domestic market is quite large in comparison with the other South Asian markets. Hence, the incentives for expanding regional trade are not very strong. While the current trend of global quest for Indian firms is likely to continue in the mid-term, the prospect of regional expansion seems more unlikely.

* * *

This study concludes with the observation that despite some of its inbuilt complexities, the Indian market, following liberalization, is poised for stupendous growth. Indeed, judged in terms of purely aggregate economic performance, India's integration into the global economy since 1991 appears to have been hugely successful. In fact, India's domestic demand for consumer goods, in particular, new Western goods, may even come as a surprise to many who think of India primarily in terms of its grinding poverty. In reality, however, a large number of people in India are able to afford upper end labels and even Mercedes cars as indicated by the evidence. But what is particularly new about liberalization is that it has given birth to a new group of middle-class elite consumers that is different from the traditional middle class.   In terms of its composition, this class comprises company executives, entrepreneurs, information technology (IT) specialists, finance and management consultants, media professionals and nouveau riches. Comprising an estimated 300 million—roughly 22 percent as against 12 percent elsewhere in the world—it also has higher income levels and spending proclivity thanks to the lucrative packages offered by transnational corporations.[6]

As Varma asserts, "The logic of economic reform, therefore dictated that the middle class now be analysed not for its lack of ideological moorings or its lack of commitment to anything but its own material well-being or its utter insensitivity to social and moral courses but for its cravings for and ability to buy what the developed

[6] E. Sridharan, "The Growth and Sectoral Composition of India: Its Impact on the Politics of Economic Liberalisation", *India Review* 3 no. 4 (2004): 405–28.

countries could sell to it...[7] Or as the newly launched *India Today* magazine pointed out:

> The economic liberalization that has been sweeping across the country for the last few years has altered the lives of a large section of India's burgeoning middle class. They have become much more international in their outlook and aspirations, more sophisticated and liberal in their lifestyle and attitudes and certainly more adventurous and demanding in terms of holiday and leisure activities". With the new Manmohanomics, there are now many more opportunities to make money and even more avenues to spend it.[8]

It is in this sense that 1991 marks a watershed in India's economic history.

---

[7] Pavan K. Varma, *The Great Indian Middle Class* (India: Penguin Books, 2007), 178.

[8] Aroon Purie, in the inaugural issue of *India Today Plus*, First Quarter, 2013.

10

Where India Is Now

Changing Economic Landscape

Going back several decades, it is generally agreed that for all his accomplishments, the principal architect of modern India, Pandit Nehru, failed in one vital area—eradication of poverty—which was central to his vision of India. In order to "feed the starving people", he imposed a combination of socialism and protectionism on the country.

One of the psychological legacies of the Nehruvian socialistic era was that the more affluent sections of society were branded as being rather vulgar and spending money to live well was considered an even greater sin. In his overreaction to the memory of colonial capitalism, Shashi Tharoor notes, Nehru created "a State that ensured political freedom but presided over economic stagnation that regulated entrepreneurial activity through a system of licenses, permits and quotas that promoted both corruption and inefficiency but did little to promote growth"[1] In the economic sphere, in other words, Nehru underestimated the need for negative liberty and ignored the consequences of curbing individual initiative. Besides, he seemed to

---

[1] Shashi Tharoor, *Pax Indica, India and the World of the Twenty first Century* (New Delhi: Penguin Books, 2013), 206–7.

forget his own realization that in modern times, "isolation" was both undesirable and impossible". His economic policies were at odds with his vision "of intimate cooperation politically, economically and culturally between India and the other countries of the world."[2]

For over three decades, after India became independent, the Indian economy grew, for various reasons, at a modest rate. Between 1956 and 1974, industrial modernization and the so-called green revolution could muster a mere 3.4 percent average annual rate of growth at a time when many Asian economies were booming. Between 1975 and 1990, the country's economic growth accelerated at a rate higher than 5 percent, then increased to more than 6 percent after 1992. Subsequently, despite some fluctuations, the Indian economy grew at 8.8 percent between 2003 and 2007 thereby transforming India into one of the fastest growing economies of the world along with China. Its rate of growth surged from a low 3.4 percent in pre-reforms period to a high of 9.2 percent in 2006–7. In 2012, India, as the IMF predicted, overtook Japan in purchasing power parity (PPP) terms to become the world's third-largest economy (Japan's GDP of $4.3 trillion did not grow in 2011 after its earthquake, tsunami and nuclear disaster whereas India's 1.3 trillion GDP, which converts to $4.06 trillion in PPP went up by at least 6.2 percent). Needless to add, this is a far cry from the pre-globalization era when India had to mortgage its gold reserves for getting foreign exchange.[3]

How did two decades of a liberalized economy transform the Indian State from being an economic laggard with a growth rate of 6 percent to one of the most rapidly growing economies in the world, averaging nearly 8 percent a year? One important reason for this is that post 1991, the Foreign Exchange Regulation Act (FERA), which had restricted foreign equity to a maximum limit of 40 percent, allowed 51 percent foreign equity in most sectors of the economy. India, consequently, received $24 billion worth of investment through the foreign direct investment (FDI) route between 1992 and 2002—an

[2] Jawaharlal Nehru, *The Discovery of India* (New Delhi: Penguin Books, 2010), 41.

[3] These figures are from the World Development Indicators, the World Bank, accessed through the National University of Singapore Library Website (accessed on August 3, 2010).

improvement on the past but a figure that China could surpass in a single year. However, Indian companies still remained largely averse to foreign investment.[4]

Some exceptions existed though, for example, Infosys (software), Bharti (communication), Wipro (software), and HDFC and ICICI (financial services). All these major firms that made it from relative obscurity to the top rungs of the Indian corporate ladder had one thing in common. They all invested heavily in the services sector, (often even ahead of such big industrial groups as Tata, Birla and Reliance), building up a substantial presence in a range of services including software, communication, retail and financial services. The IT sector, which is highly competitive, accepted the presence of foreign capital. Indian entrepreneurs such as Narayan Murthy of Infosys took advantage of deregulation and India's emerging natural comparative advantage in the software and services sector, to transform a company founded on a $250 initial investment in 1981 into a $4 billion company in just over three decades[5]. Also, the smaller companies that needed foreign capital, technology and managerial expertise in order to compete with larger entities welcomed foreign capital as joint-venture partners. For example, an increase in the foreign equity limit in Indian telecommunications was welcomed by Bharati Enterprises whose telecommunications company, Airtel, benefited enormously from its partnerships with Singtel, Warburg Pincus and other foreign companies.[6]

As a result of policy reforms, many consumer sectors today are brimming with excitement. For example, following the delicensing of the telecommunications sector in May 1994,[7] India has been transformed from a nascent market for cellular telephones into the

[4] Suresh D. Tendulkar and T. Bhawani, *Understanding Reforms: Post 1991 India* (New Delhi: Oxford University Press, 2007), 106–16.

[5] Tendulkar and Bhawani, *Understanding Reforms*, 83–94.

[6] Rahul Mukherjee, "The Politics of Telecommunications Regulation: State-Industry Alliance Favoring Foreign Investment in India", *Journal of Development Studies* 44 no. 10 (2008): 1405–23.

[7] On July 21, 1995, West Bengal's Chief Minister, late Jyoti Basu made the country's first cellphone call from a Nokia Tetstra's MobileNet service in Kolkata.

world's fastest growing one—with Nokia, Samsung, Motorola, LG, Sony Ericsson and others scrambling to build more manufacturing capacity in the country.[8] The Indian automobile industry, which came into its own precisely one decade after liberalization has not looked back since. The coming of Sony and some Asian giants such as Akai, LG and Samsung has changed the television market scenario as never before. In the audio equipment segment, till 1991, Philips had virtual monopoly of the audio market. With players such as Sony, Samsung, LG and Akai entering the Indian market, however, this product category has seen an explosion as probably in no other. In the cosmetics market, many sought after international brands which upmarket beauty conscious Indian women have always craved for are now available at the international price. While global players such as Revlon, Avon, Oriflame and L'Oreal have swept the market, local brands such as Lakme, a Tata brand and a pioneer in the post-independence Indian cosmetics market for women, has repositioned itself with a plethora of new products in a bid to beat competition.

Ranked as the country's largest private firm, the Tata Group, which already draws 65 percent of its revenues overseas, has invested more than $1 billion internationally. Its purchase of the Anglo-Dutch Company Corus Steel for $12.1 billion in 2007 was one of the largest deals in the history of the Steel industry. Other major Tata Group buys include the purchase of Tetley, the second largest selling tea brand in the world and automobile brands such as Jaguar and Land Rover. Tata Motors has also introduced a new concept in the automobile industry through its Nano, marketed as the world's cheapest car. This catapulted the Tata Group to the sixth position among the world's most innovative companies—behind Apple, Google, Toyota,

---

[8] Today there are more than 700 million mobile phone subscribers from just 2 million in 2000. According to an article published in Forbes on 6 January 2016, "India's mobile phone subscriber base crested the 1 billion users mark, as per data released recently by the county's telecom regulator". The Wikipedia article "List of countries by number of mobile phones in use" gives 1,186 790005 for India but clarifies that this is the figure for phone numbers, not for actual phones since some people have multiple SIM cards installed.

General Electric and Microsoft and ahead of Sony, Nokia, IBM and BMW.[9] And more recently, Volkswagen's merger with Tata Motors has allowed the combined company to claim the crown as the world's biggest carmaker.[10]

Conversely, the FDI and presence of multinational firms in India has also substantially increased after liberalization even though this has been a slow and gradual process. Instead of a one shot adoption of free trade, protection levels have been brought down in stages. This, however, has not deterred a large number of leading MNCs from diverse sectors from having Indian affiliates, buying out their partners in joint ventures or becoming the dominant partner and acquiring other firms. From Parle and Tomco in the early years of liberalization to the more recent cases of ACC and Ranbaxy, a number of prominent Indian firms have passed into foreign hands. In some individual industries, the extent of MNC presence has substantially increased after liberalization and they completely dominate some sectors such as passenger cars, scooters, consumer, electronics and soft drinks.[11]

What about the fact that India, a sharply stratified society, still has a huge underbelly of poverty-stricken people? This fact has been sharply brought home by a New York Times Report of December 10, 2005: "fifteen years after India began its transition from a state-run to a free market economy, a new culture of money—making it and even more, spending it—is afoot. So intense is the advertising onslaught, so giddy the media coverage of the new affluence that it is almost easy to forget that India is home to the world's largest number of poor, according to the World Bank".

Indeed, more than two decades after liberalization, even as economic growth spreads, the big questions of the future continue to be regarding the disequalizing effects of economic wealth. This is not a

[9] Nirmalya Kumar with Pradipta K. Mohapatra, Sui Chandrasekhar, *India's Global Powerhouses* (Boston: Harvard Business Review Press, 2009), 157–76.

[10] *The Economist*, Special Report, "Imagining the Industry's Future: The Road to 2033, How might carmaking look 20 years from now", April 20, 2013.

[11] WTO statistics on anti-dumping, available at http://www.who.org.

question, however, that any society, democratic or authoritarian, has been able to resolve, let alone any rapidly growing society—and certainly not China. The good news is that although the rate of growth has slowed down recently from a scorching 9 percent prior to the global financial crisis, the Indian economy is likely to continue to grow between 7 percent and 8 percent for the next couple of decades. This means that even though poverty may not vanish, the number of poor will come down to a manageable level (since 1947, the percentage of the population living below the poverty line has come down from some 90 percent to just over 30 percent making India not just home to the largest number of poor people in the world—26 percent of the global extreme poor—but also to the largest number of people who have recently escaped poverty based on a poverty line set at $1.90 per person per day).

Needless to add, a significant percentage of the Indian population still remains at the bottom of the pyramid (BOP).[12] But what is worth noting is that this segment has traditionally aspired to own international brands of repute as symbols of social class and prestige. In the future, many from this segment may well be able to afford a coveted Louis Vuitton or Hermes bag, run in their Nike, Reebok or Adidas shoes, wear an Armani or Chanel suit; and listen to music on their iPod from Apple.

From a transnational perspective, India, of course, still lacks China's vast resources. But the country, clearly, has potential. It is large (it is home to one sixth of humanity) and it is young (it has 450 million people below the age of 21 years)—and will continue to be young. It also has a well-developed legal system, a democratic political system, a mixed economy with deep-rooted capitalistic conditions, a large population of world-class companies, an educated IT—competent workforce and a relatively affluent middle-class (India has a population of 1.21 billion, 300 million of whom are middle-class consumers with money to spend), that is well-aware of global brands via exposure to the global media. Also it uses English in most cases as the language of the business world.

---

[12] C.K. Prahalad and Kenneth Lieberthal, "The End of Corporate Imperialism", *Harvard Business Review*, August 2009.

Changing Cultural Landscape

Culturally speaking, what are the consequences of economic liberalization? Although difficult to generalize, globalization undoubtedly has not just influenced the economy but also India's socio-cultural panorama. The economic reforms have expressed themselves primarily in terms of rising literacy and aspirations, economic prosperity, exposure to Western culture and a new generation breaking away from joint-family ideals, thereby leading to the rise of nuclear family, and a need for accessibility to entertainment and information at home[13]. To better understand this phenomenon, let us, once more, briefly examine here, the cultural constructs developed by Dutch management researcher, Geert Hofstede.[14]

The first of these cultural constructs, is power distance, which according to Hofstede, is defined as the extent to which the less powerful members of institutions and organizations within a country expect and accept that power is distributed unequally. India scores high on this dimension—with PDI of 77 indicating an appreciation for hierarchy in society and organizations. Today, however, Indian organizations are in many ways, becoming flatter. Thanks to liberalization and the pattern of economic growth during this period, the lowest income group in rural India has declined sharply leaving only the ultra-poor there. This segment now has higher standards of living and higher expectations as well. In many Indian urban areas, access to selected commodities, brands and services has become a means for securing upward social mobility and virtually upgrading one's societal position.[15]

Regarding the second cultural dimension developed by Hofstede, Individualism/Collectivism, the fundamental issue addressed by it is the degree of interdependence between the members of a society.

[13] S. Ninan, *Through the Magic Window: Television and Change in India* (New Delhi: Penguin Books, 1995).

[14] Geert Hofstede, *Culture's Consequence: Comparing Values, Behaviors, Institutions and Organizations across Nations*, 2nd edition (Thousand Oaks, CA: Sage Publications, 2001).

[15] Raghav Bahl, *The Amazing Race between China's Hare and India's Tortoise* (Penguin Books India, 2010).

India, with a score of 48 is more collectivist as compared to the developed Western countries, where there is more emphasis on individual freedom, and individual human rights even to the exclusion of the need to preserve community harmony and cohesion.[16] Clearly, in the Asian context, autonomy and independence are not as important or at least do not have the same connotations as in the West. The cultural codes are more about kinship, of an extended family, family obligations, joint decisions and the home as a shared space. In such situations, the actions of the individual are influenced by the opinion of one's family, neighbors and work group. Today, however, the country appears to have climbed a notch higher up the individualism ladder, the implications of which are evident in the altering perception of products, services, career choices, and even family.

Interestingly, however, the resulting change is not based on a total abolition of older traditional structures and their replacement by new patterns. Most countries in Asia are adopting new technologies but retaining their identity at the same time. Rather than becoming like the West they are developing their own forms of modernity. For instance, joint families in India still exist but have now loosened up in many ways to make room for individuality. Most young people also have radically different approaches to shopping. They want strong brands, but they get tired of them quickly; they are more likely to make their choice of brands in the store and at the point at which they are triggered into thinking about consumption. Paradoxically, this new generation of Levi's-worshipping and Coke-sipping Indian youth, is not the typically West-influenced youth one would expect going by the invasion of Western brands. In fact, the Indian youth between the ages of 20 and 35 years, who form the greatest section of the country and are also the greatest spenders, prefer the "outward trappings of Western culture" but are still very traditional.[17] A typical Indian youth may wear Nike shoes and a Lacoste shirt but is still very much Indian in his values. He respects his parents, even to the extent of marrying a spouse of their choice, lives together in a joint family

[16] Hofstede, *Culture's Consequences.*
[17] D. Bobb, "Generation Why", *India Today* 30, no. 4 (2005): 98.

and removes his Nike shoes before entering a place of worship.[18] Indian women too, in their large majority, despite modernization, are not opting en masse, for Western apparel. Instead traditional Indian wear is getting more fusion, spawning a new look that is called "East-West outfits".

As for the third dimension, masculinity, a high score (masculine) on this dimension indicates that the society in question will be driven by competition and material achievement. Work is the center of one's life and visible symbols of success in the workplace are very important. A low score (feminine) on this dimension means that the dominant values in society are caring for others and quality of life. India (with a score of 56) is a masculine society in which visual displays of success and power are considered important. Although this continues to hold true in many respects, the current trend in India is toward a reversal of traditional gender roles. With Indian women joining the workforce in large numbers, Indian men are increasingly assuming a more participatory role in terms of parenting, shopping and sharing household chores. Indeed an important consequence of globalization is the altering conjugal power relations. Globalization has generated more opportunities for Indian women to enter high-profile jobs leading to a new kind of power equation between husband and wife with the latter becoming financially more assertive than before. However, major purchase decisions, by and large, still tend to be taken by men. Traditional parent-child relations have also been impacted with parents becoming much more accommodating now vis-à-vis their children's wishes. In the case of certain purchase decisions such as cars, children above 12 years play a big role as they determine whether according to color or interior furnishings, the car is considered "cool."

This has also led advertisers to challenge the traditional role and status perceptions of women (recall the Onida and Ray Ban advertisements). Hence, it would now be just as shortsighted for a marketer conducting a survey of paper towels, disposable diapers or frozen foods to restrict the sample to the "woman of the house"

[18] Marieke de Mooij, *Consumer Behavior and Culture-Consequences for Global Marketing and Advertising* (California, London, and New Delhi: Sage Publications, 2004).

as it would be for a marketer of financial services or automobiles to restrict the sample to the "man of the house". Today many car and car-accessory manufacturers (for example, Volkswagen, Apollo Tyres and others), in fact, actively target the Indian woman who has greater affluence, independence and self-confidence than in the past. Paradoxically, however, the present trend also suggests that although the role of women at work will continue to expand, rising unemployment, social practices and technological progress will reduce the pressure on employers to change their practices to attract women who continue to bear the major share of household work and childcare. With rising global competition, Indian firms, in fact, have chosen to follow the American model with demands for extended work hours as well as attendance on weekends. This creates a time bind for both men and women where something must give.[19] Household organization therefore may likely continue to be dominated in the future by women many of whom may choose to work from their homes.

The fourth dimension, uncertainty avoidance, has to do with the way members of a certain culture feel threatened by ambiguous situations. India scores 40 on this dimension and thus has a medium low preference for avoiding uncertainty. India is traditionally a country where tolerance for the unexpected is high. Nothing has to be perfect or go exactly according to plan. Rules are often in place just to be circumvented and one relies on innovative methods to "bypass the system". A word used often in this context is "adjust" and means a wide range of things—from turning a blind eye to rules (for example, neglecting to put one's safety belts while driving) to finding a unique and inventive solution to a seemingly insurmountable problem. Today, following globalization, uncertainty avoidance, at one level, is of even lesser consequence. Young India has become much more entrepreneurial, with traditionally secure job sectors such as the civil services, engineering, and medicine being increasingly marginalized in favor of risk-taking ventures. In urban India especially, the employed salary-earner has been replaced by a growing number of

---

[19] Sonalda Desai and Anupuma Mehta, "No Economy for Women", *The Hindu*, March 8, 2017.

self-employed. At another level, however, this has created even more job uncertainty than before.

The long-term orientation dimension is closely related to the teachings of Confucius and can be interpreted as the extent to which a society shows a pragmatic future-oriented perspective rather than a conventional short-term point of view. India, with a score of 61, is to all intents and purposes, a long-term pragmatic culture. In India, time is not linear or monochronic and thus not as important as in the case of many Western societies. Typically, societies that have a high score on long-term orientation, forgive lack of punctuality and accept a changing schedule based on a changing reality as one goes along rather than an exact plan. Although these factors continue to matter, the perspectives now appear to be shortening. This is reflected among others, in the workplace where there is no longer any real job security. Earlier, the public sector in India was the most sought after employer guaranteeing job security and a host of such coveted benefits as healthcare and pension. Post liberalization and with the emergence of such new sectors as IT, the orientation has changed to more lucrative even if short-term benefits. In recent years, Business Processing Outsourcing (BPO) jobs for example, have become one of the most preferred for the urban Indian youth. The lack of focus on long-term planning is further reflected in the proliferation of products and services oriented toward instant consumer gratification—for example, in healthcare and food habits.

Changing Political Landscape

Following independence in 1947, India, as stated previously, remained for many decades a poor "Third World" country with little or no say in international affairs despite her huge population and the riches of her cultural heritage.

Since 1991, however, reaping the benefits of its far-reaching economic reforms that projected it as a new and significant market opportunity for Western companies, India progressively became less shy about engaging the world. Where once Russia was considered as the sole extra-regional friend, India now intensified its simultaneous engagement with all the major Western powers. With the collapse of the Soviet Union, China's rise as an economic power began to be seen by the Western countries as a potential threat. The expectations regarding China's adoption of market economics and capitalist processes to transform it into a liberal democracy were belied by the brutal suppression of pro-democracy demonstrations in Beijing's Tianenmen Square in June 1989. By contrast, India was seen as a successful and politically plural democracy. And now, because of accelerated economic growth, it also appeared as a major commercial opportunity rivalling China. India's nuclear tests in May 1998 may have retarded this realignment somewhat, but by the turn of the century India's relations with the US and the West in general, had begun to crystallize into a mutually benefical and substantial relationship. Indeed as the former UN diplomat Shashi Tharoor puts it "We are now in a position to graduate from a focus on our own sovereign autonomy to exercising a vision of responsibility on the world stage, from a post-colonial concern with self-protection to a new role participating in the making of global rules and even playing a role in imposing them."[20]

Although the US had been wooing India for some time and the Indo-US nuclear deal has removed a major irritant and more importantly, given India access to the high technology needed for its growth—today, given the protectionist policies of the new US government, many feel that India should perhaps invest more in other international partnerships such as with traditional ally, Russia.

In this instance, even though Russia continues to be an important partner and a significant source of advanced defense technologies and hardware for India, its focus, sadly, is no longer on India, but on China.

In the case of Europe, India and the EU had in 2004–05, forged a very strong bond based on shared values as multi-ethnic, multi-religious and multi-lingual democracies. That has changed in the past one decade thanks to the Eurozone crisis, which has muted the voice of Europe in international affairs. With Brexit this trend will likely further intensify. The fact that Germany has emerged unscathed from the crisis and is now the strongest power in Europe has only added to the existing strains. It is perhaps important to recall

[20] Shashi Tharoor, *Pax Indica: India and the World of the Twenty-First Century* (New Delhi: Penguin Books, 2013), 15.

here the fact that both India and the EU, despite their divergent approaches, ultimately stand for the same global principles of commitment toward a multipolar, rule-based democratic international order. In a world plagued by multiple challenges including Islamic fundamentalism and a radically changing international landscape, dialogue between the two must recognize their core strengths and synergies and this should be the central idea taking the relationship forward.

India's engagement with Southeast and East Asia, on the other hand, since the formulation of its Look East Policy in 1991, is already considerable and likely to grow in ways that could not have been imagined even two decades ago. Whether in terms of trade, investment or tourism, India is beginning to increasingly reconnect with Asia. Although protectionist lobbies and bureaucracy have slowed down the pace of India's liberalization and consequently, its integration into the international and ASEAN economic systems, in general terms and compared with the caution of the early 1990s, India is now a much more confident, even assertive participant on the Asia Pacific political and strategic sphere. India's trade with Southeast Asia, for example, now represents about a quarter of its total trade, outweighing that with the US and the EU.[21] This should be seen and is being seen by many of our neighboring States as all for the good. A prosperous India is good for the region. We not only need a peaceful neighborhood but also co-actively find synergy with it. India can now afford to provide easy if not duty-free access to its market, as well as to build institutions that our neighbors and friends would like to buy into. India's FTAs with Sri Lanka, Nepal and Bhutan and advances in trade relations with Bangladesh showcase the potential benefits of regional economic integration. There is no reason to believe why this cannot be extended to other countries also. At the same time, and while these initiatives are to be welcomed, they still fall short of creating a truly interconnected and interdependent South Asia, marked by a free flow of goods, peoples and ideas across the borders, as it had been for most of the region's long history. Apprehensions of domination by India are still a given among its neighbors and this

---

[21] Figures from "Trade Statistics" available at http//business.gov.in/trade/trade-stat.php.

is hardly surprising given the reality of the above-mentioned asymmetry. India, as stated previously, is the largest country in the region in terms of area, population and economic and military capabilities, larger than all its neighbors put together. Each neighbor shares some significant ethnic, linguistic or cultural feature with India but not so much with the others. It is this asymmetry, which shapes the neighborhood perception of India and vice versa. An obvious illustration of this is Nepal brandishing the China card to offset what it regards as its excessive strategic dependence on India. This being so, India's own strategic compulsions are still dictated by subcontinental concerns that override existing political divisions. India cannot insulate its security from developments within its neighboring countries. To keep its attention focused on achieving high and sustained economic growth over the next several decades, India will need to ensure a stable, peaceful and secure periphery. As the largest country in the region, it is only India that can take the lead in transcending the political divisions in the subcontinent, restore its cohesiveness and make its borders increasingly irrelevant, drawing upon its eternal sources of unity. India cannot take full advantage of the growing web of economic interaction and interdependencies bonding Asia together while being isolated from its own periphery. That is why the neighborhood must rank as the highest priority in India's foreign policy behavior. In this instance, it is perhaps worth noting that although initially a reluctant member of the South Asian Association for Regional Cooperation (SAARC), when it was first created in 1985 at the behest of Bangladesh, India today has taken the lead in advocating a South Asia Customs Union, a common currency and even a South Asia Parliament. This is the result of a growing recognition that economic integration in South Asia is indispensable for the Indian economy as it globalizes.

Can India perhaps do more in this instance to leverage its still largely untapped resources of soft power in the region? Coined by Joseph Nye Jr, the terminology suggests:

> If a country's culture and ideology are attractive, others more willingly will follow. If a country can shape international rules that are consistent with its interests and values, its actions will more likely appear legitimate in the eyes of others. If it uses institutions and

follows rules that encourage other countries to channel or limit their activities in ways it prefers, it will not need as many costly carrots and sticks.[22]

India's soft power assets, in this case, include, among others, Bollywood films which along with cricket, are a subcontinental passion, eclipsing borders and politics. Even during periods of intense hostility with Pakistan, the popularity of Bollywood movies and movie stars in that country has continued to rage unabated. This is also true of Sri Lanka, the Maldives and Afghanistan. Similarly, the love of Bangla language, literature and Rabindra Sangeet transcends the boundaries between India and Bangladesh leading to a more benign perception of India in that country over the years. While these assets may not, of course, directly persuade the South Asian countries to support India, they may still go a long way in enhancing India's intangible standing in the region. This is because soft power has assumed even greater preponderance with the advent of globalization. This was underlined, not just by Joseph Nye but also by Francis Fukuyama in his path-breaking Post-Cold War book, *The End of History and the Last Man* wherein he states that the West had won the War not because of its arms but because of its ideas on democracy and liberalization. In his words, "the collapse of the State-controlled centrally planned State-economies of the former Eastern blocs symbolizes the triumph of the West... an unabashed victory of economic and political liberalism...[and] the total exhaustion of viable systematic alternative to Western [neo]liberalism".[23]

Fukuyama's book, no doubt, contains the most accurate insight about what is new today—the triumph of liberalism and free-market capitalism as the most effective way to organize a society. But at the same time, his work also implies a finality to this triumph, which is in contradiction with the world as it appears today. In a way, both Fukuyama and Huntington's works became prominent because they tried to capture in a single catchy thought, the "One Big thing" that

[22] Joseph Nye, "Soft Power: The Means to Succeed in World Politics", *Public Affairs* (2004): 25–6.

[23] Francis Fukuyama, "The End of History", *The National Interest* (Summer 1989): 4.

would drive international affairs in the post Cold War world—either the Clash of Civilisations or the triumph of liberalism. In order to understand the post-Cold War world, however, one has to begin by understanding that a new international system has succeeded it—globalization. It is not the only thing influencing events around the world of course. But to the extent that there is a North Star and a single worldwide shaping force, it is this system, the "One Big Thing"that people need to focus on; what is old, is the politics, power, chaos, clashing civilisations, liberalism.... It is the interaction of all these elements, both old and new, that defines international relations in the Post-Cold War world of today, characterized not just by one Superpower exerting its indisputable control over the rest of the world, but by an interconnected set of relationships that reduces conflict through cooperation.

The following chapter deals with this topic, that is to say, the replacement of the wrestling matches between the two Superpowers with the sprints to economic success by the two fastest rising economies of the South, India and China.

11

The "China" Factor in Southeast Asia

This chapter has a strong focus on China reflecting my belief that China is and will remain for the foreseeable future, the one country that has a direct impact on India as far as international relations go. Managing the rise of China, therefore, geographically and strategically, qualifies both as an immediate and a long-term challenge. The threat from Pakistan is only a subset of this challenge given the strong alliance between the two countries.

Over the last 30 years or so, China, as stated previously, has experienced an extraordinary rise. It has demonstrated an average growth in excess of 9 percent annually with growth rates touching 13–14 percent in peak years. As a result, China's per capita income rose by more than 6 percent every year from 1978 to 2003, much faster than that of any other Asian country, significantly better than the 1.8 percent per year in Western Europe and the US and 4 times as fast as the world average. In terms of GDP, China, in 2005, overtook the UK as the world's fourth-largest economy; in 2007, it passed Germany to become the third largest economy, and in 2010, it crossed Japan to become the second-largest economy after only the US. This feat has made the Chinese economy, in PPP terms, the second largest in the world with a GDP of roughly $10 trillion.[1] China has also invested billions of dollars in infrastructure in every continent. Although projecting China's long-term future is not easy, it is reasonable to believe that China will continue to rise and that it will most likely overtake the US in GDP size at some point during the first half of this century.

India's economic reforms, on the other hand, which produced the recent spurt in growth, took place in the early 1990s, over a decade after China's. To date, these reforms have been neither comprehensive nor complete. China is far ahead of India in the economic league. China's officially declared GDP, a $7.3 trillion in nominal terms and $11.3 trillion in PPP terms, is about three times that of India's ($1.7 trillion in nominal and $4.5 trillion in PPP terms). China's exports at more than $1.5 trillion are nearly five times that of India and its imports are almost four times those of India. China's officially declared GDP at $7.3 trillion in nominal terms and $11.3 trillion in PPP terms is about three times that of India's ($1.7 trillion in nominal and $4.5 trillion in PP terms). China's exports at more than $1.5 trillion are nearly five times that of India and its imports are almost four times those of India. China's global economic footprint consequently, is much bigger than India's. Hence, economically speaking, even though the relationship between the two countries is flourishing, it continues to be asymmetric with a mounting trade surplus in China's favor. At the same time, the Indian economy has also grown at a rate of about 7.5 percent during the first decade of this century, thereby placing it, when measured by PPP methods, in the fourth place globally with a GDP of approximately $4 trillion.

On the political front, both countries appear, on the surface at least, to be making all efforts to resolve their differences and to cooperate amicably. However, given their long historic rivalry, in particular, the unresolved boundary, the Tibet issue and the Chinese support to Pakistan, the relationship remains a complex amalgam of competition and cooperation. As one analyst concludes, "the

---

[1] Martin Jacques, *When China Rules the World: The Rise of the Middle Kingdom and the End of the Western World* (London: Allen Lane, 2009), 192.

relationship between Asia's two great powers can best be character-ized as one of global cooperation on transnational issues especially vis-à-vis the "West," geo-strategic rivalry at the regional level in the form of growing commercial exchange and in some cases, bilateral competition.[2] This statement perhaps best captures the conventional wisdom about the dichotomy in Sino-Indian ties characterized by a broad convergence on transnational issues and a deep bilateral rivalry that persists despite the two countries' mutual and growing economic interdependence

While this chapter is concerned largely with the impact of China's growing ascendancy in the region, I have attempted to put this in the broader context of India's Look East/Act Policy and the backdrop of a newly emerging global order, which inevitably, will look somewhat different as the twenty-first century progresses. I have posited that although historically, the dominant power in the international system usually exploits the differences between two rising powers to check them, this is the era of globalization. Unlike the past, rising powers today (China and India) and the dominant power in the international system (the US) share many common interests. They also face many common threats. They have to cooperate as also compete with each other on many issues. I believe that they are more likely to engage in co-operational competition rather than open hostility.

China may of course, continue to expand its economic and military capabilities and may even become the most powerful coun-try in the world—but the world, which is emerging, will still be populated by a number of substantial powers, both old and new, including India that are unlikely to accept junior league status in a Chinese centric world. Hence, even though sections of Asian and international opinion have already begun to concede a central role to Chinese hegemony with the corollary that it is best for the rest to acquiesce to this inevitability—what a careful analysis points to, in fact, is that we are, in reality, neither in a China-centric Asia nor in a world destined to become China-centric. In the Asia-Pacific region,

<hr>

[2] Schmidt Johannes Dragsback, "India and China in Comparative Perspective—Emerging Asian and Global Powers", paper presented at the Madras Institute of Development Studies, Chennai, India, November 1, 2011.

for example, in addition to the US there is a cluster of major powers with substantial military capabilities and these may be significantly expanded in the region to a perceived Chinese security threat. India, Japan, South Korea, Vietnam, Indonesia and Australia fall in this category. Similarly, the cluster of major ASEAN powers also deploy a formidable array of security capabilities, in particular, maritime capabilities, though still modest, in comparison, to US military presence. Even without a substantial US military presence in the region, these capabilities together would easily surpass what China can deploy. Therefore China faces the same dilemma as other emerging powers in history—what Bismark referred to as *Le Cauchemar des Coalitions* or the nightmare of coalitions. There will always be a countervailing coalition to constrain a rising power.

At the same time, with 70 percent of its supply and almost 80 percent of its total trade being shipped through the Indian Ocean region,[3] China, has many a stake in the region and thereby poses many a challenge in the neighborhood. As the top trading partner of most Asian nations, it serves as the economic hub of an increasingly integrated Asian economy. Already members of the ASEAN have adopted a policy that now prioritizes balance between the US, Japan and China. In the US-China-Russia triangle, it is China that has emerged as the pivot, which means that the US pivot to Asia aimed at limiting China's strategic expansion has become less credible.

For India, these developments have profound implications. For one, the value of the US as the leading component of a countervailing coalition in Asia has diminished even though it is too early, of course, to say how developments in the US will affect global geopolitics. If the global footprint of the US and its allies diminishes, this may create spaces for other major powers to play a bigger role. We see this already in Russian activism in West Asia and the Chinese initiatives on the Afghanistan issue.

Second, would Russia be more amenable to Chinese and Pakistan calculations today given Russia's improved relations with Pakistan and the fact it even entered into a military hardware relationship

---

[3] Mohan Malik, "The Indo-Pacific Maritime Domain", in *Maritime Security in the Indo-Pacific Perspectives from China, India and the United States*, ed. Mohan Malik (London: Rowman and Littlefield, 2014), 15, 17.

with it for the first time in several decades? One element of India's strategic response has been unfolding for some time now in Japan with the emphasis being laid on the consolidation of an India-Japan partnership, which it is hoped, will help the second and the third largest powers in Asia to shape the emerging security and economic architecture in this part of Asia, now projected to replace the trans-Atlantic as the center of gravity of the global economy.[4]

India, China and ASEAN

India's strong willingness to play a greater strategic role in Asia is not new. India has always shown a desire for a greater role in this region, including as a security provider[5]. This is reflected in the large number of agreements it has signed over the years with the majority of regional players. India's Look East Policy, partly prompted by the Singaporean Prime Minister, Goh Chok Tong[6] was initially aimed at expanding India's economic cooperation with South East Asia[7] Subsequently, it was broadened to include building closer economic, institutional and defense ties across the whole of the Asia-Pacific region.[8] From a sectoral dialogue partner of ASEAN in 1992, India over the years, has progressively attained the status of full dialogue

---

[4] Ministry of Foreign Affairs of Japan, "Japan-India Relations (Basic Data)." August 4, 2014. http//www.mota.go.jp/region/asia-aci/India/data.html.

[5] See Rory Medcalf, "Unselfish Giants", Understanding India and China as Security Providers". *Australian Journal of International Affairs* 66, no. 5 (2012): 554–66.

[6] Countries like Singapore were quick to grasp both the economic and strategic potential of the end of the Cold War and India's economic liberalization programme. Senior Minister, Goh Chok Tong, played a key role in generating an "India fever" in Singapore.

[7] The partnership between India and ASEAN comprises Brunei, Cambodia, Indonesia, Laos, Malaysia, Myanmar, the Philippines, Singapore, Thailand and Vietnam.

[8] In 2003, the geographic focus and agenda of the Look East Policy was significantly expanded to include Australia and East Asia as well as broader economic and security issues.

partner, a summit partner and since 2012, a strategic partner. India is already a member of the ASEAN Regional Forum (ARF) and the ASEAN Defense Ministers' Meeting plus Eight (ADMM+8), which includes several summit partners of ASEAN. India also has a Strategic and Cooperative Partnership with China, a Special Strategic and Global Partnership with Japan and has concluded a Framework for Security Cooperation with Australia.

Ironically, however, it may be recalled that at the time the ASEAN was being formed, the Indian leadership had spurned the overtures made by its founders. This despite the fact that prior to and even after independence, India had been a staunch advocate of "Asian solidarity".[9] India finally changed its policy in 1979 when it sought observer status in ASEAN. Unfortunately India's recognition of the Vietnamese-installed government in Cambodia made the ASEAN states reluctant to accept India as a full dialogue partner. Consequently, India's admission to this body got deferred and it was not until after the end of the Cold War that India finally became a "sectoral partner" of ASEAN.[10] Twenty years later, India was made a full dialogue partner at the Bangkok ASEAN Summit. The very next year, it was also made a member of the ARF.

Since India's entry into ARF, it has steadily increased its presence in Southeast Asia and sought to foster important ties with a number of countries in the region extending from Vietnam to Singapore. In the same period that saw exponential growth of Sino-Indian trade, two-way trade with ASEAN member states has grown from approximately $US 13 billion to $US 74 billion making its trade with the region as a whole even more significant than with China.[11] Nevertheless, despite these initiatives, India's engagement with ASEAN and other major regional players remains way behind that of China's, which offers much better pre-set conditions conducive for economic investments to Southeast Asian investors.

[9] *India's "Look East" Policy: Changing the Asian Strategic Landscape*, AsiaInt Special Reports, 2001, 1.

[10] Ramesh Thakur, *The Politics and Economics of India's Foreign Policy* (London: C. Hurst & Company, 1994), 237–8.

[11] Figures from "Trade Statistics" available at http//business.gov.in/trade/trade-stat.php.

Since adopting an open to the world policy, China, in fact, has been paying special attention to regional networking. It has actively participated in and promoted comprehensive regional engagements, from the Asia Pacific and East Asia to Central and South Asia with the view to create an environment that seeks to promote economic cooperation, enhanced political trust and regional security.[12] Having taken the initiative to establish a comprehensive cooperation framework with members of the ASEAN, which facilitates trade and other economic relations immediately after joining WTO, China, today, is not only ASEAN's largest market, but the Chinese government also provides development assistance for nations in the region. The continuing reality therefore, is that the gap between China's and India's level of engagement with ASEAN remains huge.

India's engagement with ASEAN is essentially a part of its wider strategic objective to counterbalance China since China is at the core of Indian thinking. China's ASEAN policies have also been conditioned partly by the 'India factor' as Chinese scholars have called it. China also remains India's most important contender in policy initiatives in this region led by ASEAN. Whether the ASEAN countries show sympathy or antipathy toward China, China is much too strong and influential to be ignored in their perceptions and policies toward India. Indian ambitions may be great but it has to step in incrementally, facing challenges, mainly concerning its integration with other Asian countries, in which matter India has to make greater efforts. Military power is not as crucial, despite India's thinking, as economic interdependence. Without such integration, it would be premature to talk about India's role in any genuine security architecture in Asia. However, this does not prevent India from putting together the building blocks of a mature security relationship with the countries of Southeast Asia.

Although the India-China rapprochement and their common participation in various regional forums have helped to take the edge off

---

[12] For example, APEC in the Asia-Pacific, Shanghai Cooperation Organization (SCO) with Russia and Central Asia and ASEAN + Frameworks in East Asia. See Anywama Rumi, Kokubun Ryose, in Xi-De Jin, Zhang-Liping, Lu Jianren and Yunling Zhang, eds, *Making New Partnership, A Rising China and its Neighbor* (Beijing Social Sciences Academic Press, 2007), 14.

their long-standing rivalry, mutual acrimony does tend to erupt from time to time. The increase in China's influence, however, need not necessarily be at the expense of India and vice versa. Both sides have asserted that there is sufficient space to play their respective roles in regional and international affairs while paying attention to each other's sensitivities and expectations. This could be termed competition, but it can be called cooperation as well. India's strategic engagement with ASEAN need not be premised on the China factor alone. This policy also increases India's interaction with other major powers including China.

Shedding Cold War perceptions of India as linked to the USSR, the ASEAN countries are nearly unanimous in welcoming an Indian strategic presence, though there are some countries that still have some reservations. Neither Indonesia nor Malaysia for instance, are enthusiastic about a larger role for India in patrolling the Malacca Straits with or without the USA, and not all the littorals are more comfortable with an Indian as opposed to a US role. India's strength, however, lies in the fact that none of the Southeast Asian States see India as a security threat. Besides, its democracy and legal systems are attractive to Southeast Asian investors as also the fact that English is generally the language of governance and commerce in India. India will continue to retain this perceptional advantage as long as it remains an open, liberal and plural democracy. The ASEAN states, of course, accept that, for the time being, India lacks China's resources, has poor infrastructure and its decision-making process is cumbersome with a difficult bureaucracy. India also needs to bring its tariffs closer to ASEAN levels so as to make trade with the countries of the region easier. China's assertive stance on disputed territories, however, has given India the opportunity to further enhance its strategic presence in Southeast Asia and ASEAN states are increasingly looking to India to play a balancing role in the region.

Bilateral partnerships with individual ASEAN States such as Vietnam, for instance, hold out particular promise. Vietnam has been India's traditional friend in ASEAN and Indo-Vietnamese ties have been close ever since the time of Vietnam's nationalist movement.[13]

---

[13] See Anuradha Bhattacharjee, "India's Look East Policy: Relations with Vietnam", Briefing Paper, European Institute of Asian Studies, Brussels, July 2012.

To be the leading power in South Asia, India, many strategists feel, would have to prevent a Chinese advance into Southeast Asia. There is thus a convergence of Indian and Vietnamese views since both countries are concerned about checking the advance of China in a southerly direction. Vietnam has supported every move by Delhi to up-graduate its relationship with ASEAN. For its part, China sees India and Vietnam as its most probable future adversaries. Beijing is also deeply suspicious of India looking east as a move to encroach on China's strategic space and to link up with Japan, whose tense relationship with China has prompted it to reach out to India as a potential strategic partner. As the most-advanced Asian naval power and potential source of considerable technological assistance, Japan offers significant partnership opportunities as India deepens relations with East Asia.[14]

However, it is the strategic sphere of the relationship that holds out the greatest promise. With almost 55 percent of India's trade transiting through the Malacca Straits, India, understandably, does not want to see these crucial waterways dominated by a strategic competitor.[15] Hence, it is only to be expected that as China's relationship with India's neighbors in the Indian Ocean grows made easier by its relationship with Pakistan, Sri Lanka and the Maldives, the strategic relevance of India's own connections with neighboring Asian States in the Pacific Ocean will also grow. Also should China persist with its current accelerated rate of incursions along India's disputed border[16] or its presence in the Indian Ocean acquire a significant military dimension, India will likely seek a deeper relationship with critical partners such as Japan, Vietnam, Australia, ASEAN and Indonesia. Should China's assertive behavior in maritime territorial disputes in Asia continue to be regionally destabilizing, it can be expected that States in East and Southeast Asia will look more seriously

[14] See Bhattacharjee, "India's Look East Policy".

[15] David Scott, "India's Role in the South China Sea: Geopolitics and Geoeconomies in Play", *India Review* 12, no. 2 (2013): 55.

[16] Figures available from "Trade Statistics", Business.gov.in, http//business.gov.in.trade/trade_stat-php.

toward India to assume an influential role in the region's security architecture.

India, however, is likely to continue to carefully avoid any anti-China axis or coalition. There is in fact, a competitive element in India's policy—to get some kind of equal footing with China even while avoiding any direct anti-Chinese alliance, axis or coalition. Hence, although India's partners in the region can expect greater Indian involvement in multilateral maritime security initiatives particularly in the area of humanitarian assistance and disaster relief, it is unlikely that India will engage in any security initiatives that could be perceived as overtly threatening or containing China.[17]

What can be the basis of some common understanding between ASEAN, India and China? All three are developing, and share similar perspectives on most North-South issues and the challenges of globalization. They benefit from open policies on trade and investment and contacts with developed countries. They want a more fair and democratic international economic order and have a stake in the stability of the economic system. They also have similarities in Asian value systems and take pride in cultural identity, though there are differences in how human rights is viewed. And all three are faced with threats to national integration arising from separatist and communal forces as also terrorism. But they have had ideological differences, especially in the Cold War, and have divergences in threat perceptions. China supports Pakistan and India traditionally has had closer ties with Russia, and both factors have aggravated mutual hostility. Vietnam continues to harbor great suspicions of China while some members of ASEAN have close links with the USA.

The three units differ on the matter of strategic culture. The ASEAN is committed to pacific settlement of disputes and faith is placed in the role of institutions in the construction of peace. India and China on the other hand have more realist and zero sum perspectives of security. They tend to define their security interests in global terms whereas ASEAN has a narrower regional focus, and

---

[17] Alyssa Ayres, "China's Mixed Messages to India", *Forbes*, September 17, 2014.

relies mainly on self-help. To ASEAN, the Sino-South Asian ties are not seen as having much impact on ASEAN's security concerns, whereas the Sino US, Sino Japanese or Korean problems are seen as far more problematic. However the fact that India, China and Pakistan have all three nuclear weapons is certainly worrisome for ASEAN. Security cooperation therefore means confidence building measures to remove the layers of suspicion and hostility that had built up in the Cold War period.

The ASEAN's approach is pragmatic and based on dialogue. It recognizes the legitimate security of all and pursues a 'non-aligned' position when it comes to inter great power competition for influence. The proxy war that had taken place in Indochina makes ASEAN fearful of all great power rivalry. The ASEAN and India do share some concern about China's influence and power projection, but ASEAN is not engaged in power balancing against China, whatever the feelings may be in some particular ASEAN countries. In fact, ASEAN's basic principle is to encourage the development of good relations and ARF is still the only forum for all the major players in the Asia Pacific, though the ASEAN + 3 mechanism (China, Japan and the Republic of Korea) is also a contributing factor to this. There is no common ASEAN consensus on the Chinese threat perception, but there is a general concern at allowing China to grow in influence without restraint by countervailing powers or by international rules and regimes.

In recent years, China, as pointed out earlier, has begun to flex its muscles, asserting "indisputable sovereignty", claiming maritime rights over the South China Sea waters within its "nine dash line." This engulfs almost the entire sea and, snakes along the shores of the other claimants such as Brunei, China, Malaysia, the Philippines, Taiwan and Vietnam, that for decades, have contested one another's claims, occasionally even resorting to violence. Sovereignty over these territories not only serves as a source of national pride, it also confers hugely valuable rights to drill for oil, catch fish and sail warships in the surrounding waters. As the main corridor between India and Pacific Oceans, the sea carries one third of global maritime trading worth over $5 trillion each year, $1.2 trillion of it going to or from the United States. Its large oil and gas reserves and its vast fishing grounds also produce 12 percent of the world's annual catch, provide energy and food for Southeast Asia's 620 million people. Despite the enormous stakes, the US has failed to stop China. For the most part, Washington has believed that as China grows more open and engaged with the world, it would come to accept international rules and norms. Should China succeed in its endeavor, it will be poised to establish a vast zone of influence off its southern coast leaving other countries in the region with little choice but to bend to its will. At the same time, it will also have dealt a devastating blow to the United States' influence in the region. Tilting the balance of power across Asia in its own favor.

ASEAN does engage in some hedging activity. Hedging is most common when great powers are unpredictable and the global distribution of power is shifting fast—in other words, during times like today. Some countries will react to this new course of events by joining alliances intended to oppose either China or the US influence and thwart either power's aims within international institutions, Others will simply acquiesce, try to maintain ties with either China or Washington because they feel they have no other options, wish to retain certain security and economic benefits or share a sense of ideological or cultural kinship.

A hedge vis a vis China means that excellent relations with other powers need to be developed. This is primarily with the US followed by Japan, the EU, Russia and India. Several of China's neighbors have responded to its rise by welcoming a US security presence in the region but have stopped short of signing treaties to become a full-fledged US allies. Indonesia, Myanmar, Singapore and Vietnam, for example, have all adopted a variant of this strategy. The ASEAN is comfortable with the US presence in East Asia while the Taiwan and Korean issues are unresolved. The US presence diminishes the need for Japan to play a military role, which is less provocative to China and Korea. But support for the US is not evenly shared across ASEAN nor is it directed necessarily against a putative Chinese threat. For example, Singapore welcomes the US presence but as a mainly ethnic Chinese State, it is the last to feel a direct threat from China due to close trade, linguistic and cultural ties. India, most importantly, seeks a resolute American presence in the region to hedge against China while China sees the US as significantly complicating its regional goals and worries about American containment attempts.

The US, meanwhile, is determined to continue as a dominant actor in the Asian power balance but needs to co-opt regional powers to share the responsibility. Neither India nor the US wants to over-emphasize China in their shared Asian strategic objectives. India has been particularly careful to avoid sending any signals that it is attempting to contain China or intrude on China's strategic space. As such, it is likely to cautiously expand its influence in the region even while attempting to avoid any overt rivalry with China[18] To a large extent, how the two countries deal with each other and the US will determine the future. Right now, the US has better relations with China than India and China have with one another. By leaning in favour of one or the other, the US can gain a natural strategic lever-age. But what if India and China were to engage more proactively with one another? Interestingly, public opinion in India does not view China but rather Pakistan as the greatest threat to Indian secu-rity (83 percent believe that China will pose a security threat to India in the next 10 years, while 63 percent would like to see relations with China become stronger).[19]

While engagement as well as competition will likely continue to characterize the overall policy, the precise mix of India's China strategy, no doubt, will vary according to changes in the regional and global situation. There is in fact a carefully crafted pragmatism guiding bilateral relations on both sides. This pragmatism is based on the assumption that while certain political differences as a legacy of history will take time to resolve, such differences should not impact economic interaction and mutually beneficial cooperation. So long as India refrains from becoming a member of an anti-China military alliance, China has more to gain by increasing its engagement with India rather than by confronting it. It is of course inevitable that each side will continue to develop relations with the other's neighbours. India, therefore, should accord priority to its subcontinental neigh-bourhood so that it does not leave gaps that China or others can take advantage of.

[18] Ministry of Foreign Affairs of Japan, "Japan-India Relations (Basic Data)", August 4, 2014 http//www.mota.go.jp/region/asia-paci/India/data.

[19] David Brewster, "Indian Strategic Thinking about East Asia," *Journal of Strategic Studies* 34, no. 6 (2011): 848.

But even as India and China continue to grow, would they not want to progressively reshape the international system to advance their own interests-interests that may well differ from those of the United States, the established global hegemon? In answering this question, the book endorses the viewpoint that this concern is misguided for at least two reasons: first, because neither India nor China is likely to surpass the United States in power anytime soon, let alone exercise global military hegemony, and second, because both countries understand and appreciate the current global Order much more than is perhaps commonly realized. Since the end of the Cold War, both nations have come to recognize that the US led international order has created a peaceful external environment within which they can safely develop. Not only have they grown as a result of their integration into the global economic system, but they have also used that integration as a force for beneficial domestic reforms. Consequently they see globalization as a positive and to some extent, inevitable trend. On balance, neither one has also tried to overthrow the current Order, seeking rather to steadily increase their influence within it. The slow pace of recovery from the global financial crisis in advanced country markets has also conveyed to both the importance of looking at each other more closely for new economic opportunities. As a result, both countries are gradually adjusting to each other's economic rise as also coming to terms with the fact that in a globalized world, competition between them will likely be inevitable.

I would like to end on a note of hope. I would like to believe, in the spirit of the fledgling Indian Council of World Affairs that had organized in 1947, the visionary "Asian Relations Conference", that building durable peace and friendship with China is not impossible. A hallmark of Pandit Nehru's vision, it may be recalled, was his conviction that India, together with China, the "other" great Asian civilization, will lead the region in a new post-Imperial resurgence. Today, this seems almost prophetic when one considers the Goldman Sachs prediction that the three largest economies in the world in 2050, will be China, India, and the US (in that order). Hence, it is relations between the three that will likely determine the future geopolitical dynamics of the world. In other words, the power that has better relations with the other two, will, as stated previously, gain a natural strategic leverage. In the case of Sino-Indian relations, if the exponential growth of trade which grew roughly from US$ 7 billion in 2003–4 to US $65 billion in 2013–14,[20] is any indication, the two Asian countries whose rise as major world powers promises to test the established global order in the coming decades, appear, if only for economic reasons, to be making all the right moves.

The critics may, of course, be right in arguing that good trade relations do not necessarily resolve all the political problems between countries. Yet there are two counter-arguments worth making. First of all, trade contributes to the nurturing of a more positive relationship that makes political hostility less likely. More importantly, however, it ensures that the stakes involved are too high for the countries in question to contemplate engaging in any military retribution against one another. And second, unlike the past, the challenge faced by all major powers today, whether rising powers, India and China or the established global hegemon, the US—is the short term security afforded by large-scale military spending against the longer-term security of rising production and income to prevent relative decline. The new Trump slogan, "America First" is perhaps symptomatic of this changing trend in international relations.[21]

For the future—even though the international environment is favourable for India to expand its strategic goals, turning potential into reality will require time. Consistent efforts, however, within the framework of India's Look East/Act East Policy have most observers of the Indian reality hopeful.

[20] Figures from "Trade Statistics" available at http//business.gov.in/trade/trade-stat.php.

[21] President Trump's "America First" strategy, favouring trade over peace-keeping, environment, and human rights, has found broad support within the US. In foreign policy and economics, he has made it clear that the pursuit of primarily national advantages will guide his policies—apparenrly regardless of the impact on the liberal order.

12

Setting the Scene in South Asia

This chapter reflects my belief that without normalization of our relations with the countries of the subcontinent—Pakistan, Bangladesh, Nepal, Bhutan and Sri Lanka—along with our big neighbor, China, India cannot realize its full developmental potential.

Unlike the EU or even ASEAN, for that matter, which successfully define the political boundaries of a regional community of States, the developing regional political complex in South Asia, that is the South Asian Association of Regional Cooperation (SAARC), groups some of the poorest countries in the world. It is also, as per the projections of the World Bank, the world's least economically integrated region.

Historically, however, there is a great deal of commonality between the countries in the region—in dress, food habits, marriage and social customs. Indeed these commonalities should have provided a solid ground for regional cooperation. However, the efforts to build institutions to foster closer regional cooperation in South Asia have been relatively slow. The SAARC, of course, has played its part by taking certain steps, however, halting they might appear to be, to achieve its charter objective of "promoting active collaboration and mutual assistance in the economic, social, technical and cultural fields". However, much more needs to be done. In the process of strengthening SAARC, we can perhaps draw on some of the more successful regional expansions in other parts of the world. The experiences of regional cooperation in some of the developed and developing regions such as Europe (EU), Latin America (MERCOSUR) and Southeast Asia (ASEAN), for example, suggest that economic liberalization can provide a good foundation for the growth of regional cooperation, and subsequently a more prosperous and safer region. And even if these models cannot be applied indiscriminately, there are, nevertheless, a few valuable insights to be gained.

The EU's experience as a pioneer of regional integration, for instance, teaches us that historical reconciliation, is a critical element in developing the necessary political will for establishing regional cooperation. And that even former enemies can reconcile, even if only for economic reasons. Let us recall that Germany and France reconciled after World War II primarily because post-War leaders of the two countries shared a similar view of the origins of the war, the ensuing peace and the joint future of Europe. Essential for this process was an exceptional combination of co-operation, co-ordination and supranational integration by a coalition of elites willing to tranform parts of national sovereignty. The subsequent increase in trust and transparency of State behavior helped bridge the traditional political and economic disunity. The argument I would like to forward here is that if a war-devastated Europe could come together on May 9, 1950 to pool its coal and steel resources together as the first step toward a larger unity, is it not possible for South Asia with much more commonalities right from our origins, to forge a new unity despite the differences?

The Indian subcontinent is a single geo-political unit and developing interconnecting ties should be our greatest priority. Currently, all South Asian nations including India are confronting several problems: poverty and malnutrition, illiteracy and disease, disparate economic development, gender inequality and degradation of the environment. Such crucial issues can only be tackled and resolved jointly. By fostering cross-border economic and people-to-people linkages and leveraging the complementary strengths of different South Asian States, we have a far greater chance to overcome some of our mistrusts apart from of course improving the lives of our peoples. I wish, with our limited resources, we had also found the strength and unity to face the challenges, which at the end of the day, matter most to the 1.5 billion people living in one of the most crowded regions of the world.

South Asia: A Profile

South Asia or what is known today as South Asia consisted of closely inter-related kingdoms dating back to well before four millenia. The epicenter of South Asian civilization in ancient times, were the great Mohenjadaro and Harappan civilizations of the Indus Valley. The Indo-Aryan influx that took place across the Himalayan Massif around 1750 BC brought with it new religious philosophies and social institutions enriching the great Indian civilizations. The Rig Veda, the two great Indian epics—the Mahabharata and the Ramayana—the Tamil Sangam texts, as much as available, and archaelogical evidence, amply reveal the sweep and richness of the civilizations and cultures across the subcontinent, from the Himalayas through the Ganges Valley, spreading right across the islands of Sri Lanka and the Maldives. The saga of the subcontinent's cultural odyssey is seen to continue in the Upanishads, the emergence of Jainism and the teachings of the Buddha, which have profoundly shaped the way of life of many neighboring countries such as Sri Lanka. An offshoot of Hinduism, Buddhism rejects the evils of the Hindu caste system even while retaining its moral and ethical codes.

It is clear that the various South Asian societies evolved for many long centuries within a common socio-economic political and cultural framework. Diversity in ancient South Asia was not the inevitable cause of conflict it is today. The transformation of diversity from being the cultural strength of South Asia to its political weakness took place in the colonial era when the colonial rulers used and manipulated the various ethnic, linguistic and religious communities for advancing their own ends. With the Partition of India in 1947, a vast subcontinent, which had existed for long as an integrated and undivided unity, was brutally torn apart, leading to the creation of several independent and sovereign states with no shared vision of the future or of the subcontinent as a whole. The persistent challenge for India since independence therefore has been the reconciliation of its security interests, which cover the entire subcontienent with the reality of a divided policy. What is particularly noteworthy here

is that because of the many linguistic, religious and family affilia-
tions, communal tensions invariably also spill over to neighboring
countries across national boundaries.

Trade Relations: Whither India and the Subcontinent?

There are presently two reasons why we have not made any vigorous
attempts to expand regional trade. First, in South Asia, India dominates in size and population and in almost all indices of growth and
development. The market size of most SAARC countries, in comparison, is significantly smaller. Hence, there are very few incentives for
Indian firms to actively seek regional trade liberalization. In addition,
South Asian countries enjoy comparative advantage on a relatively
narrow range of products, leading to competition among the countries for the same market and the same products. For example, in
textiles and apparel, a few firms of four SAARC countries (India,
Pakistan, Bangladesh, and Sri Lanka) have reached world-class levels
of outputs. But the export of these firms to the South Asian region is
minimal. A study by Bandra and Yu shows that in the case of wearing
apparels, more than 80 percent of India's exports and 97 percent of
exports from Pakistan, Sri Lanka, and Bangladesh go to NAFTA and
the EU region, while export wearing apparels inside the South Asian
region is very small.[1] Given this dynamic, many analysts believe
that in the instance of the establishment of a FTA, companies from
Pakistan, Bangladesh and Sri Lanka will have fewer gains than their
Indian rivals.[2] Second, political tension among South Asian countries
is another important factor for the non-expansion of intra-regional
trade. India-Pakistan trade for example, is a complicated and vexed
issue. In a classic case of cutting its nose to spite its face, Pakistan
continues to shun and indeed sabotage lucrative trade and transit
links with India, both bilaterally and within the SAARC framework.
Indeed, there are lobbies in Pakistan, which resist the import of

---

[1] J.S. Bandara and Wusheng Yu, "How Desirable Is the South Asian
Free Trade Area? A Quantitative Economic Assessment", *The World Economy*
26, no. 9 (2003): 1306.

[2] Bandara and Yu, "How Desirable Is the South Asian Free Trade Area?"
1293–323.

Indian items. Strangely, Pakistan imports the very same items from other countries, especially China.[3]

Consequently, many Indian companies, have been aggressively seeking global markets—the US and the EU in particular—for their investment and industry expansion. For example, more than 53 percent of export of manufacturing goods from India goes to NAFTA and the EU, while exports of India's manufacturing goods inside the SAARC region is very small.[4]

In the face of competition from Eastern European and Central Asian countries, and the protectionist policies of Japan, North America, and Western Europe, however, not to mention their own limited structural abilities (that is, few manufacturing sectors, small gross domestic savings, and the small scale of economies), it is in the self-interest of the South Asian countries to forge deeper economic cooperation with each other. As pointed out earlier, the persistence of the global financial crisis has meant that the relatively open and liberal trading environment in the West, which allowed the export-driven economies of China and East Asia as major manufacturing platforms supplying their markets, is now under siege. In responding to shrinking markets and sluggish growth, both the US and Western economies are increasingly bringing in stringent protectionist measures in the form of non-tariff barriers, such as very strict environmental, labor or health and sanitary standards on imports. For India, (and other South Asian countries) which adopted their economic reforms relatively late, these protectionist trends come at a time when they are making efforts to establish themselves as a globally competitive manufacturing hub.[5] As a result, it very unlikely that either India

[3] *The Hindu*, March 19, 2017.

[4] Bandara and Yu, "How Desirable is the South Asian Free Trade Area?" 1293–323.

[5] There have been legitimate fears that the US-led Trans-Pacific Partnership (TTP) in the Asia-Pacific and the Transatlantic Trade and Investment Partnership (TTIP) might create a vast trading zone with restrictive norms and standards designed to keep away competition from countries like India. Although Trump has publicly announced that the US will no longer participate in the TPP and will seek the renegotiation of other free trade deals with various countries, the general trend toward more restrictive market access will no doubt continue.

(or other South Asian countries,) will be able to use their relative advantage as a low-cost country to increase trade. In other words, the extremely supportive international environment that had helped China's economic rise and which India to some extent, also leveraged in the 1991-2008 period, no longer exists. It is unlikely to revive even when the global economy fully recovers from the consequences of the financial crisis. There are longer term forces at play, which may transform global and economic and trade practices in such a way that India's investment and trade export led strategy may not deliver the expected outcomes.

On the other hand, there are complementarities and scope to revive trade within South Asia to very high levels. Why is it that official intra-regional trade within the SAARC region, to take one indicator, hovers around 5 percent of total trade of the countries of the region, while the corresponding figure for East Asia exceeds 50 percent and ASEAN 25 percent? Why should it be easier to forge an FTA with Thailand, Singapore, ASEAN and other nations than get South Asian Free Trade Area (SAFTA) off the ground? Why is it that a region with 22 percent of the world's population produces barely 6 percent of its GDP, with countries spending far more than they need to on goods they could have just easily imported from within South Asia?

The obvious answer to all these questions is that while geography determines our future, history continues to weigh heavily on our past. The bitter rivalry story between India and Pakistan needs no retelling. The two countries have much in common but more divides them. In fact, since independence, both India and Pakistan have actually grown apart in many ways and this fact, sadly, cannot be masked by about 5,000 years of common culture rhetoric.

Until and unless both countries share the same vision of things, such as the one espoused by post-War European leaders such as Jean Monnet, Robert Schumann and Konrad Adenauer, and which eventually led to the transformation of the "Others", that is France and Germany into potential consumers rather than as long-term enemies, and in doing so, they give up their "I versus You," attitude seeing themselves instead as part of a larger group or the "We" group that is responsible for strengthening the region (and this may take some time to come)—India will have to manage its adversarial relationship with Pakistan as best as it can.

India's basic weakness, of course, is that it has no real response options between the extreme choices of military retaliation and appeasement when it comes to Pakistan's sponsored terrorism. These will have to be built up gradually. In the view of this book, however, our security concerns including Pakistan's cross-border terrorism as also China's increasing inroads into Nepal, Sri Lanka, Bhutan, Pakistan, Bangladesh and the Maldives are likely to be more effectively addressed if we can invite our neighbors to build a greater stake in our own prosperity.

For the present, there are two ways that an analyst can see India restoring a coherent, unified and effective strategy for the subcontinent given its geographic, historical and cultural reality. One is by being powerful enough to impose its security perspectives on other countries in the subcontinent. The other is by developing political, economic, cultural and security policies to create a web of closer interdependencies. These approaches can help the country work around though not erase the existing subcontinental political borders. If it chooses to create a web of interdependencies, India could take advantage of its size and its asymmetrical strengths vis-a-vis its neighbours to achieve a level of interconnectedness that would render borders irrelevant. At least, that is the hope.

13

The "Automobile" Category

To illustrate the salient theme inherent to the book, that of unity in diversity among peoples and nations, this chapter focuses, in some detail, on the specific instance of the automobile industry (that is cars, two wheelers, trucks, engine oils, accessories, services related to cars and so on) in France, Germany and India.

We are discussing only one product category here because although many products can be discussed, it was felt that the ideas while illuminating the general thesis—that fundamental human needs and wants everywhere are universal—would not be rigorous enough to illustrate the conclusions. With some thought therefore, the category of "automobiles" has been chosen for the following reasons: first, this is a non-traditional item that is sold throughout the world; second, its appeal goes beyond any singular group of customers as opposed to, for instance, perfume, which is only meant to appeal to the female segment of the population or the medical profession that would focus on the health care industry. Third, the industry has a wide range of products starting from entry-level vehicles to luxury cars. Given the size of automobile companies, they also tend to place the largest number of advertisements. Fourth, advertisements in this sector tend to have a balanced mix of visual and textual elements, which sets it apart from other categories such as "Food and beverages" or "perfume," which would tend to focus on the visual.

However, there is a caveat. As far as India is concerned, at least in the early days of liberalization, very few cars were manufactured in the country, so I have also included motorcycles and scooters in this category since in India they have the same functional value as cars in Europe—the Indian population being segmented to include a "bike" segment of 25 million households in which motorbikes are present.[1]

Over 500 automobile advertisements were selected and their content analysed. By making a statistical analysis, 20 most recurring themes or product attributes that are used by advertising strategists as promises or selling propositions were put together: safety, economy, environment, utilitarian aspect, excitement/performance, quality/ perfection, relaxation, comfort, company image, responsibility, nationalism, social status, technology, social/family values, originality/ humour, supranational elements, aesthetic qualities, performance, ideology/emotions and reasoning.

For the purpose of this study, first a database of all companies operating in these three countries, France, Germany and India, was established (Figure 13.1). After some reflection, however, a second database of advertising themes in function of their frequency, was also established (Figure 13.2). This is because it was found that most advertisement copies (headlines, subhead, tagline/baseline/ logo, body copy) contained, in fact, more than just one theme. For example, the BMW tagline in India, "the luxury car where you do not have to sell your soul to safeguard your body" simultaneously emphasized the themes of social status, economy and safety. For its German market, on the other hand, BMW specifically chose the themes of safety and family values: "Your children are close to our heart" ("Ihre Kinder liegen uns am Herzen"). Similarly, terms can also have dual connotations depending on the context in which they are used. For example, the term "quality" could denote both quality of car and quality of service. "Catalyst" could correspond not just to technology but also environmental concerns. Consequently, all such words and phrases were systematically incorporated into the database in terms of multiple themes. The conclusions were based on the findings highlighted by both Figure 13.1 and Figure 13.2, that

---

[1] Sundeep Waslekar, "India can Get Ahead if Gets on a Bike", *Financial Times*, November 12, 2002, 15.

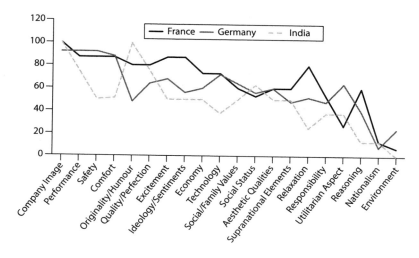

Figure 13.1   Companies
Source: Author.

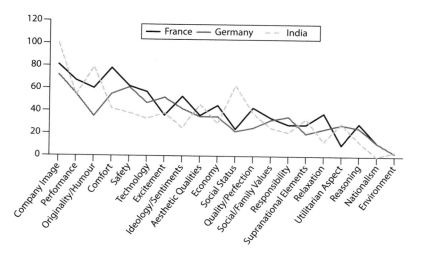

Figure 13.2   Thematic Frequency
Source: Author.

is to say, how many companies had resorted to a particular theme and how often a particular theme was resorted to. It was assumed that if a theme was used by a minimum of 50 percent of companies in all three countries, it could be taken as a basis of unity among the three countries.

Major Selling Points in India

What were the ideas used in Indian automobile advertising? In India, five major themes or selling points dominate (plus 50 percent): company image or reputation; humor and originality; quality/perfection; social status and performance. The other themes were of course present, but accounted for less than 50 percent. For example, environment, quite understandably, had higher representation in France and Germany.

1. Company image: Eight companies had resorted to this theme in their advertising: Mercedes, BMW, Rover, Daewoo Motors Bajaj Auto, Yamaha Escorts, and Vespa. This theme had appeared in 24 Indian advertisements (100 percent).
2. Humour/Originality: Eight companies had resorted to this theme in their advertising (100 percent): Hindustan Motors (Ambassador/Contessa Classic), Mercedes, Daewoo Motors, BMW, Rover, Bajaj Auto, Vespa, and Yamaha. This theme had appeared in 19 Indian advertisements (79 percent).
3. Quality/Perfection, Six companies had resorted to this theme in their advertising (75 percent); BMW, Daewoo Motors, Hindustan Motors (Ambassador), Bajaj Auto, Vespa, and Rover. This theme had appeared in 13 Indian advertisements (54 percent).
4. Social Status: Five companies had resorted to this theme in their advertising (63 percent): Hindustan Motors (Contessa Classic), Mercedes, BMW, Rover, Daewoo Motors. This theme had appeared in 15 Indian advertisements (63 percent).
5. Performance: Six companies had resorted to this theme in their advertising (75 percent): Hindustan Motors (Contessa), Mercedes, BMW Rover, Bajaj Auto, and Vespa. This theme had appeared in 13 Indian advertisements (54 percent).

The following themes, however, had an average rating of 50 percent.

1. Economy: Four companies had resorted to this theme in their advertising (50 percent): Rover, Bajaj Auto, HM (Contessa), Vespa. This theme had appeared in seven Indian advertisements (29 percent).

2. Safety: Four companies had resorted to this theme in their advertising (50 percent): Hindustan Motors (Ambassador/Contessa), BMW, and Vespa. This theme had appeared in nine Indian advertisements (38 percent).

3. Excitement: Four companies had resorted to this theme in their advertising (50 percent): BMW, Rover, Daewoo Motors, and Bajaj Auto. This theme had appeared in eight Indian advertisements (33 percent).

4. Aesthetic qualities: Four companies had resorted to this theme in their advertising (50 percent): Mercedes Benz, BMW, Rover, and Vespa. This theme had appeared in 11 Indian advertisements (46 percent).

5. Ideology/Emotions: Four companies had resorted to this theme in their advertising (50 percent): BMW, Bajaj Auto, HM and Yamaha Escorts. This theme had appeared in six Indian advertisements (25 percent).

6. Comfort: Four companies had resorted to this theme in their advertising (50 percent): Hindustan Motors (Ambassador), BMW, Rover, and Vespa. This theme had appeared in 10 Indian advertisements (42 percent).

7. Social/family values: Four companies had resorted to this theme in their advertising (50 percent): Hindustan Motors (Ambassador/Contessa), Bajaj Auto Ltd, Yamaha Escorts, and BMW. This theme had appeared in six Indian advertisements (24 percent).

8. Supranational: Four companies had resorted to this theme in their advertising (50 percent): BMW, Daewoo Motors, Rover and Mercedes Benz. This theme had appeared in eight Indian advertisements (33 percent).

Case Illustrations

This section gives some concrete examples to show how advertising strategists utilized some of the above-mentioned themes to sell their product. For instance, the HM-produced Ambassador cars began first by focusing on traditional values that did not take into consideration the quality or sophistication of the car. In one case, an Ambassador advertisement showed a father perching his two small children atop the roof of the car to enable them to have a vantage view of the traditional Dussehra fireworks display. The narrative said: "Papa, it's so crowded".—Relax.—There is no place for us to see.—I'll give you the best." A second advertisement emphasized the reliability and spacious aspects of the car; the visual showed seven adolescents standing in front of a Hindi movie poster—the Ambassador car parked directly behind them. The text, once again, was narrative: "Hey! There are so many of us." So?—How do we go?—I have my dad's car"—seven adolescents out to have some fun thanks to dad's Ambassador car—not in the least unusual in the Indian context. A few Ambassador advertisements also resorted to humor in an effort to sell better. For example, one advertisement showed an Ambassador car traveling a dusty village road with several street urchins running behind it, their faces alive with curiosity and wonder. The text says: "How long have we been traveling?"—"Five hours—Tired?—Not of the journey but your singing.—Ha ha."

As India opened up its economy, the corporate Indian CEO became important. When the Contessa, also of HM but situated in the luxury segment, first came to the market, the advertisement for it constructed the owner to be rich, powerful and a man of substance. The Contessa car therefore was linked to social status and to golf clubs. To illustrate this, the advertisement showed two men on a golf course and a Contessa parked next to them. The inordinately lengthy text read "We had never met before. I decided to size him up over a game of golf. But when he pulled up in his car, I knew I had found my business partner." The text went on to say:

> There was a spring in his step, a firmness in his handshake that I was by now expecting. As we got ready to tee off, I sensed I wouldn't need to watch out for his shortcomings. Instead I could concentrate on my handicap. After the fifth hole, I was sure. And understood just what

had impressed me when he stepped out of his Contessa. They complement each other so well. Both of them comfortable in the power they wield. Assertive but not arrogant. Distinguished, not deliberate. It is easy to know a man from him car. So when you are looking for fine men, just look inside a Contessa.

This advertisement is a good example of the fact that in a high power distance and collectivist society such as India,[2] communication is often indirect and that before getting down to business, it is often necessary to first build up a personal relationship.

According to the data, most foreign companies operating in India, such as Mercedes, Rover, BMW, Daewoo, etc. are situated like Contessa in the luxury bracket, also focused on selling social status. This is because in large power distance cultures, such as India for instance, one's social status must be made clear so that one can be accorded proper respect. Hence, the Mercedes advertisement is all about "style and power" ("The S-class from Mercedes defines style and power"). The Rover advertisements also emphasized, in bold letters, the attributes of Power and Pleasure "For men who understand real POWER—A car that spells pure success"; "For men who appreciate pure PLEASURE—A car that spells pure luxury"; BMW used such expressive terms as "automotive status" ("Setting the pace in automotive status").

The Korean Daewoo, on the other hand, used the theme of company image to aggressively sell—"Who's busy selling cars to Detroit? Daewoo. That's who." "Who's busy sending Televisions to Tokyo? Daewoo. That's who." "Who's busy reaching new heights in the world? Daewoo. That's who". "Japan's main supplier of top of the line TV sets. Korea's leading name in the high-tech electronics market comprising home appliances, personal computers and more"/"A US \$34 Billion Korean conglomerate... World's 33rd Fortune 500 Company." India, a high PDI country, understands the implied snobbery. Detroit is the hub of the American automobile industry and Japan, the market leader for electronic goods. For a Korean

---

[2] Geert Hofstede, *Culture's Consequences: Comparing Values, Behaviors, Insititutions and Organisations across Nations*, 2nd edn (Thousand Oaks, CA: Sage Publications, 2001).

newcomer to succeed in these hallowed markets is a form of status signaling. Similarly, the German BMW also used the same theme to promote itself as the market leader ("The result was a car that combines unsurpassed comfort and refinement with the same qualities of dynamism and progress that have made the name BMW great").

All this seems to suggest that automobile manufacturers generally tend to embrace the trend that suits the national culture of the country they are selling in. Interestingly, however, although the main market in India is the sub-compact economy segment, hardly any foreign company seemed to be entering it. The reason is the highly competitive cost structure. Since they cannot match the price of Maruti 800 for a similar car nor its high capacity utilization, foreign car companies seem to be preferring to operate in a segment which values attributes other than just price. As a result, this segment has been witnessing heavy competition with the entry of several foreign players.

Major Selling Points in Europe

When we look at comparable advertisements in France and Germany, we find that these themes were also used in 73–100 percent of advertisements in France, which had about 15 automobile companies; and in Germany, which had 25 companies, they were repeated in 60–92 percent of advertisements.

1. Company image: In France, 15 companies had resorted to this theme in their advertising (100%): Ford Motors, Renault, Peugeot, Citroen, Opel, Volkswagen, BMW, Audi, Mercedes Benz, Volvo, Chrysler, Jaguar, Honda, Nissan, and Alfa Romeo. This theme appeared in 47 French advertisements (81 percent). In Germany, 23 companies had resorted to this theme in their advertising (92 percent): Opel, Mercedes, Volkswagen, Mitsubishi Motors, Fiat, Peugeot, Audi, BMW, Ford, Nissan, Mazda, Toyota, Jaguar, Chrysler, Kia Motors, Land Rover, Jeep, Alfa Romeo, Renault, Volvo, Porsche, and Rover. This theme had appeared in 94 German advertisements (72 percent).
2. Originality/Humor: In France, 12 companies had resorted to this theme in their advertising (80 percent): Peugeot, Citroen,

Volkswagen, Mercedes Benz, Honda, Opel, BMW, Audi, Volvo, Jaguar, Nissan, and Renault. This theme had appeared in 35 French advertisements (60 percent). In Germany, 12 companies had resorted to this theme in their advertising (48 percent): Mercedes, BMW, Mitsubishi Motors, Renault, Opel, Rover, Volvo, Fiat, Citroen, Porsche, Volkswagen, and Peugeot. This theme had appeared in 46 German advertisements (35%).

3. Quality/Perfection: In France, 12 companies had resorted to this theme in their advertising (80 percent): Peugeot, Citroen, Audi, Honda, Renault, Volkswagen, Mercedes Benz, Chrysler, Jaguar, Nissan, BMW, and Opel. This theme had appeared in 25 French advertisements (43 percent). In Germany, 16 companies had resorted to this theme in their advertising (64 percent): Opel, Mercedes, Audi, Volkswagen, Mazda, Toyota, Peugeot, Hyundai, BMW, Ford, Nissan, Jaguar, Volvo, Fiat, Renault and Mitsubishi Motors. This theme had appeared in 33 German advertisements (25 percent).

4. Social Status: In France, eight companies had resorted to this theme in their advertising (53 percent): Renault, Citroen, Opel, Volvo, Jaguar, BMW, Audi, and Chrysler. This theme had appeared in 14 French advertisements (24 percent). In Germany, 14 companies had resorted to this theme in their advertising (56 percent): Volkswagen, BMW, Nissan, Jaguar, Jeep, Chrysler, Volvo, Fiat, Mercedes, Mazda, Mitsubishi Motors, Renault, Peugeot, and Rover. This theme had appeared in 28 German advertisements (22 percent).

5. Performance: In France, 13 companies had resorted to this theme in their advertising (87%): Peugeot, Citroen, Opel, BMW, Audi, Volvo, Chrysler, Jaguar, Honda, Nissan, Volkswagen, Ford, and Renault. This theme appeared in 39 French advertisements (67 percent). In Germany, 23 companies had resorted to this theme in their advertising (92 percent): Opel, Audi, Volkswagen, BMW, Nissan, Jeep, Volvo, Kia Motors, Lancia, Fiat, Peugeot, Mercedes, Renault, Jaguar, Mazda, Mitsubishi Motors, Rover, Porsche, Hyundai, Land Rover, Chrysler, Fiat, and Citroen. This theme had appeared in 72 German advertisements (55 percent).

6. Economy: In France, 11 companies had resorted to this theme in their advertising (73 percent): Opel, Nissan, Renault, Peugeot,

Citroen Volkswagen, Audi, Volvo, Chrysler, Jaguar, and Honda. This theme had appeared in 26 French advertisements (45 percent). In Germany, 15 companies had resorted to this theme in their advertising (60 percent): Opel, Audi, Volkswagen, BMW, Nissan, Mazda, Mitsubishi Motors, Rover, Chrysler Volvo, Kia Motors, Renault, Jaguar, Mercedes, and Fiat. This theme had appeared in 46 German advertisements (35 percent).

7. Safety: In France, 13 companies had resorted to this theme in their advertising (87 percent): Peugeot, Citroen, Opel, Volkswagen, Ford Motors, BMW, Audi, Chrysler, Jaguar, Honda, Nissan, Renault, and Volvo. This theme had appeared in 36 French advertisements (62 percent). In Germany, 23 companies had resorted to this theme in their advertising (92 percent)—Opel, Mercedes, Audi, Kia Motors, Volkswagen, BMW, Ford Motors Nissan Mazda, Jaguar, Mitsubishi Motors, Jaguar, Chrysler, Volvo, Lancia, Alfa Romeo, Land Rover, Fiat, Renault, Citroen, Peugeot, Hyundai, and Rover. This theme had appeared in 79 German advertisements (61 percent).

8. Excitement: In France, 13 companies had resorted to this theme in their advertisements (87 percent): Renault, Peugeot, BMW, Audi, Chrysler, Jaguar, Nissan, Opel, Volkswagen, Honda, Alfa Romeo, and Volvo. This theme had appeared in 21 French advertisements (36 percent). In Germany, 17 companies had resorted to this theme in their advertising (68 percent): Opel, Mercedes, Audi, Volkswagen, BMW, Porsche, Mitsubishi, Jaguar, Jeep, Chrysler, Volvo, Alfa Romeo, Fiat, Renault, Peugeot, Citroen, Nissan; and Kia Motors. This theme had appeared in 67 German advertisements (52 percent).

9. Aesthetic Qualities: In France, nine companies had resorted to this theme in their advertising (60 percent): Renault, Peugeot, Citroen Audi, Jaguar BMW, Honda, Opel and Volkswagen. This theme appeared in 21 French advertisements (36 percent). In Germany, 15 companies had resorted to this theme in their advertising (60 percent): Mercedes, Volkswagen, Nissan, Mazda, Jeep, Volvo, Kia Motors, Fiat, Renault, Mitsubishi Motors, Opel, BMW, Lancia, Jaguar, and Rover. This theme had appeared in 46 German advertisements (35 percent).

10. Ideology/Emotions: In France, 13 companies had resorted to this theme in their advertising (87 percent): Renault, Peugeot, Nissan, Citroen, BMW, Chrysler, Alfa Romeo, Audi, Opel, Jaguar, Honda, Volvo, and Volkswagen. This theme had appeared in 31 French advertisements (53 percent). In Germany, 14 companies had resorted to this theme in their advertising (56 percent): Opel, BMW, Mitsubishi, Renault, Jeep, Chrysler, Jaguar, Volkswagen, Volvo, Alfa Romeo, Fiat, Citroen, Nissan, and Audi. This theme had appeared in 55 German advertisements (42 percent).

11. Comfort: In France, 13 companies had resorted to this theme in their advertising (87 percent): Renault, Peugeot, Citroen, Opel, Volkswagen, Audi, Chrysler, Jaguar, Honda, Nissan, BMW, Volvo, and Ford Motors. This theme had appeared in 45 French advertisements (78 percent). In Germany, 22 companies had resorted to this theme in their advertising (88 percent): Opel, Mercedes, Audi, Volkswagen, BMW, Nissan, Mazda, Mitsubishi Motors, Rover, Jeep, Chrysler, Volvo, Kia Motors, Lancia, Alfa Romeo, Fiat, Renault, Citroen, Peugeot, Ford, Land Rover, and Hyundai. This theme had appeared in 72 German advertisements (55 percent).

12. Social/Family Values: In France, nine companies had resorted to this theme in their advertising (60 percent): Peugeot, Citroen, Volkswagen, Chrysler, Nissan, BMW, Audi, Honda, and Renault. This theme had appeared in 20 French advertisements (34 percent). In Germany, 16 companies have resorted to this theme in their advertising (64 percent): Mercedes, Volkswagen, BMW, Land Rover, Chrysler, Volvo, Kia Motors, Renault, Citroen, Peugeot, Nissan, Mazda, Fiat, Opel, Mitsubishi Motors, and Rover. This theme had appeared in 41 German advertisements (32 percent).

Thematic Unity in Diversity

This section attempts to interpret if indeed there is "unity" in the themes used in automobile advertisements across the three countries. According to the data, company image and originality/humour, as seen previously, are the two most frequently used attributes used to sell in all three countries. Humor, of course, is the dominant tone used by Indian advertisements. Something that is enjoyable, relaxing and fun is more likely to capture the Indian consumer's attention than other approaches. Car advertisements in India, therefore tend to be family oriented and humorous. Interestingly, humor also has high representation in European advertising. For example, 80 percent of French companies have used humor to sell. A study of thematic frequency further confirms the importance of this theme in the French (60 percent) and Indian (79 percent) contexts as compared to Germany—(35 percent) (Figure 13.2).

In France, three French companies—Renault, Peugeot and Citroen—in 17 of 22 advertisements, have used this theme in a manner reminiscent of the Indian Ambassador advertisements, using humor, and family values to sell better. Peugeot, for instance, has advertised with a series of storyboards, the slogan stating, "It's the first time that men are crazy about their wives' cars" ("C'est la premiere fois que les hommes sont fous de la voiture de leurs femmes"). The advertisement recounts humorously that when a husband begins to offer flowers to his wife, it is generally because he wants to borrow her Peugeot 106 ("Quand un mari se met a offrir des fleurs a sa femme, c'est generalement parce qu'il veut emprunter sa 106"). A second Peugeot advertisement displays a range of masculine underwear, the copy narrating humorously how Mr. Duchemin had tried simply everything to get his wife to lend him her Peugeot 106 ("Et pourtant M. Duchemin a tout essayé pour emprunter la 106 de sa femme"). In yet another instance, Peugeot has marketed its car as one "that the children recommend to their parents ("La voiture que les enfants conseillent a leurs parents").

Interestingly, a large number of German companies have also resorted to humor/originality to sell in France (11 of 21 German advertisements). Volkswagen, for instance, shows four camels inside its Golf car to illustrate the "exemplary sobriety" ("sobrieté exem-plaire") of the model that could also double, when required, as a pure thoroughbred. BMW showed a one-page-length visual of the famous Mona Lisa painting albeit horizontally so that it resembles a car. The Swedish Volvo showcases a butterfly poised on the car's engine, the text stating: "to make a butterfly emerge from its chrysal-lis state, simply place it on the engine of a Volvo 850 T-5." ("Pour sortir un papillon de sa condition d'insecte, posez-la sur la radiateur d'une Volvo 850 T-S Summum"). As for Germany—of the 130 advertisements found in that country, only 46 (or 35 percent) advertisements have resorted to humor/originality to sell. Interestingly, however, the large majority of the companies to use this theme are German—56 of a total of 130 companies have used this theme in 24 of the 56 advertisements (43 percent) in an effort to sell better. Many leading German manufacturers such as Mercedes, BMW and Volkswagen have also reiterated family values in an effort to sell. For example, the Volkswagen advertisement says—"the very name is reason enough to be Extra Happy. Golf Variant. Young Family" ("Der Name des Autos, dass extra Happy macht. Golf Variant. Young Family"). The majority of French companies operating in Germany such as Renault, Peugeot and Citroen, have also retained this theme in their advertising. In some cases, they have also sought to integrate into the German culture. For example, Citroen shows the traditional German "kuckucksuhr" or chiming wall-clock + a man with a protruding belly; the former symbolizes "time" and the latter characterizes a "chronic lack of movement" ("Bewegungsmangel"). The text says, "All those that stand still will be overtaken" ("Wer stehen bleibt, wird uberholt")—to overcome, which Citroen helpfully recommends a "sortie" (or Ausflug) in its new Evasion model.

Safety, understandably, has higher representation in the two European countries—62 percent and Germany, 61 percent. While Germany has the highest figures, this theme is also represented in India since it appears in nine out of 24 Indian advertisements (38 percent) and used by 50 percent of companies as against 92 percent for Germany and 87 percent for France (Figure 13.1). Examples include the HM produced Contessa ("powered disk brakes") and Ambassador ("comfortable, sturdy, safe and spacious"). Bajaj and Vespa advertisements also carry the term "SAFE" and the visual of a crash helmet respectively. Interestingly, BMW, presented as the "ultimate in driving safety" (slogan), is the only foreign automobile company in India to insist on absolute safety measures, often in combination with performance, company name and even technology. However, this salient theme is often also combined with performance, company name, comfort and surprisingly, technology. For

example, "torsional rigidity", highest degree of passive safety;" "com-
puter-engineered crumple zones", "intelligent side impact protection
system", "hydraulic bumper system", "front passenger airbags;" "its
smooth elegant lines disguise all-embracing safety" "optimal safety";
"unsurpassed safety"; "ultimate in driving safety combined with the
ultimate in exhilaration". Many of these terms such as "turbo", for
example, would go on to become common buzzwords. Viewed from
a certain perspective and because they reinforce certain core values
(in this case, safety on Indian roads), companies such as BMW, in
my view, can also represent a potent force for social change in developing markets.

For its European market, however, the BMW advertisements are
much more subtle. In Germany, as mentioned earlier, BMW emphasizes safety and family values through its tagline—"Your children are
close to our heart" ("Ihre Kinder liegen uns am Herzen"). In France,
on the other hand, BMW showcases a one-page visual of a tiny ladybird perched on a large leaf, the copy stating ingeniously "Imagine a
car capable of seeing something—even before you have noticed it"
("Imaginez une voiture capable de voir quelque chose. Avant meme
que vous ne l'ayez remarqué"). The other leading German manufacturer, Mercedes, also emphasizes safety in conjunction with family
values in Germany even while ignoring it for the Indian market. For
example, "And then suddenly, it was there to protect the biggest wonder of the world, your baby" ("Dann schliesslich gilt es, das grosste
Wunder der Welt zu schutzen, Ihr Baby"), the advertisement visual
showing a mother kangaroo with a baby tucked inside its pouch.

Comfort also has higher representation in Europe: France—87
percent; Germany—88 percent and India—50 percent (Figure 13.1).
A study of thematic frequency, however, shows the French, German
and Indian figures as 78 percent, 55 percent and 42 percent respectively (Figure 13.2). Interestingly the Indian figures now appear to be
more comparable with the European ones. The Indian companies to
use this theme in India are: Ambassador ("Comfortable, sturdy, safe
and spacious"), Vespa ("To make your ride even more comfortable"),
Rover ("You are entering a new world where your creature comfort
reigns supreme") and BMW, which has emphasized this theme in two
out of its four advertisements in India. For example, "The luxury car
that envelops you in exclusive comfort." "Of course we realize that

discerning drivers today demand the very best in comfort, luxurious ambience…" "If you set out to create the world's ultimate luxury car, one aspect has to be uppermost in your mind; you are entering a new world where your creature comforts reign supreme"/"And it's not just to do with the sumptuous and completely redesigned all leather seats, electronically adjustable arm back and headrest it has also to do with the feeling of relaxing spaciousness and well being…; " and "the result was a car that combines unsurpassed comfort and refinement with the same qualities of dynamism and progress that have made the name BMW great."

Interestingly, BMW uses the comfort theme widely in France also (two out of its three advertisements), thereby suggesting its resonance with the French buyer. The French advertisements, however, are much more quirky and subtle. A particularly interesting example is the BMW visual of the famous Mona Lisa painting albeit positioned horizontally so that it resembles a car—the copy querying ingenuously, "Is it a back? Is it a smile? Is it the most comfortable car in the world?"("Est-ce un dos? Est-ce un sourire? Est-ce la voiture la plus confortable au monde?"). For the German market also, BMW has used this theme in seven out of its twelve advertisements. In comparison, Mercedes has resorted to it in only two out of its 10 advertisements in that country. In India, the theme of comfort is not included in any of the four Mercedes advertisements. Instead, Mercedes focuses on selling social status ("The S-Class from Mercedes defines style and power"). What is particularly interesting is that the majority of advertising themes used by Mercedes in Germany (that is safety, quality, comfort, excitement and environment) in fact, were not reiterated for the Indian market. Is the Mercedes name so synonymous of safety, quality and so on that the company does not find it at all necessary to emphasize them in its advertising in India? Or are these themes deliberately omitted because of the Indian buyer's perceived resonance with social status?

For the excitement factor, France has shown the highest figures (87 percent) followed by Germany (68 percent) and India (50 percent). A study of thematic frequency, however, suggests a different picture: Germany (52 percent), India (38 percent) and France (36 percent). The Indian figures now appear to be more comparable to Europe. Examples in Indian advertising include the Vespa motorcycle advertisements—"New Vespa Select—Moves you stand-ing still. Thrills you on the move" + A single glimpse can quicken you heartbeat. But it is the Vespa Select riding experience that really sets your pulse racing." BMW marketed it car as follows—"And for all those who have longed for the ultimate in driving safety to be combined with the ultimate in exhilaration, it means that the time for compromise is over". For the French market, on the other hand, BMW advertised its car as one "invented to transform the rigours of work into pleasure" ("BMW a inventé la machine a transformer la rigueur en plaisir"). The visual, in this instance, showed the intricate layout of the Versailles Palace gardens, the copy stating that "it is perfectly possible to appreciate rigor. Even while retaining a child-like spirit" ("On peut apprécier la rigueur. Et avoir gardé une ame d'enfant").

For the performance factor, Germany, a country with virtually no speed restrictions on its national highway, is with 92 percent, the most "performing" of the three countries. France, with 87 percent, is a close runner up. Interestingly, India (75 percent) shows all signs of catching up soon with the two European countries. As for thematic frequency, Figure 13.2 shows France leading with 67 percent while Germany and India have similar figures—55 percent and 54 percent respectively. Indian examples highlighting this theme include the Rover Montego advertisements, which said, "This powerhouse is amazingly economical and the fastest car so far in India"/"It has a perfect synthesis of driving pleasure and styling with distinguished corporate looks"; and the Vespa advertisement that said, "the sheer exhilaration of the performance that lies under the hood". BMW, on the other hand, emphasizes the fact that when it came to creating a completely new car that would redefine the concept of moblity and performance in the world of luxury motoring, BMW took the lead. But while in India, BMW is about "exclusive comfort without sacrificing performance", for the German market, the correspond-ing advertisement visual shows a steering wheel, with the text stating simply—'Pleasure in driving" ("Freude am fahren"). In this country obsessed with speed and technology, not just BMW but practically every other company has also used this popular theme in an effort to better sell. For example, the Italian Alfa Romeo sells with the tag-line, "Boxer engines with 66 Kw (90ps) take care of the exhilaration"

("Boxermotoren mit 66 Kw (90 PS) sorgen fur Fahrspass"); The Fiat Punto Cabrio is described as a car that provides "all the thrill of driving beneath an open sky" ("Der Fiat Punto Cabrio—Der ganze Fahrspass unter freiem Himmel"). Not to be left behind, the French Renault also says, "Only thus can one experience the all-determining pleasure factor while driving" ("So kann man das entscheidende Mehr Fahrspass erleben").

The ideology/emotions theme shows a certain disparity, particularly between the two European countries: France (87 percent); Germany (56 percent); India (50 percent). However, this is somewhat compensated by the figures given in Figure 13.2: France (53 percent); Germany (42 percent) and India (25 percent). All three countries have used this theme as an important appeal, however, with certain variations. In France most of them primarily use emotions as a means to bond. For example, a Citroen advertisement says, 'if love still holds some meaning for you, you will surely buy the new Monospace Evasion" ("Si l'amour signifie encore quelque chose pour vous, vous acheterez surement le monospace "Evasion"); yet another Citroen advertisement said, "If your family and friends are very important for you, you will surely buy the Monospace Evasion" ("Si votre famille et vos amis sont tres importants pour vous, vous acheterez surement le monospace Evasion"). A BMW advertisement emphasizes the bonding between the car and its owner—"Men will always love their cars" ("Les hommes n'ont pas fini d'aimer leurs voitures.").

Interestingly, a corresponding Indian Yamaha advertisement also highlights the same bonding—in this instance, the intense if somewhat idealistic love affair between a young couple and their Yamaha motorcycle—"A love affair that never ends"; and "Two souls but a single goal. Two hearts that beat as one." There is a slight touch of humor here because contrary to what is assumed at the outset, this love affair, as one finds out in the end, is not between the boy and the girl but between the couple and their Yamaha—"You and your Yamaha. Together forever." In Germany, an Alpha Romeo advertisement described the car as one that evokes emotions." ("Ein Auto, dass Emotionen weckt..."). In France, in contrast, the same model (Alfa Romeo 145) is marketed as "palpitations guaranteed" ("Palpitations garanties") "passion in its purest form" ("Ici la passion a l état pur"). Yet another advertisement queries "You would like to share our passion for this legendary brand immersed in sportivity?" ("Vous voulez partager notre passion pour cette marque légendaire toute empreinte de sportivité?").

Social status, not surprisingly perhaps, has the highest thematic representation in India—63 percent as compared to France (24 percent) and Germany (22 percent). In terms of company representation also, India, with 63 percent, scores over both France (53 percent) and Germany (56 percent). For example, "setting the pace in automotive status" (BMW), "The luxury car that lets you judge automotive status from a wider angle (BMW) "unprecedented standards in luxury motoring" (BMW); "But then of course you wouldn't expect less from the world's most advanced luxury car" (BMW); Mercedes, on the other hand, emphasizes "The Mercedes C-Class is yours for the asking. If you are an exporter and if you appreciate true class".

This theme also has a certain resonance with the European buyer as evidenced by the fact that Renault, Opel Porsche and Volvo have all used it in their advertising in the three countries. While the Volvo advertisement is relatively, low key, due perhaps to its "low power-distance" Swedish origins[3],—"Outer sign of inner richness" ("Signe extérieure de la richesse intérieure")—the French Renault advertisement series are very similar to the Indian ones—"Vous hésitez entre dix chambres, sept salles de bains, trois salles de bals mais jamais entre deux voitures" ("You hesitate between ten rooms, seven bathrooms, three ballrooms but never between two cars"), and "Bientot, vous n'hésiterez meme plus entre le confort de vos quatorze salons et celui de votre nouvelle voiture" ("Very soon you will not even hesitate between the comfort of your fourteen sitting rooms and that of your new car"). In Germany, the somewhat lengthy Porsche advertisement targeting the aspirational values of its buyer, is reminiscent of the way Germans, in general, like to structure their lives around their well-known "agenda". The first Porsche advertisement says—18 years: the first kiss—19 years: the first car.—26 years: the first job.—42 years: the first Porsche.—isn't it wonderful that life is always upward? A second one, just as lengthy, suggests that in life, one might compromise on many things but never on a Porsche—"9.00 am Sales Meeting: Compromise with the sales targets.—10.30 am. Client

---

[3] Hofstede, *Culture's Consequence.*

meeting. Compromise with the remuneration. 12.30 pm: staff meeting; Compromise with the pay package—4. 30 pm Call made to house—Theater cancellation. 6.30 pm: Board Meeting: Endless string of compromises.—9. 30 pm. Driving back home—no more compromises".

For the "supranational" theme, the French figures lead (60 percent), followed, interestingly enough by Indian ones (50 percent) and Germany (48 percent). Thematic representation, on the other hand, shows India (33 percent) as leading followed by France (28 percent) and Germany (20 percent). In the case of India, most major foreign automobile companies have reiterated such terms as "international" "global" and "world-class" in their advertising. This does not surprise when one recalls that this was effectively the time when the Indian economy was just opening up to foreign investment. The key concepts propagated in European advertisements, in contrast, are cause-based issues that are also most likely to be universally accepted such as global solidarity, world peace, environment and human passion. Illustrating this, Citroen, for instance, shows a series of retro images of "Woodstock Music Festival" and "anti-nuclear" demonstrations in the US of the 1970s. Mercedes identifies itself with a pollution free environment through its visual of the earth (globe) surrounded by trees, animals and birds—but with no car in the picture. The copy is a subtle play of words, "In the end, it is also a question of the existence of cars" ("Schliesslich geht es auch um die Existenz des Autos").

What about motorcycles? Motorcycle advertisements in India invariably emphasized the fact that they are low cost, had excellent fuel consumption, great resale value (the common refrain is "value for money for years") and were therefore, important as an investment. Highlighting its fuel efficiency, one Bajaj advertisement, for example, said—'India's most fuel-efficient motorcycle".[4] Yet another one emphasized the many varieties available—"different strokes for Indian folks"; and another favorite of Indian buyers is—"the heartbeat of India". Indian two wheeler advertisements have also tapped into the free- thinking culture of youth. "Born free", for instance, has

---

[4] Today, this theme continues to be employed by such stalwarts of the Indian automobile industry as Maruti Suzuki. For example, "For a country obsessed with mileage, Maruti Suzuki makes India's most fuel-efficient cars".

become a popular slogan to express mobility. This is a phrase used in all three countries. In France, this concept was used, among others by Citroen—"For men that love freedom" ("Pour les hommes épris de liberté), by Chrysler—"Conceived for your freedom" ("Concu pour votre liberté") and by Harley Davidson "A legend of freedom" (Une légende de liberté); in Germany, it is reiterated by Chrysler "Where freedom begins"/'Expressions of your personal freedom" ("Wo die Freiheit beginnt"/"Ausdruck Ihrer personlicher Freiheit"); by Mitsubishi "A piece of personal freedom" ("Ein Stuck personlicher Freiheit"), and by Mercedes, "The taste of freedom and adventure" ("Der Geschmack von Freiheit und Abenteuer"). In India, the Bajaj slogan also implied breaking free of economic constraints.

Up until now, similarities or the "unity" factor among the three countries only has been discussed. What are the differences? Of the twenty themes studied, six were hugely underrepresented in one or all three countries: environment, utilitarian aspect, relaxation, reasoning, technology and nationalism. Let us first consider the example of environment. This theme, at first glance, had the same degree of emphasis in both France and Germany (12 percent). It has appeared in seven French advertisements (12 percent). Interestingly, however—all these advertisements are by the German Opel. In Germany, on the other hand, six different companies had resorted to this theme in their advertising (24 percent): Opel, Mercedes Benz, Audi, MW, Mitsubishi Motors and Mazda. It had appeared in 15 German advertisements (12 percent). Undoubtedly, this theme has special relevance for the German buyer. This was substantiated by a study conducted by Frontiers[5] in association with Research International, which found that German consumers see man as a part of the ecological system while other Europeans see environmentalism as restricted still to intellectual debate. Germans associate pollution with the air they breathe, and the French with the water they drink. Hence, while French motorists do not view the automobile as a major source of pollution, in contrast, in Germany, the demand for environment-friendly cars is much higher.[6] In the Indian case, even though environment did not feature anywhere in

[5] The Henley Centre, 2–4 Tudor Street, London EC4Y OAA.
[6] The Henley Centre, 2–4 Tudor Street, London EC4Y OAA.

automobile advertising, it appears, nonetheless, in some of the other product categories such as healthcare (five companies), industry and commerce (one company) and housing and furniture (one company). The obvious conclusion here is that just because a theme is not found in one product category, it does not automatically mean it has no place in the given society.

Let us now consider the utilitarian aspect. In India, this theme is underrepresented with only three companies having resorted to it in their advertising (38 percent). In terms of thematic representation, this theme has appeared in seven Indian advertisements (29 percent). In France also, only four out of 15 automobile companies have used this theme in their advertising (27 percent). It has appeared in six French advertisements (10 percent). Examples in the French case include the Japanese Nissan advertisement that shows a dozen blond babies crawling in and out of the open car doors to highlight the fact that its car can accommodate a large family. In Germany, on the other hand, this theme is used by as many as 16 out of 25 automobile companies (64 percent). It has appeared in 37 advertisements (28 percent) thereby suggesting that the German consumer has a special resonance with it. Examples include a Renault advertisement that attempts to integrate into the German cultural context with its tagline—"More space for your ideas" ("Mehr Raum fur Ihre Ideen"), emphasizing the German fondness, in general, for such terms as "ideas" (Ideen) and "thinking" (Denken).

As for the relaxation theme, 75 percent of all companies in India have ignored it in their advertising. In contrast to this, 52 percent of all companies in Germany and 80 percent of companies in France have incorporated it in their advertising. Interestingly, one of the few companies to use this theme in the Indian market is yet again BMW ("It also has to do with the feeling of relaxing spaciousness and well-being"). The fact that this theme has wider acceptance in France does not surprise when one considers the fact that one of the more well-known stereotypes associated with that country, is in fact, its relaxed and enjoyable lifestyle ("art de vivre"). In this regard, it is worth noting that French advertising made altogether 38 references, such as "well-being is an art" and that "one has never felt as good on earth as in an Espace with its "soft upholstery", "comfortable seats", and noiseless sound system.

Another salient theme, "reasoning" also highlights the differences, primarily cultural, between the three countries. While in India, this theme is used by only one out of a total of eight companies in the country, that is by the German BMW (13 percent), which specifically highlights "its numerous intelligent, innovations, in Germany on the other hand, 10 out of 25 companies (40 percent) have used it in their advertising. Interestingly, the French figures are even higher—nine out of 15 companies (60 percent) have used this theme in their advertising. French advertisements tend to generally describe the product as "intelligent" and "sophisticated"—a reflection perhaps of that country's own aspirational goals. The Opel advertisement, for example, says, "Intelligence without ostentation, excellence without excess" ("Intelligence sans l'ostentation, l'excellence sans l'excès"). In Germany, on the other hand, the same advertisement talks about "innovative thinking for a new age" ("Eines Neues Denken fur eine neue Zeit"); In terms of thematic representation, however, the two European countries appear more comparable—France: 29 percent and Germany: 25 percent.

What about technology? Interestingly, both France and Germany have more or less comparable figures (73 percent and 72 percent respectively), thereby suggesting that this theme, contrary to popular perception, also has a certain resonance with the French buyer. Not surprisingly perhaps, this theme is less popular in a country like India where only three companies, namely BMW, Rover and Contessa, have used it to sell their product (38 percent). It is only when high-end cars finally reached India that this theme also appeared in the advertisements. The new generation of automobiles coming in to India brought with them a different set of values, which now emphasized the technical aspects of the vehicle, such as emission control techniques, catalytic converters, and injection technology.

A trait associated especially with the French is individualism.[7] Hence, for its French market, a Jaguar advertisement has allied two favorites, "technological sophistication" and "design and style" to "individualism" to sell in that country: "We have assembled the most sophisticated technology and we have individualized them with distinction" "... behind so much elegance hides the most advanced engines ever created by our engineers... and represents the perfect

---

[7] Hofstede, *Culture's Consequence*.

symbiosis between the most advanced technology and the style dear to Jaguar" ("Nous avons réuni les technologies les plus sophistiquées et nous les avons personalisées avec distinction"/"Derriere tant d'élégance se cache la gamme des moteurs la plus perfectionnée que nos ingénieurs aient jamais créee .. et represente l'union parfaite entre les technologies les plus avancées et le style cher à Jaguar").

For the German market, however, Jaguar, like Opel, has opted to link technology with innovation and tradition—"The perfect balance between Innovation and Tradition." "The perfect symbiosis of Tradition and Technology" ("Die perfekte Balance zwischen Innovation und Tradition"/"Die Perfekte Symbiose aus Tradition und Technik"). It is also a central theme with Audi whose universal slogan is "Progress through Technology" ("Vorsprung durch der Technik"). For the French market, however, Audi, like Jaguar, has used a more "individualized" approach—"Think Audi, it will make you forget the others" ("Pensez Audi, vous oublierez les autres"). Similarly, while BMW talks specifically of the "Power of Ideas" in Germany ("Die Kraft der Ideen. It's Ti Time"), in France, the text is adapted to suggest that the car has been 'created around oneself" ("Mais ce qui surprend le plus c'est le sentiment que la nouvelle BMW Serie a été concue autour de soi"). This, once again, suggests that French buyers do not want to be inclusive; they want to be exclusive. What is particularly interesting is that the term "Technology" (or "Technik") appeared 10x in German advertising but only 1x in French advertising.

Germany has higher uncertainty avoidance scores, which often translates into verification of technological expertise, warranties and guarantees.[8] Hence, in an effort to sell better, many Asian entrants to this market such as Mazda and Nissan, have specifically used this theme. The Nissan advertisement, for example, reads—"Everything comes with the perfection and guarantee of the most advanced technology" ("Alles mit der Perfektion und Sicherheit modernster Technik"). Similarly, Renault and Jaguar have also highlighted "modernsten Sicherheitstechnik" and "modernste Automobiltechnologie."

Nationalism, interestingly enough, has the lowest representation in Germany (8 percent), a country that, ironically, was responsible for two devastating World Wars. Both France and India, on the other

[8] Hofstede, *Culture's Consequenes.*

hand, have the same scores (13 percent). In terms of thematic frequency, the Indian figures at 4 percent, are slightly higher than France and Germany that have the same scores (3 percent). One reason for this could be that since its defeat in World War II, Germany has been more focused on its economic recovery (the German economic miracle) and being a good team player in the European Community.

What are the Conclusions?

This survey illustrates the fact that global advertising appeals widely to human universals. Some interesting conclusions stand out. One is that 13 of the 20 themes, that is almost two-third, are common to advertisements in all the three countries. They have been utilized in at least 50 percent of the advertisements shown. Indeed, what is particularly interesting is that the German BMW has reiterated 17 of the 20 themes in all the three countries. The three excluded themes are: economy, environment and nationalism.

The differences are related primarily to the features that consumers of each country consider to be the most important in a car. For example, the excitement factor as well as superb engineering are considered very important in the two European countries. Therefore, advertisements in both countries focus on qualities such as engineering, workmanship, and product components, often featuring new ideas. Since both German and French cars are well made, this should not be surprising. The French also place some emphasis on the aesthetic qualities of their products. Interestingly, the French have the highest uncertainty avoidance scores, yet they demonstrate the feminine dimension and place greater emphasis on design, style and beauty. Many carmakers take this format when advertising in this market.

On the other hand, according to the data, though the German consumers are attached to the utilitarian aspect, they are not specifically attached to performance, technology or perfection as one might have expected. They, contrary to popular stereotyping, are also not totally devoid of humor although this attribute is perhaps more emphasized in French advertising, which is generally more quirky and visually appealing. Most advertisements also often provide a subtle presentation, linking the product to a place, an event, person or symbol. As a result, French advertisements are more likely to be dramatic, with implicit sales pitch and little product visibility (recall the French BMW advertisement series, which showed an entire page length visual of the Mona Lisa painting, the Versailles Gardens layout or a ladybird perched on a large leaf). Germans, in contrast, appear to be less emotional/sentimental. In other words, French advertisements use more emotional appeals while German advertisements seem to contain more information cues providing reasons why one should buy the product. Also, since German consumers like driving fast, they tend to prefer cars that are well designed and technically advanced.

In India, a country with low uncertainty avoidance, high masculinity attributes and high power distance, automobile consumers tend to invariably look for social status. Initial Indian car advertisements, in fact, have not mentioned the quality of engineering or technological sophistication. In line with this trend, most of the foreign carmakers coming to India did not bother to elaborate the qualities of their car. They took it for granted that buyers in India would know of their reputation, focusing instead on the value of their cars as status symbols. Though major German companies showcased their products in France with French license plates to suggest wide acceptance, in India, there are several advertisements showing German license plates, which emphasize the fact that they are foreign products, thereby adding to snob value (for example, BMW displayed the license plate, M-XV9894). Traditional Indian values too play an important role in Indian advertising where they are used to attach value to products (recall the Ambassador advertisements). Some advertisements are quite subtle. To push the excitement factor, a Mercedes advertisement says its "engines cannot be tamed, only managed." This is in contrast to developed markets where customers tend to look for various advanced features in a car. Now of course, with the explosion of automobile brands in India, there is a huge change in the mode of advertising.

Nevertheless and as stated earlier, two-thirds of the themes used in France and Germany are used in their Indian advertisements. It is not that the other themes are not used. For example, in Europe, since both men and women are buyers of cars, there are advertisements to appeal to women consumers. A Renault advertisement in France and Germany highlights the fact that "the modern Eve trusts only her airbag" ("la moderne Eve ne fait confiance qu'a son airbag"/"Pralles

Vertrauen schenken modern Evas nur ihrem Airbag. Sonst keinem"). Yet another one promises "a more robust sound system for the modern Eve that would bring the curtains down on boredom" ("Starker Sound fur moderne Evas. Und fur Langweile fallt der Vorhang"). A Peugeot advertisement in France shows a woman executing a series of vicous judo holds on to her husband, the text imparting precise instructions on how to make the poor man relinquish his grip on the keys of her 106 ("Maintenir l'épaule de votre mari contre le sol. Grace a votre main droite et de la main gauche tordre légèrement le poignet jusqu'a ce que le malheureux lache la clef de contact de votre 106").

In comparison, Indian advertisers do not yet emphasize the gender factor since most buyers of these vehicles continue to be men. The absence of this theme in Indian advertising, however, does not mean that "women's emancipation" has no place in this society. It merely appears elsewhere, for example, in one of the advertisements on Onida washing machine and the copy is expressed a little differently here. Acknowledging the growing financial independence of Indian women who no longer feel the need to defer to their husbands in making important purchase decisions, the Onida washing machine advertisement is targeted at the modern Indian housewife who goes out and buys herself a washing machine without consulting her husband. He takes the news rather well, saying, 'I am sold" I said, thoroughly impressed. "Let's go and get the ONIDA right away!" The kids and their mother giggled mysteriously. Something sleek and beautiful was lurking behind the curtain. Ah ha! She's already bought it! I should have guessed. "Women's liberation!" quipped my six year old daughter, as she raised the curtain with a flourish!" This Onida advertisement is a good example of the changing face of women in Indian advertising. It also emphasizes the fact that in the highly collectivist and masculine Indian society,[9] a family is a complex structure where an individual may need to take into account the opinion of all the members of the family before making any major purchase decisions. An advertisement on Ray Ban highlights the fact that Indian women are now increasingly making bold career choices. The advertisement visual shows a young Indian woman dressed in a pilot's uniform standing in front of an aircraft, the text saying just

[9] Hofstede, *Culture's Consequences*.

how much she had always wanted to be a pilot and now having finally become one, she could afford to buy a pair of her favorite Ray Ban sunglasses. Both advertisements in this case seem to suggest that the traditional roles of Indian women as wives, mothers, daughters, and daughters-in-law were now being modified to reflect social changes in the interests of giving them more consumer power.

The data further indicates that there are significant differences in the way European and Indian cultures produce advertising messages. Although advertisement in these three diverse cultures share certain universal traits, the specific content was likely to vary along major normative cultural dimensions.[10] European advertisements, for instance, tend to utilize direct rhetorical styles, individualistic visual stances, sexual portrayals of women more often than Indian advertisement, which tend to utilize indirect rhetorical styles, collective visual stances and stereotypical portrayals of women more often. Neither environment nor women's emancipation, as can be seen, are essayed in the same way in these two categories. In comparison with India (the Onida advertisement, for example), women's emancipation in Europe is portrayed in a direct manner and in relation with safety (for example, the Renault advertisements). This is because India, a high-context culture, is characterized by an indirect style of communication. The context in which the information is embedded is just as important as what is said. The advertisements therefore are often multidimensional and indirect. They go beyond the technical aspect to suggest that the customer is intelligent, powerful, and has good breeding, thus appealing to deeper emotions (for example, the Contessa advertisements). The text tends to be a little longer because the product is not yet familiar to the Indian market and specifications need to be detailed. Interestingly, however, a large number of French and German advertisements also emphasized soft-selling techniques (indirect, humorous, image-oriented content) rather than hard-selling ones (direct, strong message, argument appeals).

Some of the above-mentioned differences notwithstanding, this study concludes with the observation that the majority of the advertisements in all three countries use common themes with slight variations to account for local tastes and sensitivities.

---

[10] Hofstede, *Culture's Consequences.*

Contemporary Indian Scenario

Two Decades Later ...

Between 1995–6, the period covered in the first analysis, and 2003–4, sales of cars and two-wheelers in India more than doubled. Indeed as a New York Times report of December 10, 2005, pointed out "based on the trends of car sales of the last five years, India is one of the world's fastest growing car markets."[11] This does not surprise when one considers the fact that between now and 2025, 95 percent of the increase in the global production will be in emerging markets and their increase in consumption will be higher than that of the traditional top six developed markets. With nearly 23 percent of the global population, a study by McKinsey Global Institute (MGI) suggests that if India continues its recent growth, average household incomes will triple over the next two decades and it will become the world's fifth largest consumer economy by 2025, up from 12th now.[12] As Carlos Ghosn, the boss of Renault Nissan, put it, "the great thing about emerging markets is that they have so many people and so few cars. Whereas in Western Europe, the ratio of cars to people is one to two, in China, it is still one to 20 and in India, one to 40. Even if these countries eventually settle at say, just half the ownership levels in the rich world, the potential remains immense.[13]

According to the data, although information content (or type of cues) used to influence consumer purchase decision in India varied greatly between 1995–6 to present, certain product attributes (for example, status, family values and economy) have remained relatively constant. Fuel efficiency for example, remains the main criterion for purchasing a car in India followed by styling, interiors and price.[14] Indeed in a country obsessed with mileage (recall the popular Maruti advertisement, "kitna deti hai"?) ("How much mileage does

---

[11] Rama Bijapurkar, *We Are Like That Only: Understanding the Logic of Consumer India* (Penguin Books: 2009), 83.

[12] The full report, "The Bird of Gold: The Rise of India's Consumer Market", is available free of charge online at www.mckinsey.com/mgi.

[13] *The Economist*, "Markets and Makers, Running Harder", Special Report, April 20, 2013.

[14] Arti Sharma, "For That l'il Buggy", *Outlook*, February 27, 2012, 39.

it give?"), almost all the cars invariably emphasize fuel efficiency. The volume leaders, consequently, are those companies, which offer products with globally acknowledged best in-class fuel-economy rates. In line with this trend, the Fiat slogan in India is "BurnTyre. Not Diesel"—all the perks of a Premium Class minus the cost." Interestingly, for its French market, Fiat has retained the same theme of economy but adapted the mode of presentation. While the emphasis of Fiat's advertisement in India is on humor (visual of a worried Indian man making a comic face), the emphasis, in France, is on "more Pleasure" "less Privations" ("+ de Plaisir; – de privations"), and the visual in this case, showcases a slender feminine waistline. Yet another Fiat-owned car, the Lancia, uses the same theme (that is economy) to sell in the French market. Keeping in mind the French penchant for seduction, Lancia uses the well-known French fable of Le Petit Chaperon Rouge (or Little Red Riding Hood) in an effort to fit into the French culture. The car (in vibrant red), surrounded by a pack of sniffing wolves, is projected as an object of intense desire with, in the background, the silhouette of a very sexy young woman, her face partially concealed by the trademark red hood. Parodying the French fable, the advertisement says, "You have such an economical price". To which the car retorts—'It is to better seduce you, my pretty child".

Other companies to use this theme in India include BMW, Jaguar and others. Bearing in mind the fact that the average consumer is very price-conscious, BMW also emphasizes, for its Indian market, in India, the economic factor, that is the attractive interest rates offered. In Germany, on the other hand, BMW's emphasis is on performance and ecology ("Sport Modus" Sie Wollen schnell zum Ferien Haus. Eco Pro Modus: Sie sparen fur ein Ferienhaus"). This is because as seen previously, consumers in this country invariably tend to look for fast acceleration combined with exhilaration ("Mehr Fahrfreude"). In France, on the other hand, BMW emphasizes child-like emotions— "Joy is childlike" ("La Joie garde une ame d'enfant"), with the visual showing an elderly man standing in front of his vibrant red Cabriolet. Yet another French BMW advertisement emphasizes aesthetic qual-ities—"harmony of movement" ("l'harmonie du movement")—a theme that has a special resonance with the French consumer. The basic tagline of "Unlimited driving pleasure," however, is retained in all the three countries (this appears as "Weniger Verbrauch, mehr

Fahrfreude" in Germany and translated as "Less consumption, more driving pleasure" in India and "Moins d'emission, plus de plaisir" in France).

Likewise, for its Indian market, Jaguar prefers the theme of economy—in this instance, its "pre-budget prices." For the French market, however, Jaguar, keeping in mind the high individualism scores of the French[15] says—"sublime in all its differences ("sublime dans toute sa difference"). Hyundai also uses the same format in France—"why drive like everybody else when one can drive the new Santa Fe?' ("Pourquoi rouler comme tout le monde quand on peut rouler en Nouveau Santa Fe?").

Interestingly, design, style and comfort have also caught up with the Indian consumer, who is now looking beyond pure functionality. With the market straddling the space primarily between function-ality and aesthetics, features and accessories determine to a large extent the value perception of the car especially in the mid-to-upper segments. Bearing this in mind, Ford for example, offers a range of enhanced features such as acoustic sound lamination that cuts down on road noise, dashboard, internal aesthetics, seats, space, side panels boot space etc.; Chevrolet offers 'more style, more comfort and con-venience"; and the Maruti Ritz is "designed to keep you calm and comfortable." A Renault advertisement for its Kwid model highlights style—"Live for more style." And Volkswagen emphasizes the "look" of its new Jetta—"an aesthetic design that is both sleek and sporty enough to "loosen all self-restraint" and "reason enough to make anyone go a wee bit overboard". The visual, keeping in mind India's penchant for humor, shows Santa Claus's reindeer sleigh parked in front of the car with a sign 'FOR SALE' on it. As advertisements go, this one is certainly very original.

Interestingly, for its French market, Volkswagen has reiterated the theme (aesthetic qualities) to sell the same Jetta model—"Carosserie en design véritable" ("Bodywork in veritable design"). The French advertisement emphasizes, in particular, the "beauty, elegant silhou-ette and ingenuous design" ("belle", "silhouette élégante", "design ingénieux"). There is, however, an added emphasis on environ-ment (400 Euros de bonus ecologique), (400 Euros of ecological

---

[15] Hofstede, *Culture's Consequences.*

bonus). The logo and the tagline is the same in all three countries—
"Volkswagen. Das Auto." Yet another German manufacturer,
Mercedes, also highlighted design and performance for its German
market—"Elegant beherrste Kraft" (or "Elegant, controlled Power"),
the visual showing the sleek lines of a springing tiger; the Indian
advertisement, on the other hand, is more straightforward—it reiterated, with a simple visual of the car, the same themes of performance
and design ("exhilaration just got more enticing") but added, like
BMW, the important economic factor (in this case, attractive interest
rates) to entice the price conscious Indian buyer.

The performance factor is now also catching up in India with
many cars combining the all-important mileage factor with performance. The Chevrolet advertisement, for example, says, "India drive
khulke" ("India full-throttle). "India's most fuel efficient car". The
Porsche Panamera Diesel model is presented as "a Sprinter that can
run marathons" (recall the erstwhile Volkswagen advertisement in
France, which showed four camels squeezed inside the car's interior
to illustrate the "exemplary sobriety" of the model that could also, on
occasion, double as a "race horse").

An especially important development in India, in recent years, has
been the growth of the luxury segment. As India emerges as a nation
with the highest growth rate of Ultra-High Networth Individual
(UHNIW) among the BRICs nations, it is increasingly becoming
"the destination" for many luxury carmakers (recall that in the initial
years of liberalization, this was limited to only a handful of top car
manufacturers). Across income, car segments, regions, a key factor
is how the vehicle is perceived vis-à-vis a sense of achievement. The
present trend suggests that the demand for upmarket models will be
sustained in the medium term. What is especially encouraging for
companies is that first-time time car-buyers are buying further up the
value-chain and not necessarily from the cheapest category. With the
profile of first-time buyers in India getting younger, there is also a distinct shift in preference toward more modern cars that are slightly more
expensive.[16] To tap this segment of Indian yuppies with a higher
consumption index a Toyota advertisement uses the tagline "My

[16] Jonathan Ananda, "Cars Get the Axe as India Turns Younger", *New
Sunday Express*, December 12, 2017.

First". Honda emphasizes the fact that is is "Born of Luxury". The new Renault Fluence advertisement says—"Status Redefined" (recall the erstwhile BMW advertisement, "automotive status"); Honda targets the status conscious upwardly mobile Indian buyer with the tagline—"You've always wanted to outperform in life. You've always wanted to move ahead. With advanced Honda technology, you can do just that"; the Skoda Superb is "designed for the ambitious and determined"; the Chevrolet Cruze is marketed as "Incredibly luxurious" and Volvo is marketed as a car that—"comfortably beats other luxury cars. Even before you turn on the engines".

In a high PDI country like India that is also collectivist, some carmakers such as Toyota, for example, have focused on both luxury and family values—"Luxury that brings joy to your family". Interestingly, since France is also a high PDI country, Toyota has retained the same theme of social status for this market also. Its Corolla model is marketed as a "car that one can be proud of" ("une voiture dont on peut etre fier"). The advertisement visual shows the car parked in front of a luxury hotel—La Jatte Palace—and two liveried door men kneeling on a red carpet in front of a partially opened frosted glass window to receive the car keys dangling from the (concealed) owner's hand. Unlike Toyota, however, Volvo, owing perhaps to its Swedish low power distance and feminine dimension, uses the themes of ideology/emotions and safety for its French and German markets. In Germany, the Volvo advertisement shows a young man standing in front of the car with a huge bunch of red roses in his hand. The text says, "When the car is not the most important thing in your life" ("Wenn das Auto nicht der wichtigste Teil ihres Lebens ist"). In France, a country that coined the popular term "joie de vivre", Volvo emphasizes the fact that life has much more to offer than just a Volvo ("La vie offre bien plus qu'une Volvo"). Yet another Volvo advertisement emphasizes safety, marketing the car, interestingly, as the "third eye" (Le troisieme oeil)-recall the erstwhile French BMW advertisement, which had described the car as one that anticipated the danger even before the driver did. The logo and tagline, "Volvo for life", however, is retained without change in all the three countries.

The present trend suggests that the demand for upmarket models will be sustained in the medium term. At the same time, the trend is also toward smaller cars. At present, about 75 percent of India's automobile industry is small car oriented, with Maruti holding on to its status as the largest-selling car brand in the country. Says Nigel E. Wark, Executive Director, Marketing, Sales and Services, Ford India: "Traditionally, people go to larger and larger cars globally. In India, we see something different. There is an aspiration to drive and enjoy a good product without going to a big car. So you will get the technology, the driving experience, the positioning and prestige of a big car in a smaller car."[17] This is due as much to economic reasons as the lack of proper roads. Says Hormazd Sorabjee, Editor, *Autocar India*: "Indian car owners are cost-conscious. They will look at the running cost of a car—and increasing fuel costs have not helped. On top of that, Indian roads are bad and congested making it difficult to run larger cars. Many companies are looking at this option now."[18]

Interestingly, two decades ago, technology had little or no representation in India. Now with the explosion of international automobile brands in the country, most advertisements also emphasize "leading technology". The Ford Fiesta for example, is marketed with the tagline, "So full of technology, it has got everybody talking." The new Skoda is all about driving "a masterpiece of technology without worrying about the fuel". The Hyundai slogan "New Thinking/New Possibilities" is aimed at constant reinvention to introduce cutting-edge global products that are technologically advanced. Similarly, Audi has combined the Germany fondness for technology—"Power of Ideas" with the Indian fondness for social status—"We are the Number One because it's not about the number of cars you put on the road. It's the number of ideas you put in the car." At the same time, design is not forgotten—"Bold yet beautiful, they comprise Audi's revolutionary engineering with stunning design." The French Audi advertisement copy, on the other hand, is more straightforward—"Le rythme du progres/L'avance par la technologie." In the case of the German market, Audi visually highlights the various car components since Germans, as we know, tend to look for more verification such as technological expertise.

[17] Arindam Mukherjee, "That Familiar About-Turn", *Outlook*, January 16, 2012.

[18] Mukherjee, "That Familiar About-Turn".

Interestingly, once again, the rationality aspect has also gained ground in recent years. In view of the ageing population around the world, most cars now also tend to emphasize the "intelligent" factor. In India, Volkswagen, for example, speaks of "intelligent gear shift prompt" and "intelligent ABS"; and Ford is all about "First class intelligent steering technology". In France, this aspect is highlighted by Rover (Stop/Start Intelligent System) and Nissan, "Intelligence attracts intelligence" (L'intelligence attire l'intelligence).

The utilitarian aspect, which was also very much underrepresented twenty years ago (recall that the concept of "space" had the greatest resonance in Germany), is now emphasized by most car-makers coming to India. The Toyota visual, for example, shows the car's interior stuffed with several teddy bears to drive home the fact that the car can accommodate a large family (recall the French Nissan advertisement, which had used the same theme by showing several toddlers crawling in and out of the car).

The other important trend in India is the greater emphasis on the environmental factor as Indian advertisers slowly integrate this aspect also. The Volkswagen Passat for example, is advertised not just as "fuel efficient and intelligent" but also as "eco-friendly." Other leading automobile companies in India such as GM, Honda, Toyota, Mahindra and Nissan have also incorporated environmental concerns into their advertising. The Mahindra Micro Hybrid for example, is presented humorously (and in green) as a car that "drinks less and smokes less." As with India, in France too, most major automobile manufacturers whether Toyota, Volvo, Audi, Volkswagen, or Honda now use the environmental theme more extensively than before—(recall that at the time of the original survey, only the German Opel had used this theme in that country. Toyota for example, markets its Avensis D-4D Clean Power model ("Le Diesel propre par Toyota") by showing the car in lush green surroundings and around it several birds and animals (recall the erstwhile Mercedes advertisement in Germany, which had showed a similar visual with the tagline, "Schliesslich geht es um die Existenz des Autos"). The universal English slogan—"Today Tomorrow Toyota", is retained albeit with the mandatory translation—"Aujourdh'ui, Demain Toyota." Honda also marketed its new CR-V Diesel i-CTDi model as one that combines respect for nature (respect de la nature) with one of the lowest carbon dioxide emissions (niveau d'emissions e CO_2 le plus faible de sa categorie). The new Suzuki Alto (Way of Life) is marketed not just as more economical (super bonus of 700 Euros)—but also as more ecological (CO_2 103 g/km/ ecological bonus). Similarly, Rover also emphasizes environmental concerns—7% of less CO_2 emissions", (7% d'emissions de CO_2 en moins"). However, although the rise of greener hybrid vehicles is a globally evolving phenomenon, India, based on current trends, is still some years away from this trend becoming mainstream.

What of the erstwhile gender divide? Indian women ostensibly have come a long way since the 1990s and enjoy much more financial independence today. This has led many companies to target them exclusively as buyers. Examples include an Apollo Tyres advertisement that combines safety with family values through its visual of a young solo female driver and in the passenger seat, a baby. The text says "Makes everyone feel safe the way you do". Yet another Apollo advertisement also showed a young, solo female driver, the text saying "Safety never looked so gorgeous." This is in stark contrast to the early years of liberalization when not a single advertisement targeting this segment, was found.

What of motorcycles/bicycles? Despite the proliferation of automobile brands, dropping prices and rising income, the trend in India does not seem to indicate that the humbler versions of everyday transport have been relegated to the background. On the contrary, their consumption has increased, particularly in the rural market, which is expected to be the primary driver for 100cc bikes over the next decade.[19] In the case of urban dwellers, there is now a very high degree of ownership and usage of both two-wheelers and cars in the household, the idea being to optimize status signaling as well as fuel consumption. Currently, however, although India is the second largest market in the world in volume terms—with three-fourth of the market currently dominated by Hero Honda, Bajaj and TVS Motors—household penetration of two-wheelers, at 36 percent, is lower than many other emerging markets such as Brazil, Indonesia and Taiwan. The numbers are worse when urban

[19] David Aaker, *Building Strong Brands* (New York: The Free Press, 1996), 21.

and rural areas are compared, with large cities having nearly three times more bikes than villages.[20]

While the Yamaha advertisement two decades ago was focused on selling emotions/ideology, today the Yamaha FZ-S, is advertised (in green) as "Yamaha FZ-S in a Black Cyber Green for the super stylish". In contrast, Hero Honda's Splendor targets the conformists—buyers essentially seeking security, value for money and social acceptance. Style, however, is not forgotten. The Hero Honda Passion PRO for instance, focuses exclusively (in Hindi) on style— "Ab sirf style hi bolega." ("It is about style only"). A second Honda ad for its Aviator model says—"Style Tip # 1". Yet another Honda product—the Honda Dio, is marketed as "Live free" (recall the erstwhile Bajaj advertisement "Born Free").

Bicycle buyers still comprise the lower-income villagers but the age profile has become younger and the school and college-going proportion increased. Thanks to liberalization and the pattern of economic growth in that period, the lowest income group in rural India has declined sharply. The erstwhile lowest income has moved slightly up the income ladder but since the price gap between the two-wheelers and bicycles is still large, they remain perforce bicycle buyers but now they have higher expectations. The mindset, even in rural India, is no longer about the cheapest possible bicycle to buy but about getting better quality for a slightly higher price. Illustrating this trend, a Hero Cycles advertisement says, "Best quality bikes year after year."

To recapitulate

Over the last two decades, the Indian industry has moved from a supply-constrained seller's market to a demand-driven buyer's market with different car brands competing on different strategies. Increased competition and customer orientation have also led advertising agencies to become more adept at reading the Indian consumer who are more informed, more sophisticated than before. Urban consumers especially are more demanding due to overseas travel and exposure to Western lifestyle. This shift in perception is due in part to the

---

[20] Aaker, *Building Strong Brands*.

increased consumption power of Indian middle class consumers as compared to the prior decades.

In practical terms, however, there really is not much to choose from between the different cars. Consumers everywhere may try to buy rationally on price—"it is cheaper", on quality—"it lasts longer"; on service—"they will not let you down when things go wrong". Sometimes, of course, it is genuinely possible to make rational choices when buying things. Mostly though, it is not about rationality but emotions because products and services are increasingly similar in their rational characteristics. If they are of poorer quality or more expensive than a direct competitor's, they simply fade away or die. Ultimately, price for price, at each level of the market, there is not much difference between the top German automobile manufacturers such as BMW, and Mercedes and the rest of them. In other words, on rational factors, there is not much to choose from. Most cars look very much the same, they perform very much in the same way and even dealer service is very much the same.

So apart from going to the dealer that gives him the best margin, how does the consumer choose really? The real questions before the consumer are: "which car suits my image best? what does it do for me? And "do I want to be seen in it? As the Tata Nano failure demonstrates, buying a car is essentially about the aspirational values of the consumer. A man buys a car for what he wants to be. Not what he is. The higher up the value chain we go the more important are these questions. Car companies know this. They also know that they have to offer something different from each other to customers, something, which is not rational but is emotional. Their strategy subsequently is more likely to be associated with the emotions or fantasies derived from consuming a product—a successful brand not only provides the customers with functional benefits but also emotional and self-expressive benefits. For example, Harley Davidson stands for the rugged independence of Western America; and BMW is essentially about fun, about enjoying life, about showing off. Audi, on the other hand, talks about the best technology money can buy, which it emphasizes by saying in German—"Vorsprung durch Technik." French carmaker Renault has also adopted a global French tag line, "Créateur d'automobiles."

("Creator of Automobiles"). Yet others have tapped into popular culture and society to make their brands a part of the community. For example, Lancia uses the Fable of the Red Riding Hood to resonate with the French consumer and Hyundai shows the Indian Red Fort and national tricolor to resonate with the Indian consumer.

In other words, these highly successful car companies have developed an emotional as well as a rational appeal, which they have thought through and which they use everywhere. At the same time, the brand personality tends to differ in different countries. In France, for example, it is more quirky, more subtle. Even when it uses explicit language, tongue-in-cheek humor, understatement and word games are some of the other characteristics of French advertising. German advertising, on the other hand, is generally unambiguous, direct and factual. Indian advertising seems to have imbibed certain characteristics from the developed world even while retaining a few traditional and cultural values common to all its communities.

This is what advertising is really all about. Advertising employs symbols that are related to the owner's self-identity to portray the desired lifestyle. It subconsciously creates an awareness and liking for a brand, which eventually turns into loyalty. Ultimately, at the heart of all marketing strategies is the need to satisfy consumers and to establish a loyal customer base.

Finally, a word of caution. Even though car ownership in India is still relatively low as compared to Europe (car ownership in Europe is about 600 per 1000 people), there has been, as seen, an unprecedented rise in car-ownership in India since the opening up of the economy. This is due as much to rising affluence as the need for status signalling. Even at the current low density of car ownership, we are still battling traffic gridlocks, bad infrastructure and road rage even as pollution from emissions poses a major health hazard. In the present scenario, if we were to achieve even a fraction of the European figures regarding car ownership, our imports of oil, investment in roads and high-ways and parking facilities would probably outstrip every other claim on resources. And yet, as per the present trend in advertising, car-ownership in India continues to be projected as a badge of economic success and social status to be proudly displayed. The sooner precious financial resources are deployed to dissuade private car-ownership and instead invested heavily in more efficient public transportation, the more sustainable will our economic development be.

Conclusions

Few expressions of globalization are as visible, widespread and pervasive as the worldwide proliferation of internationally traded consumer goods. Advertising, we have seen, is not only a good index to measure the level of globalization in a market but also a catalyst through which globalization spreads. Global trade, as seen through advertising, is developing a common global corporate culture that is sensitive to the local market without losing its main corporate identity. Logically therefore, as the world moves to more integrated markets, it will accept a common global corporate culture. This will be a vital ingredient in softening the jagged edges of political and cultural conflict. As more and more MNC products (designed in one place, financed from many sources and manufactured in several countries) reach out to the world, our common tastes and way of life and hence our "culture" will become more intercultural, sweeping away, I hope, some of the prejudices and stereotyping of the past.

We cannot say that this is inevitable—but then, who would have thought, only a few years ago, that the two most populous and formerly colonized nations of the East, India and China, would move in the inexorable direction of globalization and thence to the center-stage of global power as part of the economically powerful BRICs nations? How things have changed. The age of empire is over. The Ottoman Empire has gone. The Austro-Hungarian Empire has gone. The British Empire has gone. The Russian Empire has both come and gone. The US, a nation which was once in debt and financed largely by the city of London is now the most powerful nation in the world. Europe is wholly different, building unity on the back of 1,000 years of war, it has established the richest and largest free trade area in history—from Ireland in the West to the very borders of Russia in the East. Looking back at this, we can see just how much and how quickly the world has changed. Hence, powerful as many of the counter arguments are, I believe they do not alter the direction in which we are heading.

We are, in the main, moving toward an interdependent world pushed by the demands of global trade and commerce that necessitates the acceptance of differences while building commonalities. These demands are shaping not only a corporate global culture that will eventually influence how we look at things around us but perhaps, more importantly, also at the "Other". The point the book makes is that "Made In" is not a fixed but rather an evolving reality. Its contours have changed significantly over the past few decades. This is testified by the fact that a war-shattered Germany has undergone a radical change in the way it was perceived since World War I when all German exports were obliged to carry the words "Made in Germany" as punishment and as a means of helping consumers in the rest of Europe and North America avoid products from the former enemy. The stigma, however, did not prove to be lasting. Today, "Made in Germany" is a sign of high quality that suggests that Germany is seen as the prolific producer of some of the world's finest products.[1]

The label "Made in Mexico" too has gained tremendous ground since NAFTA, with the establishment of world-class manufacturing plants by local and global manufacturers to supply world demand. Similarly, Japan also went within a very short period from being considered "shoddy" to "high-tech". Where an earlier generation had blamed Japan's (and China's) backwardness on Confucianism, following its economic success, the Japanese work culture came to be viewed as the key to understanding the Japanese miracle. And more recently, as for the first time since 1820, the majority of world growth looks set to come, not from the West but from the East, the

[1] Barry Silverstein, "German Engineering Drives Global Brand Success", November 24, 2008, http://www.brandchannel.com/features-effect.asp?Pf_id=451.

global focus has shifted to Asia and more specifically, toward India and China[2]. P. Guerlain expresses this well:

> One day culturalists claim that Japanese culture explains the economic successes of Japan and then a few years later, culture also explains the setbacks. Soon everyone is likely to explain Chinese success by some cultural characteristics of China, though these same cultural traits were there too when China was written off as a communist basket case. Indeed if tomorrow Indonesia or Brazil came to be major international players, their culture, indeed, their diversity—which is no less than the American one—would become an explanation and a model for others countries to emulate.[3]

The German philosopher Arthur Schopenhauer puts it more baldly—"All truth goes through three stages: first, it is ridiculed; second it is violently opposed. Finally, it is accepted as self-evident". The important conclusion here is that globalization, a complex phenomenon hard to describe and almost impossible to define, is not a fixed but rather an evolving reality. Launched initially as a hegemonic process of unilateral flow of trade and capital from the developed to the underdeveloped nations, it is today a multilateral flow of investment and services from the developing to the developed world also. The greater focus on interdependence between nations does not, however, imply a simple leveling out of advantages and disadvantages on a global scale. Nor do these arguments, in any way, entail the idea of a "decline of the West" and the inevitable "rise" of any other power no matter how tempting it is to speculate about the rise of India and China as incipient superpowers. In the short term at least, most of the emerging countries of the South will continue to be marginalized by globalizing technologies. The US is and will continue to be

---

[2] I.S. Baird, M.A. Lyles, and R. Wharton, "Attitudional Differences between American and Chinese Managers Regarding Joint Venture Management", *Management International Review* 30 (Special Issue) (1990): 103–20.

[3] P. Guerlain, "The Ironies and Dilemmas of America's Cultural Dominance: A Transcultural Approach", *American Studies International* 35, no. 2 (1997): 30–51.

the most dominant economic and military power in the world and source of cutting-edge technology.

But to look beyond this, what these trends suggest is that what is happening in globalization is no longer a process solely in the cultural grip of the West. What some of the aspects of globalization that we have seen here represent is a rapidly growing context of global inter-dependence, which "unites" us all, if only in the sense of subjecting us to certain common global influences. Whatever the risk of chaos, the advantage of this state of affairs is that inputs of all cultures are pooled together, thereby opening up incalculable prospects for the future. The global future therefore is much more radically open than what the thesis of homogenization and Cultural Imperialism would have us believe. Authors such as Huntington, cannot, of course, be faulted for highlighting the differences in cultures. They can, how-ever, be questioned for believing that these differences will inevitably lead to a clash. Such a clash, in my view, will occur only if we perceive our differences to be irreversibly adversarial.

I wish to conclude on a somewhat hopeful note. We have seen that globalization has brought about multicultural advertising—a recog-nition of sorts that large sections of people everywhere understand the same symbols, texts and images. There is thus a growing congruence of values. I would like to ask the following question: can multicul-turalism be used as a tool to reduce conflict, and more importantly, to develop understanding between peoples? If multiculturalism can be such an effective tool in the pursuit of financial gains and conse-quential acceptance of other cultures and faiths, why cannot it be used to bring people together directly? Why cannot it be taught in our schools for example? Is it not possible that our teaching institu-tions make more use of intercultural themes to dilute and to correct prejudices and stereotypes? After all, thousands of our students go to foreign universities where they are exposed to foreign influences and develop a far greater understanding, and, indeed acceptance of multiculturalism thereby becoming global citizens. Why cannot we start at home? If started sufficiently early, our children can surely grow up to see a harmonious whole consisting of a mosaic of cultures rather than as unbridgeable divides.

This is particularly important in a country like India stratified as it is between castes, creeds and religions.

Index

About the Author

Anuradha Bhattacharjee works as a consultant (marketing & strategy), faculty, and cross-cultural trainer for multinational corporations in India and abroad. She has a PhD from the Sorbonne University, Paris. She has worked with UNESCO and in many multicultural business environments, most notably Freudenberg in Germany and Ogilvy & Mather and Ford in India. She has been associated as a lecturer and researcher with the University of Leicester, CERI-Sciences Po and the University of Westminster, Diplomatic Academy of London.